National Academy Press

The National Academy Press was created by the National Academy of
Sciences to publish the reports issued by the Academy and by the
National Academy of Engineering, the Institute of Medicine, and the
National Research Council, all operating under the charter granted to
the National Academy of Sciences by the Congress of the United States.

Rethinking Urban Policy
Urban Development in an Advanced Economy

Royce Hanson, *Editor*

Committee on National Urban Policy
Commission on Behavioral and Social Sciences and Education
National Research Council

NATIONAL ACADEMY PRESS
Washington, D.C.   1983

National Academy Press • 2101 Constitution Avenue, NW • Washington, DC 20418

This project received support from the U.S. Department of Housing and Urban Development, the U.S. Department of Commerce, the Ford Foundation, and the German Marshall Fund of the United States.

Cover: Computergraphics courtesy of Skidmore Owings & Merrill

Library of Congress Cataloging in Publication Data

Main entry under title:

Rethinking urban policy.

   "Committee on National Urban Policy, Commission on Behavioral and Social Sciences and Education, National Research Council."
   Bibliography: p.
   Includes index.
   1. Urban policy—United States. 2. Urban economics—United States. I. Hanson, Royce. II. National Research Council (U.S.). Commission on Behavioral and Social Sciences and Education. Committee on National Urban Policy.

HT123.R456   1983   338.973'09173'2   83-19422
ISBN 0-309-03426-4

Printed in the United States of America

To Harvey S. Perloff (1915-1983)
scholar, educator, planner, and inspiration to those
who would make cities better places to live

COMMITTEE ON NATIONAL URBAN POLICY

Preface

The Committee on National Urban Policy, established by the National Research Council (NRC) in 1981 with support from the U.S. Department of Housing and Urban Development, the U.S. Department of Commerce, the Ford Foundation, and the German Marshall Fund of the United States, was charged with responsibility for evaluating past urban policies, continuing review of current policies, examining the experiences of other advanced nations with urban policy, and developing policy options and recommendations for the future.

During the earliest stages of its deliberations, the committee decided that it could contribute most to the discussion of urban policy by addressing basic conditions or trends that seem likely to shape the future course of urban development and raise issues that public policy must face. Traditional approaches to urban policy that deal with a series of functional problems—housing, neighborhood and commercial district deterioration, transportation, urban poverty—have often failed to produce unified and lasting policies not because the problems are unimportant, but because they often tend to be derivative of more fundamental social and economic forces at work in cities and suburbs. It is also important to view urban areas as whole economic entities rather than solely in terms of political jurisdictions.

The first task of the committee, therefore, was to identify and describe those fundamental issues that we believed would shape the ways in which urban areas will develop over the next two decades and would frame the issues with which urban policies must contend. We also believed that national urban policy had to comprehend actions that could be taken at the state and local as well as at the federal level of government. This approach was reflected in the first major report of the committee, *Critical Issues for National Urban Policy* (National Research Council, 1982a). That report discussed five issues that will shape urban policy in the years to come: (1) the mobility of people and jobs, (2) the rise of an urban underclass, (3) changes in the allocation of responsibility for urban programs in the federal system, (4) changing relationships between the public and private sectors of the economy, and (5) the condition of urban infrastructure. The committee has also published a background paper, "The Evolution of National Urban Policy, 1970-1980" (Hanson, 1982), and a report on an international conference it conducted, *National Policy and the Post-Industrial City* (National Research Council, 1982b). Together these reports laid a foundation for this study, which is concerned with how urban policies might respond to the substantial changes that have occurred in the structure of the national economy.

The impact of structural change on urban areas was identified at the outset of the committee's work as perhaps the most important single issue with which urban policy must grapple in the coming years. While various aspects of the subject have been widely discussed—particularly the problems of shifting investments from some parts of the economy to others and of retraining the labor force to adjust to these shifts in investment—there has been relatively little treatment of how these shifts affect the urban areas in which the employment centers and workers are located. Fortunately, there is growing scholarly and public interest in this matter, and there is an expanding literature in industrial economics, technological change, urban economics, and local labor markets from which to draw information and insights.

Early in our deliberations we recognized the importance of the growth of the service sector, and of changes within that sector, as crucial to our inquiry. A small group of committee members met in May 1982 with Thomas M. Stanback, Jr., Wilbur Thompson, Richard Knight, and Daniel Garnick to assay the state of knowledge of services in the American economy and to identify major policy issues. Work by Stanback and his colleagues at the Conservation of Human Resources project at Columbia University has been of great help to the committee in understanding both the services as such and the ways in which urban areas are adjusting to structural changes in their economies. The committee is also indebted to Daniel Garnick, for help in developing useful data on these changes, and to Richard Knight, for preparation of a special paper on transition strategies. Special thanks are due to Gordon L. Clark, who, during the development of this study, was an NRC fellow attached to the committee.

His several papers on urban labor markets contributed important conceptual and empirical support to the committee's work. His recently published book, *Interregional Migration: National Policy and Social Justice*, was initially prepared as a special issue paper for the committee and was of great help in the preparation of Chapter 6.

Many others have contributed to the work of the committee. John Rees, who became an NRC fellow in January 1983, has made a number of contributions to the committee's work. Judith May of the Office of Urban Policy, U.S. Department of Housing and Urban Development, has been especially helpful and supportive of the committee's work. Susan Ingraham, Julie Goldflies Quinn, and Kim Hong Lethi wrote background materials or special papers used to prepare this report. A number of others read earlier versions of the report and offered helpful criticisms and comments. They include Ian Dawson, Henry Doll, Eli Ginzberg, Peter Hall, Philip Hammer, Don Hicks, Debbie Matz, Thierry Noyelle, Charles Orlebeke, and Ralph Widner.

No report could be produced without the hard, essential, and accurate work of the editors and administrative staff, and the committee is grateful to members of the staff of the Commission on Behavioral and Social Sciences and Education. Christine L. McShane edited the manuscript and gave valuable advice on how to make the report a clearer and more effective statement of its ideas. Diane L. Goldman, Ann G. Polvinale, and Sarah M. Streuli prepared the original typescripts and innumerable changes and redrafts as the report passed through its many stages. The committee also enjoyed the consistent support of the executive director, David A. Goslin; the associate executive director, Heidi I. Hartmann; and the associate director for reports, Eugenia Grohman. Rose S. Kaufman kept our accounts and gave frequent help on administrative matters. The work of each one is deeply appreciated.

Our thanks to all who helped are profuse. But those cited and each member of the committee know that our greatest debt of gratitude is owed to Royce Hanson, study director of the project. With minimal resources at his disposal and with a committee far-flung and diverse in its membership, Royce more than anyone else gave the project its energy, substance, and coherence.

As this report was being readied for publication, Harvey S. Perloff died. Harvey was the moving force behind the creation of the committee and served as chair until his health required him to step aside in 1982. He remained an active member, however, and this report carries the imprint of his guidance and thought. As an educator, planner, and activist, Harvey was never content to accept existing ideas—even his own—as adequate for tomorrow's problems. From the outset of our work he insisted that the role of the committee should be to rethink and reconstruct the basis for urban policy. To the extent that this report meets that test, it reflects Harvey's intellectual spirit.

The committee fully appreciates that no study that makes policy proposals can claim to be completely objective or that the recommendations are inevitable conclusions from the data and information. Policies represent choices; our proposals for urban policy are no different, and some of our choices will no doubt be controversial. We have made them not to reject other alternatives as unsound but as a statement of preference about which reasonable people may disagree. Our purpose, therefore, is not so much to offer a prescription as it is to stimulate a more vigorous and informed dialogue about the role and purpose of urban policy in the spectrum of national economic policy.

Paul N. Ylvisaker, *Chair*
Committee on National Urban Policy

Contents

Tables and Figures

FIGURES

Rethinking Urban Policy
Urban Development in an Advanced Economy

1 Overview

A FRAMEWORK FOR POLICY

Powerful and deeply rooted structural changes in the national and international economy are transforming urban areas and the economic functions they perform. A new urban system is emerging, with a growing polarization between the places where corporate headquarters and producer services are concentrated and those that are more specialized in the production of goods or in services for consumers.

Shifts in employment from manufacturing to services and toward more white-collar jobs, combined with the increasing segmentation of the labor market, confront urban areas of all types and in all regions of the country with difficult problems of economic adjustment and adaptation.

The future of individual urban areas is closely tied to the growth and decline of sectors of the economy—that is, groups of related industries and occupations. Policies that seek to improve or accelerate the adaptability of urban areas to these changes should therefore be closely coordinated with policies that affect the performance of sectors of the economy and with general economic policies that strive to influence the overall rate and direction of national economic growth.

This coordination requires a framework for national urban policy that is simultaneously concerned with policies that accelerate and broaden the mainstream of economic change and policies that address the problems of adjustment for the people and places left behind by changes in the economy.

1

General mainstream policies should be primarily concerned with facilitating the transformation of the national economy and making it more competitive in international markets. Such policies should concentrate on capital and human investments that reinforce and build on structural changes. The committee recommends five basic policies.

1. Sectoral policies or strategies that recognize the consequences of macroeconomic policies for different sectors of the economy, policies that encourage capital to flow to the development and modernization of those sectors that promise to be strong competitors in international markets or that are essential to the nation's defense and economic well-being.

2. Policies that promote the construction and maintenance of a system of urban infrastructure—public facilities, energy and communications systems—to support and serve the national interest in economic development and conserve the nation's existing, useful urban capital stock.

3. Policies that encourage investment of private capital in activities that accelerate transitions in local economies.

4. A national policy on labor mobility that facilitates the matching of workers and jobs and reduces barriers to worker mobility.

5. Policies that promote investments in urban education systems to improve the basic skills and work habits of new entrants to the labor force and investments in continuing and higher education to develop and maintain a labor force that can adapt more readily to continuing structural changes in the economy and to new ways of working.

Such policies, taken by themselves, however, could exacerbate the distress and dislocation in some urban areas and regions of the country. The policy framework, therefore, should also be concerned with stabilizing those places during the transition period so that they can make a smoother adjustment. For these places in transition, the committee recommends five major policies.

1. Planning by firms and worker organizations, in cooperation with federal, state, and local governments, to help workers in declining industries, occupations, and communities prepare for more rapid and smooth transitions to other jobs, whether in their communities or elsewhere.

2. Particular attention to education and training for urban minorities and the economically disadvantaged so that more of them can move into the economic mainstream.

3. Gradual restructuring of fiscal transfers within the federal system to equalize the fiscal capacities of states—that is, their ability to finance a minimum level of public services and facilities at effective tax rates set

near the national average—and to encourage states to reduce urban-suburban fiscal disparities.

4. Development of community-based centers that employ and train minorities and other economically disadvantaged workers.

5. Selective use of public employment as part of a general strategy of improving the quality of local labor forces and the quality of public services in support of economic development.

Because every metropolitan area has some features that are unique in its mix of occupations and industries, in its political and social culture, and in its stage of urban and economic development, urban policy needs to be sufficiently flexible that appropriate strategies can be tailored to meet specific circumstances.

1. Particular attention should be given to fostering institutions at the local level that have the capacity to manage the economic transition. These institutions must include the private sector as well as nonprofit organizations.

2. There is a particular need for an intelligence system in each urban area to conduct research and provide information that helps local leaders understand economic changes, assay resources, and formulate strategies for local economic development.

3. A relatively stable local fiscal climate is needed to create a more rational atmosphere for decision making.

4. Public-private development institutions and nonprofit institutions are needed that can design and carry out long-term strategies.

Ultimately, urban policy should not be a discrete package of programs— a shopping list of federal grants and loans—but rather a long-term strategic perspective on a wide range of public policies at each level of government. Specific programs for housing, transportation, crime fighting, neighborhood revitalization, and other matters can be built from that strategic base. The policy options discussed in this report are therefore not proposed as a program. Rather they are offered as illustrations of the direction that urban policy might take. The speed with which it is possible to move depends, of course, on budget priorities and resources at each level of the federal system. The allocation of responsibility for various actions to different levels of government and between the public and private sectors should continue to be a matter for national debate. Our aim is to stimulate that debate.

The appropriate degree and level of government intervention in market choices is an issue that pervades this report. We offer no easy formula for resolving that issue. We do not think that there can be a workable doctrinaire response. Some of our specific suggestions will doubtless be too interventionist for some; others will feel that we have shrunk from proposing policies demanded by the logic of the conditions we describe. We have sought a middle course precisely because we do not know all that we would like about how events will unfold. We know only that economic conditions are likely to differ substantially from those that urban areas faced in the past. This lack of omniscience commends some caution and the deliberate use of an incremental, experimental approach to national urban policy. We have therefore sought to make the general directions relatively clear and to offer specific recommendations more tentatively as reasonable ideas to be tested by experience and to be perfected through debate.

Historically, the relationship between urban policy and national economic policy has not been close. Urban policy has often been viewed as little more than a few measures designed to ameliorate the local adverse effects of "natural" changes in the economy and the inadvertent consequences of policies that advanced broader national interests, or as a political palliative for powerful interest groups, such as the housing industry, minorities, or big-city mayors. National macroeconomic policy, for the most part, has been concerned with aggregate levels of employment and efficiency. In this sense it has been relatively indifferent to how it affected particular places. Urban policy has seemed often to resist or offset national trends and the effects of other policies on cities.

Urban policy is place oriented. But it has an important role to play as an integral part of a national strategy for adjusting to the economic transformation that is now well advanced. It is concerned with the pattern of investment and income among the nation's regions and urban areas. In this sense, urban policy can complement national tax, fiscal, employment, monetary, and international trade policies, which are concerned primarily with aggregate national economic performance, and sectoral policies, which are concerned with the performance of clusters of related industries. Working together, these three branches of policy—national, sectoral, and urban—are concerned with how much is done, what is done, and where it is done, as closely related aspects of the economy. All three are needed in a time of widespread and rapid change in the economies of advanced nations, although they may not involve explicit federal intervention.

The nation's urban areas supply most of the physical infrastructure and social institutions on which the economy is built. Their economic and fiscal health is not separable from that of the nation. Serious economic hardship in a substantial number of urban areas operates as a drag on aggregate performance of the economy. The perception of wide disparities in urban and regional economic opportunities also creates a political brake on policies that could advance other worthwhile objectives. In this context, urban policy can operate to inform and modify national policy and to support national policy objectives. It is time to reconsider its role in the national political process.

The remainder of this chapter reviews the major themes of the report.

FLEXIBLE POLICIES FOR CHANGING CITIES

The New Urban System

Technological, institutional, and demographic forces are currently transforming the national economy, bringing about changes in the location of economic activities and affecting the size and density of urban areas. The physical, social, and economic changes in urban areas reflect adjustments to two fundamental and closely related structural shifts in the economy. The first is the shift in employment from extractive and transformative industries to service industries. The second is the shift from blue-collar to white-collar occupations in almost all sectors of the economy.

These structural changes are contributing to the emergence of a new urban system dominated by a set of "command and control" centers, in which corporate and producer services—banking, law, accounting, and the media—are concentrated. These metropolitan areas provide the most important services for the rest of the system—the "subordinate centers," which are more specialized in consumer services, the production of goods, or military or extractive industries.

Because of their greater diversity, the autonomy of their economic institutions, and their strong existing base for development of a service-oriented economy, the command and control centers have shown greater capacity to adjust to the structural changes in their economies than have the subordinate centers. The subordinate centers, particularly the traditional manufacturing cities, have been far less adaptive. For these cities, structural change is not merely a transitional challenge; it is a long-term problem. Continued decline, however, is not inevitable. A number of areas have demonstrated that it is possible to perform new functions and adapt to the requirements of an advanced economy.

Basic Concepts for Urban Economic Strategy

We suggest four basic concepts or criteria in examining strategies for investing in urban physical and human capital, for stabilizing urban areas as they undergo economic transformation, and for developing local institutions and national policy processes that can facilitate the transition to new national and urban economies.

1. Because each type of metropolitan area in this new urban system has different problems in adjusting to structural change, no single, uniform approach to urban policy will work equally well for all places. National policy should therefore be flexible enough to allow for variations in approach that are tailored to the requirements of specific urban areas.

2. An effective urban economic strategy must operate at both local and national levels. Traditional economic policy has been concerned primarily with the formation of capital in the aggregate. The role for both sectoral and urban policies is to focus national concern on the allocation of capital to economic activities, places, and people in a manner that not only contributes to overall economic efficiency and wealth but also provides for broad distribution of opportunity and avoids unnecessary waste of human and physical resources.

3. In making policies and strategies for urban adjustment to structural change, the transitional period is particularly sensitive. The problem is often the delicate one of simultaneously stabilizing the community while accelerating and smoothing out the process of change.

4. Given the power of the economic forces at work, attempts to shore up declining industries and vanishing occupations are unlikely to succeed, especially in the long run. Thus, it is vital to focus on activities that can broaden economic growth and thereby include more of the places and people who otherwise would be left behind.

Investing Private and Public Capital in the Urban Future

Since broad national economic policy is not and probably cannot be neutral in its effects on sectors and places, it is important that it be designed with these consequences in mind. A sectoral perspective on economic policy, which looks at how policies affect clusters of related industries and occupations, should help ensure that capital is available to modernize a number of important industries and stimulate promising, competitive sectors by facilitating the shift of capital and workers to them from declining sectors. It could both reinforce market choices and provide a better system of advance warning of economic trouble spots. A clearer national sectoral strategy could also help urban areas identify the parts of their local economies that have more potential for growth in market shares and jobs.

Sectoral policy alone, however, does not address many complex urban development issues, and it could in fact exacerbate the economic problems of some urban areas. A complementary place-oriented perspective is therefore needed, but with a shift in the focus of such policies from distress to opportunity. Leverage capital for urban economic development is often needed to equalize return to investors, especially in higher-risk investments in emerging industries and in older sections of cities. The committee suggests consolidating various federal capital leverage programs into a single urban economic development fund or bank from which local public-private development institutions could draw to carry out economic development strategies formulated to address local conditions.

Because public capital investments are important aspects of economic development, there is a national interest in ensuring that urban public facilities such as transportation and sanitary systems are in place to support economic growth and that they are maintained in good working order. While the bulk of new investments in urban public facilities (or infrastructure) will come from state and local treasuries, acceptable levels of service in many urban areas are not likely to be achieved without some federal support. A system of national and state infrastructure banks could help raise capital for public investment and provide a more flexible form of financial assistance than traditional federal capital grant programs have provided.

Basic elements of urban economic development strategy include leveraging available resources, improving capital and operating budgeting, using joint development techniques, using regulations more effectively, improving urban design, and avoiding ineffective incentives, such as indiscriminate tax breaks.

Investing in the Future of the Urban Labor Force

Improving the quality of urban labor forces is a critical element in a strategy for adjustment to structural change. The recessions of the mid-1970s and early 1980s have accelerated the decline of weaker industries; when the current recession ends, urban areas in which these industries are located can expect to continue to experience long-term unemployment.

Labor markets for skilled and unskilled workers who are displaced by structural change are more localized than markets for professional workers. A national labor information system is therefore recommended. It would involve a computerized job information system linked to worker retraining and interview and relocation assistance, which would facilitate the movement of structurally dislocated workers to communities where there are jobs they can fill.

An even more serious problem is posed by the economically and educationally disadvantaged young people just entering the labor force, who are not prepared for work in an advanced economy. If employed at all, they will be confined to low-level service occupations with low wages, high turnover, and poor benefits. They present a long-term challenge to the quality and resilience of the local labor force and the ability of urban areas to compete for economic growth and to adjust to structural change.

The urban education system is the foundation for labor market strategy, both national and local. While the principal burden for providing basic education and training is likely to continue to fall on public education systems, the private sector can be productively engaged in the education process through a variety of programs. It may also be useful to experiment with such alternatives to traditional approaches to providing educational services as vouchers for postsecondary training and contracts with private firms.

In the years ahead, workers may need to be retrained frequently or continue their education in order to keep abreast of the knowledge and skills necessary to do their jobs and to be eligible for career advancement. Thus, redundancy planning—the anticipation of changes in the economy, markets, and technology and how they affect patterns of employment, together with the development of retraining and relocation programs—should become common practice. Joint programs in which federal, state, and local governments cooperate with unions and employers could help both workers and communities adjust more readily to changes that cannot be avoided.

Community colleges and urban universities, particularly those that are state- and city-supported, can play important roles in urban labor market strategies. Making special efforts in higher education for urban minorities, improving primary and secondary education in the urban school systems from which higher education institutions draw most of their students, and developing continuing education programs for the retraining and advancement of professionals, managers, and technicians are all appropriate functions for urban higher education institutions.

Effective urban development strategies will require major new investments by individuals, firms, and federal, state, and local governments in the quality of all parts of the education and training system. A city's investments in its education and training systems will be more important to its long-term economic prospects than its infrastructure and industrial parks.

Stabilizing Metropolitan Economies

As structural transition occurs, many people cannot or will not move to new jobs in the local economy or in other areas. While voting with one's feet may in theory be an attractive response to unemployment, moving is not without cost for workers and their communities. And the sense of community is an important public value that warrants consideration along with economic efficiency. Since there are no immutable economic laws or forces dictating that most capital must locate in particular urban areas, in many cases it is easier for capital to move to an available work force than it is for workers to migrate, following capital.

The retention and creation of local jobs in basically sound businesses are important parts of stabilization strategy. Notwithstanding the widespread use of new technology, many manual and low-skilled jobs will still exist. They can be important sources of employment and of entry into the labor force for poorly trained workers, particularly if there is a community strategy for and a commitment by firms to worker education and upward mobility. If the public provides assistance to such firms, then there is every reason to expect a return on that public investment in the form of such things as first-source employment of local disadvantaged workers and cooperation in worker education and training programs.

Because any jurisdiction facing fiscal crises or default has little capacity for strategic thinking, intergovernmental fiscal transfers should be redesigned to equalize the abilities of states and local governments to pay for an adequate level of services, so that the level of services in different places does not vary so widely. Fiscal equalization, combined with the reallocation of certain functions of government, such as the federalization of welfare, could substantially assist states and local governments in their ability to devise and carry out long-term economic development strategies.

In some urban areas, expanding public employment may be both a necessary and a desirable way to approach local economic development and labor market problems. Such jobs can help the urban poor and dislocated workers who do not find work with private employers. Even more important, however, public employment programs should be carefully designed primarily to provide basic urban services and facilities. This concentration on adequate good-quality services and facilities can increase the attractiveness of an area to private business, thereby aiding economic development. In addition, one proper function of public employment is to train workers so they can compete for nongovernment as well as better public jobs. Public employment can also be used to avoid the most serious consequences for dislocated workers who otherwise are likely to face extended unemployment and for others who have no other realistic way of entering the work force.

Fostering Local Institutions to Manage the Transition

Sustained public-private leadership at the local level is necessary for economic development and job creation. Considerable emphasis should be placed on establishing a strong capacity for research and information, so that an urban area can get a better understanding of its assets, its comparative advantages, its vulnerabilities, and the opportunities that are likely to be within reach. A national network of such intelligence systems could help provide a constant infusion of new ideas and reliable information. The federal government could contribute by improving the quality of its regional and urban statistical reporting and in continuing to support research on urban indicators and the urban development process.

The growth of public-private cooperation is a promising development. Several models for such cooperation are available. The cities classified as command and control centers appear to have advantages over other places in developing effective partnerships, because of the greater autonomy and resources of the corporate officers headquartered there and the greater sophistication of political leaders and public officials. Where local leadership potential is weak, state involvement may be necessary to mobilize public resources and to induce private business leaders to join in a common development effort. Particular attention should be given to nonprofit organizations as sources of seed capital for experimental, high-risk urban development and service programs, as catalysts for cooperation and program management, and as sources of support in developing and maintaining such urban institutions as libraries, theaters, museums, health facilities, and cultural centers.

RETHINKING URBAN POLICY

In light of these considerations, this report urges that a major effort be made to harmonize national interests and those of individual urban areas in economic development. This will involve introducing both sectoral and urban perspectives into national and local economic policy-making processes, which will require closer cooperation between governments at all levels and between the public and private sectors.

Urban policy need not be a zero-sum game, in which some cities are able to win only if others lose. Where there are serious disparities among the urban economies of the country, the winners will continue to pay for the losers. Just as local interests are advanced by a strong and growing national economy, the national interest is advanced by strong local economies.

2 The Economy and Cities

INTRODUCTION

Cities reflect the economy and express the culture of a nation. Urban areas create demands for technology and are in turn shaped by it. The mill towns of the Industrial Revolution were distinctive in form, dense and compact so workers could reach their jobs on foot or by horsedrawn public transportation. Business activity was centrally located to facilitate transactions. The city was limited by its technology for transportation, communications, building, and disposal of waste. The replacement of water power with coal and the development of railroads and public sanitary systems increased options for industrial location, expanded markets, and made feasible larger and more dispersed factories and urban settlements (Tarr, 1984).

Later, major innovations in industrial technology—electricity, petroleum, chemicals, and, ultimately, the automobile—were matched by new urban technologies—steel girder construction, the elevator, the electric streetcar, and the bus—and fostered further changes in the way cities were built and functioned (Eberhard, 1966). The rise of the business corporation, the industrial trust, national and regional financial institutions, private philanthropy, labor unions, free public education, and the municipal civil service represents the beginnings of the modern service sector. Initially, business services were often appended to local industrial parents; gradually they expanded to serve industrial empires, a region, or an industry.[1] As cities and the industrial economy matured, their economic, political, and physical relationships changed. New methods of production, distribution, and marketing as well as improved personal mobility and inexpensive suburban housing contributed to the dispersion of urban areas at the same time that metropolitan economic and social opportunities attracted waves of rural and foreign immigrants.

Now a new generation of computer, energy, communications, bioengineering, and other technologies, complemented by the internationalization of business institutions and markets and by substantial demographic shifts and cultural developments, is again transforming cities to meet the needs of an advanced economy.[2] The economically advanced nations are experiencing similar changes in their economies and in their cities, although there are significant differences among them based on each nation's stage of industrialization and urbanization. With the mechanization of agriculture early in this century, workers moved from farms to cities to work in factories and stores. In more recent years the important shifts in the United States, Canada, and Europe have been from the extractive and transformative sectors toward services (Renaud, 1982; Singelmann, 1978). This shift accelerated during the 1970s in the 24 countries belonging to the Organization for Economic Cooperation and Development (Renaud, 1982).

Projections of the labor force distribution in seven major industrial nations to the end of the century, shown in Table 1, suggest that this process of change is not over. Some industry analysts suggest that projections based on past trends do not adequately account for the discontinuities in technology, the organization of work, and the internationalization of capital and labor markets. They expect that soon after the turn of the century, manufacturing employment in leading industrial nations will decline almost to the levels that agricultural employment in the United States reached by 1950—less than 10 percent of the labor force (Drucker, 1981:237).

In a general sense the same technological, institutional, and demographic forces that have contributed to the restructuring of the national

---

[1] Several major financial institutions, such as the Morgan Guaranty Trust, the Chase Manhattan Bank, and the Mellon Bank, were started as means of providing banking and holding company services for the industrial organizations of their founders (Collins and Horowitz, 1976; Nevins, 1976; Sinclair, 1981; Trescott, 1982).

[2] Throughout this report, we have used the term *advanced economy* rather than *postindustrial economy* (Bell, 1973) because the evidence indicates that manufacturing will continue to play a major role in the future economy but in a different way and in different places than in the past (Knight, 1977, 1982b). A more accurate, although also more cumbersome characterization would be an advanced industrial-service economy.

TABLE 1   Labor Force Distribution, by Industry Sectors for Seven
Industrialized Countries, 1970 and Projected to 2000

Industry Sectors	United States and Canada		England and West Germany		France and Italy		Japan	
	1970	2000	1970	2000	1970	2000	1970	2000
Extractive	7	5	5	4	19	10	20	5
Transformative[a]	32	28	47	40	41	35	34	40
Distributive services	23	20	17	16	15	15	23	20
Producer services	8	12	5	10	4	10	5	10
Social services	21	30	18	25	15	25	10	20
Personal services	9	6	8	5	7	5	8	5

NOTE: Percentages may not add to 100 because of rounding. For a description of industry sectors, see Chapter 2, footnote 5.

[a]Includes most manufacturing industries.

SOURCE: Adapted from Singelmann (1978:Table 3.1).

economies of advanced nations have also led to changes in the location of economic activities and therefore to substantial alterations in the size and density of urban areas. Contrasting the current situation with the earlier period of industrialization and urban concentration, one observer of urban development has concluded that ''there now appear to be negative returns to urban scale: larger urban areas are either increasing much more slowly than smaller ones or are actually declining'' (Hall, 1981:1). This observation should be tempered by the fact that the advantage of scale depends on the kind of activity located in an urban area. The populations of many of the largest metropolitan areas are still increasing, although at a much slower rate. Even though individual areas are growing more slowly or even contracting, the proportion of the total population living in all metropolitan areas, and even in ones of a million people or more, continues to remain nearly constant due to the graduation of slightly smaller areas into larger population-size classes (Thompson, 1980:31-33).

Advantages from the agglomeration of similar economic activities that formerly were important functions are no longer as significant for certain kinds of manufacturing and other activities, such as routine office functions (Sternlieb and Hughes, 1975). Increasingly, such functions can be located in the suburbs, in smaller nonmetropolitan areas, or even in other countries. That these activities can be dispersed in order to take advantage of lower land costs, lower labor costs, less labor-intensive production processes, and better market access has also accelerated the decentralization of other sectors of the economy, such as retail and distribution centers. None of these trends is absolute. They are matters of degree and are affected by types of industries, relative wage levels, transportation systems, changes in styles of living, and many other factors.

Concentration Amidst Decentralization

Although urban settlements are generally becoming more decentralized, it is a mistake to assume that all economic activities benefit from decentralization. Some appear to continue to benefit from a high degree of concentration and from location in the largest urban areas. Thus, at the same time that manufacturing, retailing, back office operations, and distribution centers are decentralizing, the headquarters functions of the economy are becoming more highly concentrated in a relatively small number of urban areas, albeit not always in traditional central business districts. Ironically, the internationalization of business has contributed to increased agglomeration of world and national corporate headquarters and the services on which they depend (Cohen, 1979b). The development of corporate strategy requires a concentration of highly specialized services in banking, law, accounting, advertising, and economic analysis. Urban areas in which both corporate headquarters and such advanced service firms are concentrated have become "more than just centers for a widely dispersed network of production operations. They have become . . . centers of corporate planning and strategy formulation for large corporations" (Cohen, 1979b:451; see also Conservation of Human Resources, 1977). As this new concentration of headquarters and strategic services has evolved, some of the places that once contained nationally significant concentrations of specific industries have diminished in importance, and others, such as Los Angeles and Houston, with a major base of such services, are emerging as important international centers (Cohen, 1979a:467).

Demography and Urban Change

Several important changes in national demography complement and reinforce the impact of changes in the economic structure of urban areas. The slowing of population growth and the consequent aging of the population, the increase in women's participation in the labor force, smaller households due to declining birth rates, delayed marriages, the increased number of divorces, and greater longevity have affected cities in several ways. The population density of the older urbanized areas has declined in both central cities and close-in suburbs.

There has been an apparent movement in recent years to nonmetropolitan areas. Again, this process is not unique to the United States. It is closely associated with the changes in the economic system, such as improvements in transportation and communication, the technological and space requirements of industry, and the growth of services that are not bound to central locations (Long, 1981). This current trend in deconcentration of urban areas and of the population nationally is different in character from prior great migrations, such as the rural-metropolitan migration of the midtwentieth century in which people changed their basic style of living as well as their places of residence. In many respects the current dispersion is a continuation of the urbanization of the population, rather than a return to rural or small-town life as such. It should be viewed as an organizational adaptation to changes in technology, the economy, and social organization (Long, 1981:35, 99).

One important difference in current and past demographic trends is the slight overall decline in intermetropolitan mobility for all age groups (Bureau of the Census, 1982).[3] This decline has occurred even though there has been considerable deconcentration in the population at the same time. While mobility for all age groups has declined, younger and more educated people continue to be the most mobile (Bureau of the Census, 1982). Because the population is aging, the generations that will replace the postwar baby boom generation are smaller, different regions and urban areas have substantially different age profiles and fertility ratios, and significant differences are developing among the labor forces of urban areas and regions of the country (Berry, 1981; Jackson et al., 1981).

Another demographic factor that reinforces the economic forces restructuring the economy is increased levels of education. Higher educational attainment accelerates the capital intensification of work by increasing pressure for higher wages and for ''more interesting'' work by a larger proportion of the labor force (Drucker, 1981).

While these trends indicate the general tendency of population changes, it is important to remember that the averages do not tell the entire story. Although the population in general has been dispersing and cities are becoming less dense, the concentration of the poor, minorities, and immigrants in central cities has been increasing (Bureau of the Census, 1978, 1981; Greenwood, 1980), reflecting the greater ability of more prosperous

---

[3] Mobility within metropolitan areas, however, apparently increased between 1975 and 1980. An analysis of *Current Population Survey* data on interhouse moves from 1970 to 1975 and 1976 to 1980 shows an increase of 1 percent for all age groups. There is also a considerable difference in mobility among different regions of the country (*New York Times*, March 2, 1983).

people, including minorities, to move from central areas, leaving the poor behind. It also appears to be related to the loss of jobs in manufacturing and their replacement, if at all, with some service jobs that require higher levels of skill (U.S. Department of Housing and Urban Development, 1982) and other service jobs that employ different workers, such as women instead of black men. The result has been a simultaneous increase in rates of unemployment, nonparticipation in the labor force, and welfare dependency for central city minorities (Kasarda, 1982), raising concerns about the development of an urban underclass that lives outside the mainstream of economic life (National Research Council, 1982a).

There are also other selective countervailing trends to the general deconcentration of the population. Particularly in those cities in which headquarters functions are concentrating, a growing number of single-person and other small households with few children have been attracted back to the central city, producing gentrification in close-in, architecturally interesting neighborhoods that have good access to transit and work, good-quality housing, and a varied physical and social environment (Berry, 1982).

This brief look at what has happened shows that cities have already made many adjustments to shifts in economic structure and demography. To understand the full significance of the adjustments and of the capacity of cities to make them successfully, we need to examine more closely two fundamental structural changes that are likely to continue well into the next century. The first is the shift in the principal source of employment from the extractive and transformative industries to service industries. The second is the shift from blue-collar to white-collar jobs in almost all sectors of the economy.

THE SHIFT TOWARD SERVICES

Understanding how these prospects affect cities requires a closer examination of the services themselves. While more and more people will be employed in services, the future of all services and of employment in them is not the same. The differences among the services have important implications for urban areas and urban policy.

Classifying Service Industries

Detailed study of the service sector is relatively recent. It is impeded somewhat by the way in which statistical information about industries and occupations is classified and reported. One of the most serious gaps in knowledge has been the lack of a satisfactory system for the classification of service industries.[4] Two reasonably comparable systems have been developed in recent years.[5] The list on page 18 indicates how the standard industrial classification (SIC) codes have been reorganized in the most recent of these systems, which is used in this report.

Distinguishing among the different types of services is valuable to the development of urban policy for several reasons. Close examination of the characteristics of each class of industries can lead to clues about the

---

[4] Various attempts have been made to classify industries into a manageable number of broad categories in order to trace changes in the distribution of employment and income over time. One of the most widely used industrial classification systems was devised by A. G. B. Fisher (1935) and Colin Clark (1940). Their model distributed industries among three sectors: (1) primary industries—agriculture, forestry, fishing, mining; (2) secondary industries—manufacturing, construction, utilities; and (3) tertiary industries—commerce, transportation, communications, services. The Fisher-Clark model has limited usefulness in studying trends in service industries because it lumps all services together in the tertiary category. The industries in this category, however, are quite heterogeneous, differing as to size, capital requirements, output, productivity, and location in cities and regions.

Despite the model's shortcomings, most empirical studies of the labor force have continued to use the three-sector scheme with only minor variations, such as the separation of transportation and communications from other services. Where more detailed information is needed, it is usually restricted to the 10 groups of the standard industrial classification (SIC) developed by the U.S. Department of Commerce, Bureau of Economic Analysis: (1) agriculture, forestry, fishing; (2) mining; (3) construction; (4) manufacturing; (5) transportation, communications, public utilities; (6) wholesale trade; (7) retail trade; (8) finance, insurance, real estate; (9) services; and (10) government. While this classification system is an improvement, the services class remains heterogeneous.

[5] The first of the new systems, developed by Browning and Singelmann (1975), uses the traditional classification for the first two sectors, which they call extractive and transformative industries. They divide services into four classes: (1) distributive services—transportation, communications, wholesale and retail trade (except eating and drinking places); (2) producer services—finance, insurance, real estate, professional and business services; (3) social services—health, education, welfare, government; and (4) personal services—domestic, lodging, repair, entertainment. Distributive services reflect the next stage (after extraction and transformation) in the development of goods as they move "from the most undifferentiated primary form to their distribution to the ultimate consumer" (Singelmann, 1978:30). While the other sectors do not follow this sequential flow, they do comprise distinctive groups of industries.

Producer services mainly include industries that provide services to producers of goods or that are concerned with property matters. Like distributive services, the industries in this category provide intermediate services between the extractive and transformative industries or between them and other sectors. Social services include public, private, and nonprofit "collective" goods or services, while personal services are characterized by their orientation to the individual consumer.

Stanback et al. (1981) have slightly modified Browning and Singelmann's scheme. They divided the nonservices into two categories: agriculture and extractive and transformative industries. Their six classes of services are (1) distributive services—transportation, communications, wholesale trade; (2) retail services, which are separate because they have different locational characteristics from the other industries in the distributive services; (3) producer ser-

Sectors	SIC Codes
Nonservices	
Agriculture	01, 01, 07-09
Extractive and transformative	
Mining	10-14
Construction	15-17
Manufacturing	20-39
Services	
Distributive services	
Transportation, communications,	
utilities (TCU)	40-49
Wholesale services	50-51
Producer services (including headquarters)	
Central administrative office	From each of the 10 basic SIC codes
Finance, insurance, and real estate (FIRE)	60-67
Business services	73
Legal services	81
Membership organizations	86
Miscellaneous professional services	89
Social services	83
Nonprofit services	
Health	80
Education	82
Retail services	52-59
Consumer services	
Hotels and other lodging places	70
Personal services	72
Auto repair, services, and garages	75
Miscellaneous repair services	76
Motion pictures, amusements, and recreation	
services	79, 84
Private households	88
Government and government enterprises	91-97

SOURCE: Adapted from Noyelle and Stanback (1983).

kinds of places in which they are most likely to locate. Understanding the differences in their growth rates and occupational composition is also important in formulating economic development strategies, in forecasting the performance of local economies, and in identifying opportunities or problems for the growth of particular industries or sectors.

By using this system of classification, the structural changes that have already occurred and can be expected to continue to take place can be

---

vices (virtually the same as Browning and Singelmann); (4) nonprofit services, established as a separate category from government-provided social services because it allows a closer look at a variety of activities, particularly health services; (5) government and government enterprises, which contains the remainder of Browning and Singelmann's category of social services; and (6) mainly consumer services, a category that corresponds to the personal services class of Browning and Singelmann. For a full discussion of the system and the reasoning behind it, see Noyelle and Stanback (1983:Ch. I).

more readily understood. Figure 1 illustrates what has happened since 1948 to the share of total national employment in each sector of the economy. What is immediately clear, beyond the common generalization of the continuing shift away from extractive and transformative industries, is that there are substantial differences in the performance of the different service sectors. The shares of jobs in some sectors, such as distributive and retail services, are stable or declining. Consumer services, which are often assumed to have grown rapidly in response to the increased affluence of American consumers, have not in fact done so, although some growth is projected for this sector in the 1980s (Personick, 1981).

Nonprofit and Government Services

The growth of nonprofit services reflects the rapid expansion of education services in the 1950s and 1960s. That trend slowed in the 1970s, and an increase in the rate of growth for medical services occurred. Education and health services are particularly susceptible to demographic trends, which in the current period tend to be mutually offsetting. A decline in the numbers of school-age children tends to reduce growth in education. Health services, however, can be expected to grow in the United States because of an aging and more health conscious population. Even faster growth should occur in other parts of the world as both advanced and developing countries develop or modernize their health systems (Ginzberg and Vojta, 1981:51).

The share of employment in government services dropped in the last decade. When they are combined with nonprofit services, one can see a slowing of the rate of growth for services aimed at collective consumption. It is debatable whether the decline in government services is the beginning of a long-term trend. To the extent that it reflects a reduction in the numbers of education employees due to smaller public school enrollments, the trend probably is long term. Some jobs could also shift from government to private sectors as a result of the "privatization" of some public services. Government involvement in an increasing range of complex problems, however, suggests that some growth in this sector remains a possibility, especially if the private sector cannot maintain full employment in an advanced economy.

As the economy of the nation and its urban areas has been restructured, the significance of government has increased, especially as a regulator of the economy, even though government plays a smaller role in the total gross national product (GNP) than it did in 1950 (Ginzberg and Vojta, 1981), and there has been no increase in employment. Most of the growth of government employment in recent decades has been due to the expan-

20

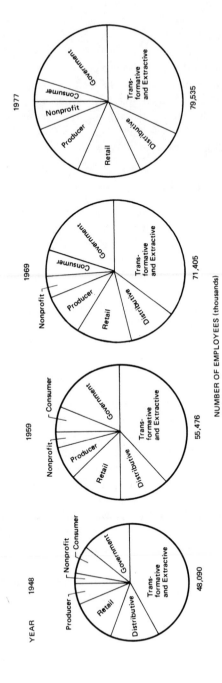

FIGURE 1 Percentage distribution of full-time-equivalent employees among industries, 1948-1977. SOURCE: Adapted from Stanback et al. (1981).

sion of state and local governments, not the federal government. Throughout the economy, and particularly in the urban economy, government is not only an employer but also the provider of a wide range of services on which other sectors depend (Knight, 1980). Education and health services are particularly dependent on government financial assistance. If we view the urban economy in a slightly different way, government and other nonprofit services are an important part of the local sector—those parts of the economy that serve local residents and businesses as contrasted with the traditional export sectors that send their goods and services elsewhere and bring money from other markets into the local economy. Like many producer services, nonprofit and government services produce income and provide amenities that are essential to the health of the export sectors (*Business Week*, 1981a; Ginzberg and Vojta, 1981). Where government is the principal activity, as in the case of Washington, D.C., and a number of state capitals, it acts as the export industry. Taxpayers in the rest of the state or nation "buy" its services. Government expenditure levels act as a multiplier in the economy, creating markets for other services, construction, and some manufactured goods.

The Growth of Producer Services

The most important finding from this examination of the changing structure of the economy is that producer services play a major role in the expansion of the service economy. Producer services include those industries that provide intermediate services to firms producing goods or other services. Such services include the planning, management, financing, marketing, legal, and accounting services that are essential to large-scale business enterprise and to government. An important development in the expansion of producer services is the growth of international markets for services that once relied primarily on domestic demand. International demand for banking, insurance, and telecommunications is expected to outpace domestic demand in the next decade. Producer services' share of the labor force has grown by over 50 percent since 1959. The share has grown faster in the last decade than that of any other sector and by 1990 will account for 38 percent of the net increase in the share of total employment by all services (Personick, 1981; Stanback et al., 1981). The nonprofit sector has been responsible for a larger share of the shift, but while the rate of nonprofit growth is projected to almost stabilize, the producer services sector is the only one projected for more than a 10 percent increase in the current share of employment by 1990 (Personick, 1981). There is some evidence to suggest that producer services are already growing at a faster rate than shown in these projections (Stanback et al., 1981).

In many respects, producer services have become an important part of the export base of the nation and the cities in which they are located. In 1980, for instance, a $30 billion commodities trade deficit for the United States was offset by a $35 billion trade surplus in services. When the clearly classifiable producer services are added to similar activities carried on within the extractive and transformative industries but not reflected in the data reported by industrial classification, it is apparent that a major change is needed in how we think about urban economies. Headquarters and producer services, together with nonprofit and government services, have begun to replace manufacturing as the economic base of many urban areas. These services generate wealth by exporting knowledge and services to regional and international markets. They also have a multiplier effect on the rest of the local economy.

The magnitude of growth in these producer, or "advanced," services in some cities has been substantial. Figure 2 illustrates this by showing the change in the structure of the Cleveland economy over a 22-year period, where most of the growth in the net number of new jobs can be attributed to the growth of these important intermediate services. In the figure, advanced services are roughly equivalent to producer services. The figure also indicates a considerable replacement in transformative industries of production jobs—those directly involved with the making of goods—with nonproduction jobs in corporate management, marketing, and research. Many of these jobs are similar to those classified as producer services (Knight, 1980; Stanback and Drennan, 1978).

Consumer Services

When a closer look is taken at consumer services, some similar trends appear. The consumer services that have grown steadily are those most susceptible to large-scale centralized management but decentralized delivery of a standard service, such as hotels, food franchises, and travel services. With consolidation of control in such industries has come geographic specialization of supporting services. The headquarters, accounting, and warehousing functions are rarely located with the consumer outlets (Stanback et al., 1981).

BLUE-COLLAR CITIES, WHITE-COLLAR JOBS

The second major structural shift, from blue-collar to white-collar occupations (see Table 2) is also more complex than meets the eye. Services

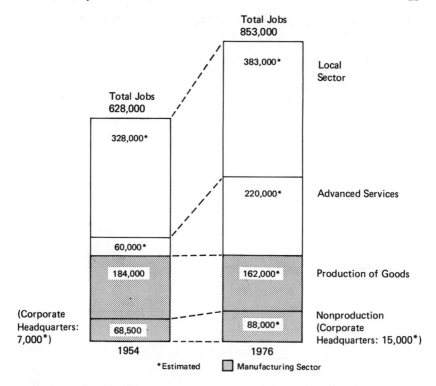

FIGURE 2 The transition in Cleveland, 1954-1976. SOURCE: Adapted from Knight (1977).

employ a larger percentage of white-collar workers and service workers than the nonservice sectors, but it would be a mistake to assume that every white-collar or other service job requires a high degree of knowledge. Many are routine, repetitive, and require primarily manual skills. There are also important differences in the occupational profiles of the different services. Some have high ratios of managerial, professional, and technical occupations, while others employ predominantly low-skilled workers (Stanback and Noyelle, 1982:29-51). Another factor that affects the occupational profile of an industry and of the economy as a whole is the impact of technology. One of the causes for the decline in the proportion of blue-collar jobs is the substitution of capital for labor, first in agriculture, mining, and manufacturing, and more recently in services. The introduction of computers, industrial robots, and other automated equipment into both manufacturing and service industries may not reduce the number of jobs in the aggregate (it may even increase the total number available in

TABLE 2   Percentage Distribution of Employed Population, by
Occupational Group, 1960, 1976, and 1982

Occupational Group	1960	1976	1982
White-collar workers	43.1	50.1	53.7
Professional and technical workers	11.9	15.2	17.0
Managers and administrators	8.6	10.6	11.5
Sales workers	7.6	6.5	6.6
Clerical workers	15.0	17.8	18.5
Blue-collar workers	38.5	32.4	29.7
Craft and kindred workers	14.1	12.6	12.3
Operatives	19.3	15.2	12.9
Nonfarm laborers	5.1	4.6	4.5
Service workers	11.6	14.4	13.8
Private household workers	2.8	1.8	1.0
Other service workers	8.8	12.6	12.8
Farm workers	6.7	3.2	2.8
Farmers	4.2	1.7	1.5
Farm laborers	2.5	1.5	1.3

NOTE: Distributions may not add to 100 percent because of rounding.

SOURCE: Bureau of Labor Statistics (1983), Rumberger (1981).

the whole economy), but it does change, often radically, who fills those
jobs and where they are located. Traditional blue-collar jobs in the nonservice industries are replaced by servicelike functions—management,
research, advertising, etc. (Stanback and Noyelle, 1982). This helps produce the anomaly in many metropolitan areas of a surplus of production
workers and a shortage of technical and professional workers, such as
computer programmers, engineers, and chemists (Doolittle, 1982).

Increasing the Proportion of "Knowledge" Jobs

Table 3 shows the distribution of occupations for manufacturing, construction, and various categories of service industries in 1980. Great differences exist in the occupational profiles of each sector. What is significant
is that services employ more "knowledge" workers—that is, workers
whose jobs require a high degree of skills and training—than nonservices,
and those services that are growing the fastest (producer services, nonprofit
services), as well as government services, tend to have the highest proportions of professional, technical, and managerial occupations. While
these sectors have traditionally had a large clerical component, three factors should be kept in mind: clerical jobs generally pay less than crafts or
operative jobs, they are heavily dominated by women, and they are not

TABLE 3 Percentage Distribution of Employment Among Occupations for Each Industry and for the United States, 1975

Sector	Professionals	Technicians	Managers	Office Clericals	Nonoffice Clericals	Sales Workers	Craftsmen	Operatives	Service Workers	Laborers
Nonservices										
Construction	2.5	1.5	14.0	3.9	1.7	0.3	53.9	7.0	0.3	14.9
Manufacturing	5.4	5.2	11.5	6.2	5.1	2.8	14.9	42.2	1.9	5.0
Services										
Distributive services	3.3	3.5	17.0	9.7	11.6	9.5	15.2	21.3	2.0	7.0
Transportation, communications, and utilities	3.8	5.0	12.4	7.0	14.3	0.6	20.5	26.3	2.8	7.4
Wholesale services	2.5	1.3	23.6	13.5	7.7	22.4	7.5	14.2	1.0	6.3
Retail services	1.1	0.9	18.6	4.8	11.6	18.0	8.0	6.7	24.8	5.4
Producer services	13.5	9.0	17.3	21.3	12.8	11.7	2.6	2.2	8.2	1.5
Finance, insurance, and real estate	5.2	5.6	21.6	22.7	16.9	18.8	1.9	0.4	5.4	1.5
Corporate services	24.6	13.5	11.6	19.4	7.3	2.2	3.4	4.7	11.9	1.4
Consumer services	0.5	7.2	7.4	3.0	4.2	0.9	13.8	11.7	44.0	7.3
Nonprofit services	36.0	12.9	4.0	11.6	6.3	0.2	2.0	1.1	24.8	1.0
Health	12.9	24.2	4.4	12.8	3.9	0.1	2.2	1.7	37.1	0.7
Education	51.0	5.7	3.7	10.8	7.9	0.2	1.9	0.8	16.9	1.2
Government	10.2	25.1	12.0	15.2	18.3	0.1	7.2	2.0	6.5	3.7
Total U.S.	10.3	6.9	13.6	8.7	8.2	6.0	11.7	15.0	13.3	6.4

NOTE: Each row sums to 100 percent.

SOURCE: Bureau of the Census (1976).

growing as rapidly *in these industries* as technical jobs requiring higher skills or training. In addition, changes in office technology could substantially change the demand for clerical workers in all sectors. The large number of service workers in the nonprofit sector reflects subprofessional jobs, which for the most part are not on career ladders that allow promotion into professional ranks (Stanback et al., 1981:66-88).

There is some evidence that a substantial amount of "de-skilling" is taking place through division of some of the most complicated jobs in the economy into components that require less skill or training (Rumberger, 1981). Thus, some managerial and professional jobs have been divided into a number of technical or subprofessional positions. Between 1970 and 1976 this de-skilling resulted in a decline in the percentage of the most highly skilled jobs (Rumberger, 1981:585).

These major transformations of work pervade both the service and nonservice sectors. As we have indicated, many of the services are being restructured through new corporate forms (e.g., nationwide banking, national food service corporations), the replacement of labor with capital (e.g., computerization of offices), increased knowledge requirements for some occupations, and the segmentation of labor markets.

Technology and the Future of Work

On one hand, technology plays an important part in simplifying many tasks, thereby reducing the level of skill that workers need to perform them (Braverman, 1974). On the other hand, technological advancement creates demands for more sophisticated tasks and very high-level workers to perform them; new technology challenges us to use it.

Because the interaction of technology and jobs is so complex, there is as yet no conclusive evidence of the effect of technological changes on the number and distribution of occupations in many service industries. There is considerable debate about whether new technology will create or eliminate jobs and the kinds of jobs that will be affected (Levitan and Johnson, 1982; Schwartz, in press). In part this debate occurs because growth rates in various occupations are difficult to trace to specific technological or market causes. Part of the problem stems from inadequacies in our system for classifying jobs and occupations. In some industries, what may appear to be a shift toward higher- or lower-status jobs may only reflect the stage that industry has reached in its development. A new industry may currently be very knowledge-intensive. Once it has developed, however, some of its jobs will be simplified. This has already occurred in such industries as computer chips as they have moved from product or service development to mass production. At the same time, however, the ratio of nonproduction to production workers is increasing in almost all goods-producing industries. And there are some disturbing signs that technology could indeed eliminate many kinds of service jobs that have previously been taken for granted, particularly in clerical occupations (Schwartz, in press).

Segmentation of the Labor Market

As employment shifts to services, the structure and behavior of the labor market of the service industries become increasingly important. Not only do services employ fewer craftsmen and operatives than manufacturing industries, but also lower-level jobs in services tend to pay less and be less sheltered (for example, they lack retirement plans and union contracts) than lower-level jobs in manufacturing (Stanback and Noyelle, 1982). A much higher proportion of them are part-time jobs, as shown in Table 4, and a very large proportion are filled by women. As one moves toward the bottom of the occupational hierarchy, service jobs are increasingly filled by black women (Treiman and Hartmann, 1981). Nonwhites generally have had more success in finding employment in certain services (for example, food service, education, public administration), but even in these industries they are not well represented in the higher-level occupations. A particular problem for those concerned with the implications for urban areas is presented by the fact that while black female participation in the labor force has been increasing, the participation rate of black men has been declining and will probably continue to decline slightly unless the economy enjoys a period of extremely high growth (Fullerton, 1980).

Table 5 projects growth in each occupational class from 1978 to 1990. While the overall profile of occupations is projected to remain fairly stable during the decade, the greatest rates of growth are expected in professional, technical, and related occupations and in service workers. Operatives and laborers, the traditional entry points to the labor market, show the least growth. These trends, particularly when read together with the occupational structure of the services that seem most likely to experience high future growth rates, suggest that a dual labor market could be emerging, "with a growing separation between relatively good jobs and relatively bad jobs" (Stanback et al., 1981:50).[6]

---

[6] For further discussion of this problem, see Beck et al. (1978), Berger and Piore (1980), and Bluestone (1970). For an extensive discussion of the debate among labor economists about the existence of a dual labor market, see Cain (1976).

TABLE 4   Percentage Distribution of Less-Than-Full-Time, Full-Year Employment Share in Each Industry Occupational Subgroup in the United States, 1975

Sector	Profes-sionals	Techni-cians	Mana-gers	Office Clericals	Nonoffice Clericals	Sales Workers	Crafts-men	Opera-tives	Service Workers	Laborers	All Occu-pations
Nonservices	13.1	16.4	17.0	30.8	26.8	54.2	41.4	42.7	39.8	61.8	37.1
Construction	7.4	14.8	24.4	47.3	21.6	33.9	57.9	59.3	75.7	71.0	52.3
Manufacturing	13.1	15.0	10.4	27.0	27.4	54.6	26.1	42.0	37.3	46.4	31.9
Services	38.3	36.2	17.6	40.9	48.0	47.7	25.6	46.4	66.3	63.5	43.5
Distributive services	12.4	25.5	11.4	35.0	26.2	17.8	14.8	39.3	55.8	45.2	26.3
Transportation, communications, and utilities	11.6	27.3	11.2	25.7	22.3	23.1	13.0	39.2	50.2	42.9	25.9
Wholesale services	14.2	15.2	11.5	42.0	36.4	17.6	21.7	39.6	78.8	49.3	26.8
Retail services	27.0	50.4	21.3	47.1	66.7	62.3	31.0	56.9	74.6	70.4	54.6
Producer services	20.6	29.2	15.6	40.3	38.7	30.5	32.4	53.2	55.4	70.2	32.8
Finance, insurance, and real estate	17.4	15.4	15.2	35.2	31.2	30.1	32.3	38.5	45.0	73.1	28.3
Corporate services	21.5	36.8	16.4	48.3	61.6	35.7	32.5	54.8	61.6	66.0	38.8
Consumer services	41.3	72.1	23.1	59.5	68.8	74.6	35.3	53.9	76.9	87.8	63.9
Nonprofit services	47.2	47.5	23.3	45.9	66.2	45.2	27.5	40.5	55.4	59.4	48.4
Health	27.7	41.6	15.4	40.7	39.0	55.8	15.5	32.5	45.3	38.6	39.0
Education	48.4	63.6	29.4	49.8	74.9	42.2	36.8	51.2	69.7	67.5	54.4
Government	15.8	12.0	11.1	27.0	21.7	42.4	22.1	24.7	48.3	41.3	20.7
Total U.S.	34.7	32.2	17.4	38.9	44.6	48.4	34.9	43.9	65.3	62.5	41.4

SOURCE: Bureau of the Census (1976).

TABLE 5 Percentage Distribution of Civilian Employment in Occupations With 25,000 or More Workers

Occupation	Actual 1978	Projected 1990	Change 1978–1990
Professional, technical,	16.0	16.7	30.3
and related	(15,570)	(20,295)	
Managers, officials,	9.0	8.8	21.3
and proprietors	(8,802)	(10,677)	
Sales workers	6.6	6.7	25.4
	(6,443)	(8,079)	
Clerical workers	18.3	18.6	26.37
	(17,820)	(22,519)	
Crafts and related workers	12.0	12.1	25.6
	(11,679)	(14,668)	
Operatives	14.6	13.7	16.8
	(14,205)	(16,584)	
Service workers	14.8	15.8	33.3
	(14,414)	(19,220)	
Laborers	6.0	5.8	19.9
	(5,902)	(7,078)	
Farmers and farm workers	2.8	2.0	− 16.3
	(2,775)	(2,327)	
Total, all occupations	100.0	100.0	24.4
	(97,610)	(121,297)	

NOTE: Numbers in parentheses represent thousands of workers. Percentages may not add to 100 because of rounding.

SOURCE: Carey (1981).

This problem can be illustrated by the medical and health occupations, which have been among the fastest growing services and are expected to continue to expand rapidly during the next decade (Carey, 1981; Sekcenski, 1981). There is a clear separation of the market levels of pay and degree of shelter between credentialed professionals (doctors, nurses, technicians) and paraprofessionals (nurses' aides, practical nurses) and service workers (orderlies, food and laundry workers).[7] This structure offers little chance for mobility between occupational categories and very short career ladders within each occupational group. That may not differ markedly from the situation in manufacturing in which few shop workers ever

[7] During the last decade, the proportion of professional and technical workers in the health industries increased. Clerical workers also increased, but the proportion of service workers declined. Women make up 75 percent of all workers in health services, but throughout the industry they earned less than men in equivalent occupations. About 20 percent of all health employees work part time (Sekcenski, 1981).

become executives. The difference is that shop jobs are paid well and have fringe benefits, security, and protection from unfettered managerial discretion. By contrast, many health service jobs have low pay, few fringe benefits, and little security.

It could be argued that health services have traditionally had a highly segmented employment pattern and are not typical of the occupational structure of the services. There is at least tentative evidence from early research on banks and department stores in New York City that these industries, which traditionally offered long career ladders that progressed from sales or teller positions into the management hierarchy, are increasingly developing two separate career tracks. Entry into the management track depends on college or higher-level professional education prior to entry. Sales and clerical positions are viewed as being on a separate track, with little opportunity to move into a management position unless one enters these positions as a college trainee.[8] Thus increased college attendance by minorities has been important in offsetting the tendency toward a dual labor market.

In contrast to manufacturing and construction jobs, which in the past provided entry into the labor market for a large proportion of workers, entry-level jobs in the services today tend to be poorly paid and poorly sheltered and to offer less opportunity for future income and occupational progress. These jobs are often part time and are more likely to employ minority women than minority men (Stanback and Noyelle, 1982).

Intermediate-level jobs are not necessarily drying up; they are, however, changing. Access to them from lower occupations is not as common as it was in the past in the manufacturing industries or in many of the traditional service industries, such as retailing, distribution, and banking.[9] The one sector in which career ladders have been long and open is government. Public employment traditionally has been important in the occupational mobility of minorities. For the short term, however, the reduction in the growth rate of public sector jobs may reduce the access of minorities to middle- and higher-level occupations (Harrison, 1972; Jones, 1979).

---

[8] Progress report on research, presented by Thomas M. Stanback, Jr., at the meeting of the Committee on National Urban Policy, Woods Hole, Massachusetts, July 25, 1982. Also see Bluestone (1981).

[9] In some cases, this results in the imposition of higher skill or knowledge requirements than some jobs actually require, because of the rising educational levels of much of the population (Berg, 1971).

Summary

The complex shift from blue-collar to white-collar occupations reflects not only the shift of employment from manufacturing to services but also important changes in the nature of the work being done in all industries. An increasing proportion of the jobs in manufacturing requires education and training acquired before entry or acquired off the job. There are fewer jobs for low-skilled manual laborers. At the same time that the average level of knowledge required for employment is increasing, some jobs are being broken into components that demand less skill or are being routinized, while the knowledge requirements for other jobs are increasing. In many of the services there also appears to be a tendency for the labor market to divide between occupations that require higher education or special training and those that do not. The higher-level occupations offer better incomes and opportunities for advancement and are sheltered in other ways. The lower-level occupations tend to be part time, less sheltered than either the high-level service jobs or traditional manufacturing jobs, and filled by women.

These changes in the structure of employment produce problems, both of entry into the labor market and in career advancement for those who are poorly trained or educated. In light of our history of racial, ethnic, and gender-based discrimination, they pose special problems for the employment of minority men and for the equality of women in the labor force. The number of intermediate-level jobs is not necessarily declining, but the requirements for access to those jobs are different in an advanced economy than they were in an earlier time. An economy based heavily on services seems less likely to offer unskilled workers the same expectations of rising incomes and benefits that were once common in growing manufacturing industries. Thus there is some possibility that an advanced economy could produce sharper class distinctions than have existed in the post-World War II period.

THE CONTINUING IMPORTANCE OF MANUFACTURING

In discussing fundamental structural shifts toward services and white-collar employment it is important to keep in mind that while the transformative and extractive industries will employ a relatively smaller proportion of the work force, their contribution to the gross national product will not necessarily decline correspondingly. As Figure 3 shows, the share of GNP of the nonservice sectors has fallen over the last 30 years but at a much slower rate than their share of employment. The Bureau of Economic Analysis long-range projections even show a gain in the nonser-

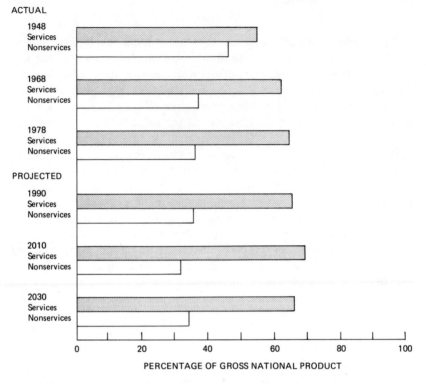

FIGURE 3   Shares of the gross national product for services and nonservices, 1948-1978 and 1990-2030. SOURCE: For 1948 and 1968, Ginzberg and Vojta (1981); for 1978 and projections, Bureau of Economic Analysis (1981).

vices' share of the economy in 2030. This implies that the earnings per worker in manufacturing will rise faster than average; thus, those people and places that can survive in the contracting manufacturing sector will be well rewarded. Also, while the proportion of the labor force employed in manufacturing can be expected to decline, the absolute number of jobs in manufacturing industries may increase slightly (Bureau of Economic Analysis, 1982; Personick, 1981:38-39).[10]

---

[10] Even the low-growth scenario of the Bureau of Labor Statistics projects actual growth in all major sectors except private household employment (Personick, 1981:38). We caution again, however, about reliance on projections. There is need for closer study of changes in the workplace and of the behavior of firms and employees as new technology is introduced.

Several things are important in interpreting this information. First, the new jobs are not likely to be of the same kind as in the past. Second, within each industry there will continue to be replacement of blue-collar, manual-labor jobs with white-collar and other jobs requiring a greater knowledge. Over 35 percent of all employees in nonservice industries already are in nonproduction occupations. Third, the slow growth in manufacturing jobs also reflects displacement of labor with robots and other machines. Thus, a smaller proportion of the work force will be engaged in actually making things, and a greater proportion will be managing, planning, selling, and inventing the things that are produced. Fourth, those aspects of manufacturing that remain labor-intensive will increasingly be performed by workers in other countries (Drucker, 1981).[11] While the trend toward overseas production of labor-intensive goods may be retarded by stringent legislation restricting imports, it is unlikely to be fully prevented.

Clearly the demand for labor is changing in both national and urban markets. Almost all urban areas have some jobs that the local labor force cannot fill and some workers who cannot find jobs that can use their skills (Cetron and O'Toole, 1972). Because of the historic concentration of specialized industrial production in particular urban areas, the restructuring of manufacturing produces local labor surpluses, whether the direct cause is technological change within an industry or product substitution in the marketplace, as in the replacement of steel with aluminum and plastics in construction and manufactured goods. Other areas of the country that house a higher proportion of new or expanding industries may experience a temporary labor shortage (Ballard and Clark, 1981; U.S. Department of Housing and Urban Development, 1980). This analysis assumes that the shift from manufacturing to services will continue at a moderate rate, in national terms. If imports of manufactured goods increased sharply, however, the decline in U.S. manufacturing employment could be massive and could strip many areas of their sources of export types of jobs. New jobs and skills could not be substituted fast enough to prevent the stagnation and even significant contraction of some areas. The widespread alarms of economic collapse, however, rarely are realized. "Doomed" Altoona, Pennsylvania, for example, still exists. Moreover, in 1980 it still had 97 percent of its 1940 population.

[11] For an illustration of this process, see "U.S. Auto Makers Using More Mexico Plants," *New York Times*, July 7, 1982, p. 1.

REGIONAL GROWTH AND DECLINE

Structural changes in manufacturing have had their most dramatic effect in the old-line industrial areas. As factories closed or reduced their work forces, urban decline began to replace uncontrolled urban growth as the major concern of public policy (Bradbury et al., 1982; Hanson, 1982). Even without the recession, structural changes were producing high levels of unemployment in some industrial areas. Physical deterioration and fiscal stress in such places are also common (Bradbury et al., 1982; Burchell and Listokin, 1981).

There has been a tendency to interpret the redistribution of population and employment among the multistate census regions of the country that has accompanied these developments as a zero-sum game between Sunbelt and Frostbelt regions. It has also been suggested that the decline of older cities and the rise of newer ones are inevitable as the inexorable forces of change in a postindustrial society work themselves out (Hicks, 1982; President's Commission for a National Agenda for the Eighties, 1980; U.S. Department of Housing and Urban Development, 1982).[12]

Some important interregional adjustments are taking place. The principal generator of employment growth in the Sunbelt, however, has not been the migration of firms from the older Frostbelt cities. The principal source of new jobs in the southwestern and mountain regions has been the expansion of existing firms (Armington and Odle, 1982). The low rate of job formation in the Frostbelt stems from low rates of large firm expansion, high rates of large firm contraction, and high rates of firm death (Armington and Odle, 1982; Garnick, 1978). Thus the differences in regional employment growth (or decline) stem principally from differences in rates of expansion and birth of firms (Armington and Odle, 1982; Birch, 1981; Norton and Rees, 1979; Rees, 1979a). While firms as such may not have moved, capital in the form of liquid assets has moved and has been used to start new firms in new places instead of reinvesting in older firms and communities (Bluestone and Harrison, 1982).

Another important factor in the decline of manufacturing jobs in many Frostbelt cities is that older industrial plants located in those places are often the least productive because of obsolete equipment, manufacturing processes, and plant designs. When shut down for cyclical reasons, they

---

[12] Interestingly, *The President's National Urban Policy Report, 1982* (U.S. Department of Housing and Urban Development, 1982) argues that the most serious urban economic problems stem from structural changes in the economy, but the report recommends that policy rely primarily on a cyclical remedy: the economic recovery program of the administration.

are the least likely to reopen. If they are modernized, they become more capital-intensive and do not recall all of the laid-off work force. The key factor, however, is not regional location but obsolescence, as the shutting of steel mills in California and Alabama illustrates.

The geographic concentration of energy industries and the growth of military-related employment, influenced by national policies that have encouraged flows of capital and labor into these industries, have also been significant forces in the development of Sunbelt cities.[13] Other factors are also important: the migration of older people with considerable amounts of retirement income to more benign climates offered by Sunbelt states, higher fertility rates, lower participation rates for women in the labor force (although the rates are quite high in some regions, such as the South Atlantic), and the presence of large numbers of immigrants who provide a pool of labor at relatively low cost for some kinds of enterprises.[14]

The factor almost uniformly overlooked in the Frostbelt/Sunbelt controversy is that the Frostbelt has consistently captured more than its share of corporate headquarters and producer services (Stanback et al., 1981:98-99). In fact, during the 1970s many of the Frostbelt cities appear to have reinforced their comparative advantage in producer services. This seems due in large part to the existence of a strong base for a service economy because of the historic concentration in the major Frostbelt metropolitan areas of the most highly sophisticated of those services, such as international banking, stock exchanges and other financial services, specialized law firms, accounting headquarters, and advertising and mass media firms (Stanback and Noyelle, 1982). Part of the reason for overlooking this phenomenon is the statistical illusion created by the way in which the service sectors are reported. By combining many producer and consumer services into one aggregate service category, some of the fast-growing producer services are offset by the more slowly growing consumer services. In addition, the employment data on the manufacturing sector nor-

[13] Much of the new growth in manufacturing in the Sunbelt has also been in new industries, such as energy, aerospace, and electronics. Perry and Watkins (1977) identify six dominant growth industries they believe to be primarily responsible for the growth of Sunbelt cities: agriculture, defense, advanced technology, oil and natural gas, real estate and construction, and tourism and leisure.

[14] See Jackson et al. (1981:36-46) and Bureau of Economic Analysis (November 1981) for a discussion of these trends in different parts of the country. The availability of low-wage, low-skilled labor was found significant in studies of specific Sunbelt labor markets in which there has been growth in manufacturing and retail employment. See particularly the discussion of Phoenix in Stanback and Noyelle (1982:102-104).

mally do not break out the internal services from the production work. Since consumer services tend to follow trends in population growth and disposable income, the high growth rate for services in Sunbelt cities disguises major qualitative differences among cities in the kind of service growth they are experiencing (Stanback et al., 1981).

There are urban areas in every census region that are undergoing severe stress from structural changes in their local economies. The problems of troubled cities in the South, such as Birmingham and New Orleans, and exceptions to regional decline, such as Columbus and Akron, Ohio (Schriber, 1982), and Boston, suggest that the industrial mix and the diversity and quality of the metropolitan labor market may be far more important factors in the capacity of local economies to adjust to structural changes than is mere regional location (Rees, 1980). All regions have growing, stagnant, and declining urban areas. Those urban areas that have historically functioned as national and regional centers for major corporate headquarters, branch offices, or division offices; as regional distribution centers; and as centers of banking and information are making a smoother transition to the new economy, whether they are located in regions that are growing or declining. In contrast, those urban areas whose economies have depended more heavily on a single manufacturing industry or a narrow range of industries are having the most difficult time, regardless of their region (Noyelle and Stanback, 1983). This is not to say that some of the most service-oriented cities are without economic problems. They may rank high on various indices of urban distress. A city with a substantial base for local expansion of sectors that are strong in national and international markets is more likely to make the transition to a new set of functions than a city that lacks such a base.[15]

The difficulty in generalizing about cities in census regions is partially illustrated by Figure 4, which compares the economic performance of metropolitan areas with the geographic regions within which they are located. Only in the East South Central region do all cities exceed the average performance of the region's economy. While some regional attributes are indeed important in the growth and decline of specific urban areas, it is important not to overstate their significance. In general, where a city is located seems less significant in forecasting its economic condition than what it does. It is therefore more useful to define regions as working urban market areas, rather than as static statistical areas. These dynamic

---

[15] Size also makes a difference (Noyelle and Stanback, 1983; Stanback and Noyelle, 1982).

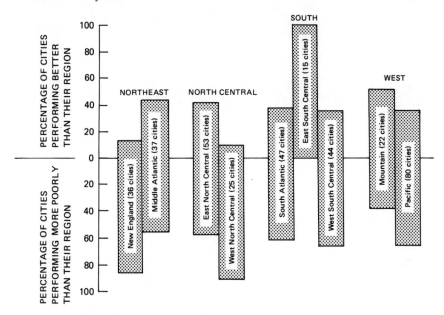

FIGURE 4   Economic performance of cities and their regions. SOURCE: Southern Growth Policies Board (1981:32).

regions are constantly changing. Once primarily influenced by their transportation networks, they are now experiencing a new set of changes made possible by the substitution of communications for some kinds of transportation. The economy of an urban area, as subsequent chapters discuss, may therefore depend for its vitality on invisible relationships that reach far beyond political boundaries, local markets, and commutation patterns.

3   The New Urban System

A CLASSIFICATION OF URBAN AREAS BY FUNCTION

A new urban system is emerging. It is both the product and the producer of a convergence of resources, capital, labor, technology, and institutions. It requires us to think about cities and urban policies differently than we have in the past.[1]

The new urban system is characterized by the growing dominance in corporate and producer services of a relatively small number of national and regional "command and control" centers. In these centers, strategic economic and political decisions are made that affect both these cities and the rest of the urban system. The centers contain high concentrations of corporate and government headquarters, producer services, and higher education and cultural resources. The remaining urban areas are more

---

[1] In the development of this section of the report, the committee acknowledges its debt to a number of scholars whose theoretical and empirical investigations have been extensively used, in particular, Berry (1974), Cohen (1979a), Dunn (1980), Perloff (1981), and Pred (1977).

The urban system described here closely follows that developed by Noyelle and Stanback (1983). Their work is the most extensive empirical investigation of the effect of structural changes on cities. Together with other studies by them and their colleagues at the Conservation for Human Resources Project of Columbia University, a rigorous analysis of the service economy and its consequences for cities has begun to appear. The committee is also grateful to Thomas M. Stanback, Jr., Richard V. Knight, Wilbur Thompson, and Daniel Garnick for their willingness to share their research and ideas with the committee and to participate in committee workshops to explore the issues and ideas discussed in this chapter.

specialized in their economic functions, which tend to be subordinate to the decisions made in the command and control centers, and they can be grouped by their primary orientation as consumer service centers or production centers. Figure 5 illustrates the classification on which this chapter is based. We fit the 140 largest metropolitan areas into four classes: (1) diversified service centers, (2) specialized service centers, (3) consumer-oriented centers, and (4) production centers. Each group contains subclasses based on size and type or degree of specialization.[2] Table 6 lists these 140 metropolitan areas within the four categories and gives indications of their size.

We have become used to thinking of urban systems as discrete physical places, such as metropolitan areas. While metropolitan areas are physical realities, they do not capture the full urban system in an advanced industrial economy. The new urban system transcends the metropolis and even the megalopolis (Gottman, 1961) of contiguous metropolitan areas.[3] It is perhaps best to think of it as consisting of an increasingly interdependent group of major cities containing firms and agencies with overlapping and fluctuating spheres of influence that extend beyond their immediate metropolitan areas. In some cases these spheres of influence extend into other regions, in some cases to other nations. The parts of the system are linked not only by transportation and communications systems but also by corporate structure and business relationships. This functional interdependence often conflicts with political pushes toward more sharply defined localism (Berry, 1974; Greer, 1965).

One should keep in mind that few if any of the metropolitan areas listed in Table 6 are pure examples of the class in which they have been placed. Because the system has evolved from existing cities, many of which may have performed different functions in the past, it is quite possible for a city in one of the subordinate categories to house the headquarters function for a firm or industry. No place performs only a single function. The purpose of the classification is to help us gain a better understanding of the center of gravity of the economies of different places. In urban form the most recently developed areas, such as Phoenix and Dallas, are more likely to mirror the physical impulses of the technology and business

---

[2] The classification system was developed by calculating the "location quotient" for each standard metropolitan statistical area (SMSA). Briefly described, this technique measures the difference between the national profile of employment, by sector, and that of each SMSA. For a full explanation of the methodology and tables showing the results of the calculations for each SMSA, see Noyelle and Stanback (1983:86-106 and Appendix IV-1:346-364).

[3] Gottman is also of the opinion that the new urban system cannot be neatly confined to traditional physical forms (lecture at University of Maryland, March 26, 1982).

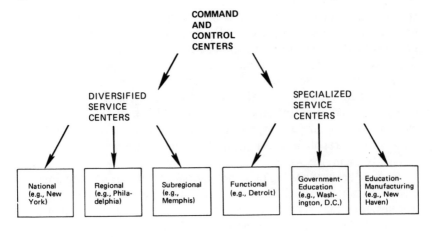

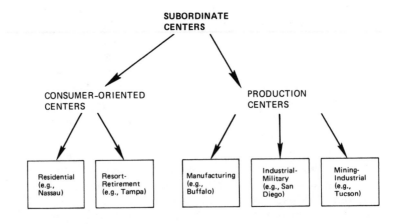

FIGURE 5   Classification scheme of the 140 largest metropolitan areas.

organization of an advanced economy, much as Lowell, Massachusetts, and Wheeling, West Virginia, reflect those of the industrial eras during which they experienced their most rapid growth.

This system of classification, using the metropolitan area as the unit of analysis, also does not focus on the distinction within each metropolitan area between the subeconomy of the central city and that of the suburbs or of the total urban area. Those distinctions are particularly important in addressing problems that have a jurisdictional and political basis, such as the concentration of blacks and poor people in central cities. It is important to recognize that these noneconomic facts of life often have a profound

TABLE 6   The 140 Largest Metropolitan Areas Classified by Type and Size, 1980

	1980 Population Rank	1980 Population- Size Group[a]
1. Command and control centers		
Diversified service centers		
National		
New York, N.Y.	1	1
Los Angeles, Calif.	2	1
Chicago, Ill.	3	1
San Francisco, Calif.	7	1
Regional		
Philadelphia, Pa.	4	1
Boston, Mass.	6	1
Dallas, Tex.	10	1
Houston, Tex.	11	1
St. Louis, Mo.	12	1
Baltimore, Md.	14	1
Minneapolis, Minn.	15	1
Cleveland, Ohio	17	1
Atlanta, Ga.	18	2
Miami, Fla.	21	2
Denver, Colo.	22	2
Seattle, Wash.	23	2
Cincinnati, Ohio	26	2
Kansas City, Mo.	28	2
Phoenix, Ariz.	30	2
Indianapolis, Ind.	32	2
New Orleans, La.	33	2
Portland, Oreg.	34	2
Columbus, Ohio	35	2
Subregional		
Memphis, Tenn.	41	3
Salt Lake City, Utah	45	3
Birmingham, Ala.	46	3
Nashville, Tenn.	52	3
Oklahoma City, Okla.	53	3
Syracuse, N.Y.	58	3
Richmond, Va.	65	3
Charlotte, N.C.	66	3
Omaha, Nebr.	69	3
Mobile, Ala.	91	4
Little Rock, Ark.	101	4
Shreveport, La.	106	4
Des Moines, Iowa	110	4
Spokane, Wash.	114	4
Jackson, Miss.	120	4
Specialized service centers		
Functional centers		
Detroit, Mich.	5	1
Pittsburgh, Pa.	13	1
Newark, N.J.	16	1
Milwaukee, Wis.	24	2

TABLE 6   Continued

	1980 Population Rank	1980 Population-Size Group[a]
San Jose, Calif.	31	2
Hartford, Conn.	36	2
Rochester, N.Y.	38	3
Louisville, Ky.	40	3
Dayton, Ohio	44	3
Bridgeport, Conn.	47	3
Toledo, Ohio	50	3
Greensboro, N.C.	51	3
Akron, Ohio	57	3
Allentown, Pa.	62	3
Tulsa, Okla.	63	3
New Brunswick, N.J.	67	3
Jersey City, N.J.	70	3
Wilmington, Del.	75	3
Paterson, N.J.	78	4
Knoxville, Tenn.	86	4
Wichita, Kans.	96	4
Fort Wayne, Ind.	100	4
Peoria, Ill.	103	4
Kalamazoo, Mich.	137	4
Government-education centers		
Washington, D.C.	8	1
Sacramento, Calif.	39	3
Albany, N.Y.	48	3
Raleigh-Durham, N.C.	77	4
Fresno, Calif.	81	4
Austin, Tex.	82	4
Lansing, Mich.	84	4
Oxnard-Ventura, Calif.	85	4
Harrisburg, Pa.	88	4
Baton Rouge, La.	89	4
Columbia, S.C.	99	4
Utica, N.Y.	111	4
Trenton, N.J.	112	4
Madison, Wis.	113	4
Stockton, Calif.	117	4
Education-manufacturing centers		
New Haven, Conn.	54	3
Springfield, Mass.	64	3
Tacoma, Wash.	90	4
South Bend, Ind.	100	4
Ann Arbor, Mich.	140	4
2. Subordinate centers		
Consumer-oriented centers		
Residential centers		
Nassau, N.Y.	9	1
Anaheim, Calif.	19	2
Long Branch, N.J.	76	3
Resort-retirement centers		
Tampa, Fla.	25	2

TABLE 6   Continued

	1980 Population Rank	1980 Population- Size Group[a]
Riverside, Calif.	29	2
Ft. Lauderdale, Fla.	43	3
Honolulu, Hawaii	55	3
Orlando, Fla.	68	3
West Palm Beach, Fla.	79	4
Albuquerque, N.M.	95	4
Las Vegas, Nev.	108	4
Santa Barbara, Calif.	122	4
Production centers		
Manufacturing centers		
Buffalo, N.Y.	27	2
Providence, R.I.	42	3
Worcester, Mass.	59	3
Gary, Ind.	60	3
Northeast Pennsylvania	61	3
Grand Rapids, Mich.	71	3
Youngstown, Ohio	72	3
Greenville, S.C.	73	3
Flint, Mich.	74	3
New Bedford, Mass.	80	4
Canton, Ohio	92	4
Johnson City, Tenn.	93	4
Chattanooga, Tenn.	94	4
Davenport, Iowa	98	4
Beaumont, Tex.	104	4
York, Pa.	107	4
Lancaster, Pa.	109	4
Binghamton, N.Y.	115	4
Reading, Pa.	116	4
Huntington, W.Va.	119	4
Evansville, Ind.	124	4
Appleton, Wis.	125	4
Erie, Pa.	131	4
Rockford, Ill.	134	4
Lorain, Ohio	136	4
Industrial-military centers		
San Diego, Calif.	20	2
San Antonio, Tex.	37	3
Norfolk, Va.	49	3
El Paso, Tex.	87	4
Charleston, S.C.	97	4
Newport News, Va.	102	4
Lexington, Ky.	121	4
Huntsville, Ala.	123	4
Augusta, Ga.	126	4
Vallego, Calif.	127	4
Colorado Springs, Colo.	128	4
Pensacola, Fla.	132	4
Salinas, Calif.	133	4

TABLE 6   Continued

	1980 Population Rank	1980 Population- Size Group[a]
Mining-industrial centers		
Tucson, Ariz.	83	4
Bakersfield, Calif.	105	4
Corpus Christi, Tex.	118	4
Lakeland, Fla.	129	4
Johnstown, Pa.	135	4
Duluth, Minn.	138	4
Charleston, W.Va.	139	4

[a]1980 population size group: (1) more than 2 million (17 SMSAs), (2) 1–2 million (19 SMSAs), (3) 0.5–1 million (39 SMSAs), (4) 0.25–0.5 million (65 SMSAs). The 126 SMSAs of less than 0.25 million are not included in this table. Most of these smaller SMSAs would fall into the subordinate classes, although a few could be considered as specialized service centers because of concentrations of government and education functions.

SOURCE: Adapted from Noyelle and Stanback (1983).

influence on such economic decisions as where to invest in an urban area. Our purpose in using the metropolitan area as the basis for classification is not to obscure this harsh reality but rather to focus on the central economic characteristics of urban areas as a basis for both national and urban strategies that may provide more leverage for overcoming some of the historic difficulties in fashioning urban economic development policy.

The classification system describes the most prominent economic role of each metropolitan area in 1980, the year it was calculated. No area is permanently or necessarily consigned to a particular class. An area can undergo transformation over time from being one type of place to being another type. This transformation has already happened in many places, and there are signs of its being in progress in others. The process can be slow or rapid, depending on the circumstances. There are some strong indications, for example, that Houston may soon join the national centers (New York, Chicago, San Francisco, and Los Angeles) as its international banking and other producer services expand. Miami may be moving in the same direction, having already gone through a transformation from a residential and resort center to a regional center. Boston's role as a regional center has become more pronounced in recent years as its role as a production center has diminished. Cities like Akron have recently strengthened their roles as specialized centers as their production roles have declined, and places like Pittsburgh and Cleveland are undergoing obvious transformations from specialized service centers to diversified regional centers.

There seems to be a tendency for cities in the producer-oriented and consumer-oriented classes to increase their degree of specialization (although there is also some tendency for diversification in the large consumer-oriented areas). This reflects the growing tendency of business organizations to restrict the different phases and functions of producing goods or providing services to specialized centers. Insurance companies, for example, are increasingly relocating their records maintenance functions in smaller metropolitan areas and nonmetropolitan areas that may be some distance from the home office.

COMMAND AND CONTROL CENTERS

The metropolises we have called command and control centers include two basically different types of places: diversified service centers and specialized service centers. Each category can be divided further by size and function.

Diversified Service Centers

The 39 metropolitan areas identified by Noyelle and Stanback (1983) as diversified service centers include three subgroups: national, regional, and subregional centers. In some respects they perform a hierarchy of service functions, the largest national centers providing the greatest agglomerations of corporate complexes and the most sophisticated producer services. They hold a virtual monopoly in some services, such as international banking and mass communications.

The regional centers tend to have smaller corporate complexes, although many of them have been growing rapidly. They do not, as a group, offer as large or as sophisticated an array of producer services as the national centers, but along with the subregional centers they are growing in relative importance as distribution centers and as locations for branch and division offices of major corporations.

Almost all the diversified service centers are served by large airports. The national and regional centers have 11 of the 13 largest international airports in the United States (Honolulu and Washington, D.C., are the others; Newark's airport is part of the greater New York region's transportation complex) and account for over 85 percent of all international passenger air traffic in the nation (Noyelle and Stanback, 1983).

National Centers

The most distinguishing characteristic of the national centers (New York, Chicago, Los Angeles, San Francisco) is the increasing concentration of banking and financial services there. Of the nation's 50 largest commercial banks, 20 (including all but 3 of the top 20) have their headquarters in these 4 places, and 25 of the 50 largest diversified financial companies are also there (*Fortune*, July 12, 1982:134, 138). These institutions are the most prominent providers of banking services, including both business and consumer credit. Their influence in the regional centers has grown in the last decade through the use of loan production offices. They are in strong positions to develop branches as banking is deregulated. They virtually control the market in municipal securities and have spearheaded the development of foreign banking in the United States.

This heavy concentration of banking services in the national centers means that there are almost no other places in the country to which one can go for large-scale financial services. These cities contain the institutions with the money and the other highly specialized expert services needed to put financial deals together. The largest and most highly specialized law firms, the headquarters of the largest accounting firms, and the largest array of other consulting services in management, advertising, economics, and public relations are located there. They also are almost exclusively the U.S. headquarters for transnational corporations and banks with North American branches (Cohen, 1979a; Conservation of Human Resources, 1977). Because of their concentration of services, even major corporations that have their headquarters offices in other cities often maintain offices in the national centers to improve their access to the services that are provided there.

Regional Centers

The 19 regional centers are not as sophisticated as the national centers in the range of producer services they provide, but they are both more highly diversified and more specialized than other cities in the system. Many of these areas contain important service firms and headquarters of national corporations. They contain 13 of the 50 largest diversified financial firms in the country, 21 of the 50 largest commercial banks, 16 of the 50 largest insurance companies, and 12 of the 50 largest diversified financial companies (*Fortune*, July 12, 1982:132, 134, 136, 138). A number of them, such as Philadelphia, Boston, Atlanta, Miami, and Houston, have aggressive commercial banks that increasingly are operating on a national and international scale. As some of these places increase the scale and sophistication of the producer and banking services they offer, they may move into the ranks of the national centers.

Regional centers serve as headquarters for 22 of the 50 largest utility companies (*Fortune*, July 12, 1982:146). With the national centers, they serve as the major distribution centers for the rest of the urban system.[4] These centers are characterized by large concentrations of regional sales headquarters of large corporations. They are often headquarters for less internationalized firms than those found in the national centers but are closely tied to large-scale consumer markets. Thus, large food products firms (Minneapolis, Atlanta, Dallas), retail sales firms (Cincinnati, St. Louis, Minneapolis, Dallas), transportation firms (Seattle, Kansas City, Houston, Denver, Dallas-Fort Worth), and utilities firms (Atlanta, Columbus, New Orleans, Portland, Phoenix, Baltimore) locate their headquarters in the regional centers. Some of these cities are also strong research, education, and health care centers and centers of management control for specific lines of industry (Noyelle and Stanback, 1983).

Subregional Centers

The 13 subregional centers are less diversified in producer services than the regional centers but are strongly involved in distributive services. Noyelle and Stanback (1983) found that many remain closely tied to agricultural markets. While many have been attempting to become more diversified, they have had less success than the regional centers, apparently because they are smaller and they start from a narrower base of functions in the urban system. It has been harder, therefore, to develop strong education and research institutions or headquarters offices of major firms.

Transformation in the Diversified Service Centers

One of the problems in developing a clearer understanding of the current and future roles of any part of the urban system has been the persistence of the belief that population growth as well as growth of manufacturing jobs is essential for the economic health of a metropolitan area. This has been a special problem in dealing with the economies of the diversified service centers. The growth rates of the areas in this class vary considerably. Some of them have lost population in absolute terms. Most of them, at least those outside the Sunbelt, have experienced a loss of manufacturing jobs, particularly from the central cities. Except in the newest places, such as Houston and Phoenix, shares of population and jobs have been lost by the central cities to the suburbs and nearby nonmetropolitan

---

[4] Of the 50 largest transportation companies, 15 are located in regional centers, along with 10 of the 50 top retailing firms. The role of the regional centers vis-à-vis the national centers in distributive services is increasing (Noyelle and Stanback, 1983).

areas.[5] Concentration on these indices, or on such things as the movement of the number of headquarters or firms into or out of a central city or metropolitan area, often does not reveal how a place has been transformed or its new or changed role in the urban system (Conservation of Human Resources, 1977).

The diversified service centers have retained strong and growing service economies. New York, for example, netted 135,000 new private sector service jobs during the mid-1970s. All but 13,200 of these jobs were located in Manhattan; only two other boroughs showed any net gains in jobs, and those gains were very small. At the same time there was a sharp decline in manufacturing and retail employment and a decline in the growth of personal services and tourism. The greatest growth was in producer services, such as advertising, management, consulting, computer data services, and research and development. Such service jobs now make up almost 10 percent of all jobs in New York City, and 87 percent of them are concentrated in Manhattan (*New York Times*, October 16, 1981; March 13, 1982). At the same time producer services were growing and increasing their centralization in Manhattan, many corporations were shifting their routine clerical operations to the suburbs or to distant smaller cities as rising Manhattan rents made moves desirable and technology made it feasible (*New York Times*, November 21, 1981).

New York is of course unique among the nation's cities in its scale and its international functions. The same processes, however, are at work in most of the national and regional centers. Although some of them, such as Houston, Dallas, Denver, and Atlanta, are continuing to increase the number of manufacturing jobs, even these cities are experiencing a faster rate of growth in producer services. Older regional centers, such as Cleveland, St. Louis, Boston, and Cincinnati, lost manufacturing jobs but gained more than an offsetting number of service jobs in the last decade (Bureau of Economic Analysis, 1981). Most of these metropolitan areas are decentralizing manufacturing, distributive services, and personal services but increasing the concentration of producer services, either in a single center or in a few centers of activity.

Particularly in the national and regional centers, the firms headquartered there have a high degree of autonomy in making decisions that are of great consequence for their own metropolitan areas as well as others. The national headquarters group usually has no higher authority to consult within the company when considering whether to move the headquarters

---

[5] Some of these places would also show losses of population and jobs but for their ability to annex adjacent areas.

itself, decentralize some operations, or expand in place. But the national centers are not wholly at the mercy of firms because there are relatively few places in the nation that contain the agglomeration of other services on which these large national and international corporations depend to function effectively. Thus, the national and regional centers also have a source of autonomy and power in dealing with their economic futures. Developments in corporate structure are important to such places. To the extent that multinational conglomerates are able to internalize the producer services they need through headquarters staffing and aquisition of service firms, they increase their independence from the city itself.

The subregional centers generally enjoy less autonomy, either in the power of branch offices or in collective economic action. Distribution firms and sales offices are also limited in the choices that are available to them. What is lacking in many of these places is a sufficient concentration of producer services to provide long-term stability and to cushion the effect of the loss of a single large firm or office.

Specialized Service Centers

The 44 specialized service centers identified by Noyelle and Stanback share command and control functions in the urban system with the diversified service centers. They differ primarily in the degree to which the services they deliver tend to be specialized in major economic activities— a particular industrial group or sector, education, and government. Because of their higher degree of specialization, firms located in these places tend to rely on the national and regional centers for the most highly specialized services, such as international banking and advertising. There are three subgroups of specialized service centers: functional centers, government-education centers, and education-manufacturing centers. These subgroups have some obvious differences, but they share two important common characteristics. They all specialize in delivering relatively high-level services to either the private or the public sectors, and they all contain strong educational and research complexes (Noyelle and Stanback, 1983).

Functional Centers

The 24 functional centers house national and international corporate complexes in one or more industries. These places are comparable in size to the national and regional centers and contain central management, research, and production groups from the core industry and subsidiary or related industries. Their service sectors accordingly tend to be large but more narrowly specialized than those found in the diversified service centers, and they are rooted in a long-standing industrial tradition that is reflected in the composition of the work force, the housing stock, and the physical form of the metropolis.

The older functional centers, such as Pittsburgh, Detroit, Rochester, and Wilmington, were built around their particular leading industries, and the form of each city reflects the way in which those basic industries related to their urban environments. Central business districts tend to be weaker than in comparably sized diversified service centers, often because the headquarters of the leading corporations were initially located with the production facilities outside the central business district, and competitors put some distance between themselves. Each corporate complex often generates a competing center of urban activity. Housing for a large blue-collar work force tends toward lower densities, reflecting the high wage levels of unionized labor. The same multinuclear structure tends to be even more pronounced in the newer functional centers, such as San Jose, Wichita, and Tulsa, because their economies are based on newer or expanding industries and technologies and because they have developed in the automobile age.

The functional centers may also serve as distribution centers on a national or international scale, but, unlike the regional and subregional centers, they tend not to be closely linked to their regional markets. Because many were established in the period of manufacturing expansion in the United States, they are burdened with a high ratio of obsolete manufacturing plants that suffer from both domestic and foreign competition. The heavy investment in these areas by their major industries, however, gives them considerable staying power. Absent a merger into a corporation headquartered elsewhere, there is often relatively little inclination to move the central administrative offices. Where it is feasible, management may be willing to modernize some old plants or convert them to new uses and even build some new facilities in the area. This also allows the industry to take advantage of a local skilled labor force in which it has a major investment.

While modernizing existing facilities and closing the most unproductive old plants have resulted in the displacement of large numbers of blue-collar workers, there has often been considerable growth in the administrative and research components of the industries. Even during a period of substantial reduction in production employment in the functional centers, there was an increase in jobs in headquarters-related and producer services (Noyelle and Stanback, 1983). Thus, while it appears that production will probably remain an important part of the economies of the functional centers (Gurwitz and Kingsley, 1982), its role is diminishing relative to nonproduction activities.[6] As a result, the character of what they export to the rest of the economy has been transformed.[7] Instead of exporting as high a percentage of the world's tires as in the past, for example, Akron now exports expertise as the major international center for management and research in the rubber industry (Schriber, 1982).

The linkage between these activities and local manufacturing within an industry is also important in that it provides a base for stability that is not present, as we shall see, in the places that are more narrowly specialized in the production phases of an industry. Thus, although there have been and will probably continue to be substantial losses of blue-collar employment in the functional centers due to technological changes and the decentralization of manufacturing activities to other areas and to foreign countries, there is likely to be greater long-term stability for blue-collar workers once the major transition has occurred (Stanback et al., 1981:101). This strength, of course, depends on the continued strength of an area's industrial specialty in the national economy.

There is also an additional factor that seems important in assessing the future of the functional centers. The presence of the home offices of major industrial corporations has meant, for many of these places, a historically strong commitment of the corporate leadership to the community and its nonprofit sector. This has produced a wide array of educational, health-related, and cultural institutions, which in themselves have become important assets of the metropolitan economy. There is evidence that such institutions benefit from the economics of agglomeration. Not only are they important factors in attracting and supporting the development of a service economy, but they also may develop into significant exports or export substitutes for the local economy.[8] Education institutions are an important part of this nonprofit complex. They provide an export substitute, since they bring money from nonresidents into the local economy.

---

[6] While Gurwitz and Kingsley deal with a particular regional center, many of their observations on the continued role of manufacturing apply to functional centers.

[7] For all functional centers, manufacturing employment's share of their economies fell from 39.0 percent in 1969 to 33.6 percent in 1978. During the same period, however, finance, insurance, and real estate services rose from 4.4 to 5.1 percent, and services rose from 16.9 to 20.0 percent (special tabulation from OBERS-BEA Regional Projections, prepared for the Committee on National Urban Policy by the Bureau of Economic Analysis, U.S. Department of Commerce; hereafter referred to as OBERS-BEA special tabulation).

[8] Noyelle and Stanback (1983) show that employment in nonprofit organizations is one of the fastest growing sectors in the functional centers. For additional insights into the economic significance of nonprofit firms to urban areas—although the study does not deal with functional centers—see Reiner and Wolpert (1981) and Wolpert and Reiner (1982).

They are important to the functional centers not only as employers but also because they have an important nexus with the administrative and particularly the research components of the industrial group headquartered in these centers. Where the universities have strong research and development capabilities, as in the San Jose, Detroit, and Pittsburgh areas, they can become a part of the process of invention and innovation that seems crucial to the long-term capacity of an area to adjust to changes in the industry that it houses (*Science*, August 6, 1982).[9]

Other Specialized Service Centers

The 20 metropolitan areas included in the government-education and education-manufacturing centers include Washington, D.C., and the capitals of 12 states. Others are university towns. All contain large private or public universities, often the state university or a branch of it. Some house a complex of several universities. Employment in these places is concentrated in the government and nonprofit sectors. While both sectors grew rapidly in the past two decades, they have slowed in recent years. State government can be expected to maintain a fairly steady, if slower, rate of growth in most states, particularly if its role increases in relation to the domestic functions of the federal government. In states with high growth rates, such as Texas, a considerable increase in government employment seems likely, especially if the state has previously maintained a relatively modest level of public services.

One factor that is hard to forecast is the impact of new office technology on the growth of public employment, since a large proportion of government employees are clerical workers. The concentration of government offices, however, also tends to attract government-related businesses and nonprofit activities. Much of the growth of the Washington, D.C., economy in the past decade has come from these sources rather than from any expansion of government employment. It is quite possible that expansion of the government-related private sector will become more important in state capitals as well. This possibility may be lower in states in which the bulk of state offices are in the state's major metropolitan centers rather than in the capital city.

---

[9] Carnegie-Mellon University, for example, is engaged in a major research and development program in robotics with Pittsburgh-based industries. A similar program is under way at the University of Michigan with Detroit's automobile companies. The fruitful relationship between research programs at Stanford University and Silicon Valley electronics and computer firms has been an important factor in the economic growth of the San Jose area.

Although the growth of a more knowledge-based economy would seem to demand an expansion of higher education, such a necessity is offset by the decline in the size of the college-age population in the years ahead. Some university systems overextended to meet the demands of the baby boom cohort and now must reduce their work forces. In addition, cutbacks in public support of research and development activities affect universities. In the education-manufacturing centers the relationship between university research and product or service development may be an important factor in the economic future of the area. The presence of government and universities tends to build a metropolitan labor force that is concentrated in professional and administrative occupations, making it an attractive market for some service industries. Such factors as these suggest a mild increase in diversification of these centers without overwhelming their primary specialization.[10]

SUBORDINATE CENTERS

Consumer-Oriented Centers

Only 12 of the 140 largest metropolitan areas are primarily consumer-oriented centers. A few smaller areas, such as Reno, would also fit this description. The three residential centers shown in Table 6 are linked economically to the New York and Los Angeles SMSAs. The remaining resort-retirement centers are built around rising consumption of mass-marketed recreation, such as theme parks, and growing retirement incomes and benefits.

The economic mix of such places is not broad. They tend toward concentration in consumer services and government. Some have attracted various light industries, some the headquarters of large firms, and some decentralized office facilities, building on a base of community amenities, good education and health systems, recreation facilities, and a professional labor force. They do not, however, have a large low- and middle-income work force, which seems to be a necessary complement to the professional work force (Frankena, 1981). In some cases, as in Orlando, the sheer rate of growth has helped produce demand for a wide range of economic activities that cannot be served by other metropolitan areas in the general region. Most of these areas do not seem to be good prospects for the development of a strong corporate complex or a producer services base.

---

[10] Noyelle and Stanback (1983) anticipate slower growth than in the last two decades.

It should be remembered, however, that because the economies of the resort centers are specialized in consumer services, they perform more as export sectors than as local sectors.

Production Centers

The final broad category of places in the new urban system is the production centers—almost a third of the 140 largest metropolitan areas. In addition, there are a large number of smaller areas with economies dominated by manufacturing or mining. Nearly all of the large manufacturing centers are in the old industrial heartland of the Frostbelt, but only two of the industrial-military centers and mining industrial centers are outside the Sunbelt.

The 25 manufacturing centers in Table 6 are different from the functional centers in several significant respects. They generally are smaller; most have fewer than a half million people.[11] They are less likely to contain major corporate headquarters, and the producer services sector is relatively small.[12] Instead they are often the sites for specialized branch plants of manufacturing industries. Their losses in manufacturing employment have not been offset, for the most part, by increases in headquarters employment and producer services (Noyelle and Stanback, 1983).

The labor force in these areas is largely composed of lower-skilled blue-collar workers. Plant managers in such places have relatively little autonomy in determining policies within their own plants, let alone in making major decisions about such things as closing, expansion, modernization, and relocation. These metropolitan areas are the most vulnerable of all parts of the urban system to the structural changes we have described. Because the plants located there are often among the oldest in the industry, they are the first to shut and the last to reopen in response to business cycles. They generally are the least productive and are therefore subject to permanent closing. There is little other strength in the economy to attract alternative employers.

---

[11] Buffalo stands apart from the rest of this group, due to its size and the strength of its financial institutions. It contains only one major corporate headquarters, however, and its economy is based in two troubled industries: automobiles and chemicals. It has had great difficulty in diversifying its economy and developing a strong service sector. Its distributive services sector has also been in decline (see Stanback and Noyelle, 1982:101-102).

[12] Their finance, insurance, and real estate category of industries, for example, provides a smaller proportion of total employment than does any other class of cities (from an unpublished 1982 OBERS-BEA special tabulation).

Because these places tend to depend on regional centers for major financial services, there is often a weak pool of local capital available for reinvestment in the community. Very few have strong public or nonprofit sectors.[13] They have greater susceptibility than other cities to "self-aggravating processes in city decline" (Bradbury et al., 1980, 1982) as one economic weakness triggers another.

The industrial-military centers developed rapidly from World War II into the early 1960s. Except for San Diego and more recently San Antonio, they have been heavily dependent on the flow of military funds and have not, as a group, experienced much diversification of their economies. This narrow base makes them highly vulnerable to budgetary decisions made in Washington. The mining-industrial centers have grown substantially in the last decade in the wake of the energy crisis, but like the military centers, their firms tend to be subject to external economic control (Noyelle and Stanback, 1983). They are also highly susceptible to fluctuations in world commodity markets. Because the production costs of fuels and minerals are higher in the United States than in many other countries, a slackening of demand tends to shut down American capacity first.

IMPLICATIONS OF THE NEW URBAN SYSTEM

The urban system we have described is characterized by an increasing polarization of the command and control centers and the subordinate centers (Noyelle and Stanback, 1983). The tendency of the most vital services sector—corporate complex and producer services—to concentrate in the command and control centers is well established. The result is to give these centers a high degree of economic autonomy and to place them in the mainstream of urban economic development. While many of these places, especially the functional centers, can expect to retain a substantial presence of manufacturing industries, the role of manufacturing in their overall economies is being displaced by producer services. In addition, within the manufacturing industries located in these places, the occupational profile is shifting from production to nonprodution occupations.

The size of the command and control centers, the diversity of their labor forces, the existence of strong educational institutions, and the presence of sophisticated political and civic leadership and local governments

---

[13] Flint, Michigan, is an exception. There the Mott Foundation has a well-supported and active program in community economic development. It is limited, however, by the lack of strong political institutions and the concentration of employment in a single industry, automobile manufacturing (G. Clark, 1983).

increase their resilience in adjusting to changes in economic structure. Although structural unemployment among manufacturing employees is a serious problem in a number of them (especially the functional centers), in those metropolitan areas with concentrations of old-line industries, such as steel, automobiles, rubber, and heavy machinery, it is more likely to be a transitional problem rather than a permanent one. While some of these areas are growing very slowly, as measured by net population increase, most are evolving quite rapidly toward a strong economic base. The long-run prognosis for their economic health is encouraging. Particular attention may need to be paid, however, to the health of their central cities or other older jurisdictions within the metropolitan area.

While the command and control centers are characterized by a high degree of economic and political autonomy, a smaller proportion of the remaining centers are as fully in control of their own destinies. A few, however, show signs of building strong, independent service economies to substitute for the erosion of blue-collar manufacturing jobs. Some are even attracting more blue-collar jobs. Others, such as Orlando, are expanding their basic service activities and are also succeeding in developing a more diversified economy. As a result, as the mix of industries and occupations changes, such cities are likely to join the command and control centers. As a group, the subordinate centers have not experienced an absolute loss of jobs, but their new service jobs tend to be consumer-oriented rather than in producer services.

The capacity of a metropolitan area to adjust to structural changes is heavily influenced by the mix of industries and occupations that it has built up over the course of its history. The size and the diversity of the command and control centers contribute to their resilience. By contrast, the production centers and the consumer-oriented centers tend to lack readily adaptable labor forces or a sufficient contingent of professionally and technically trained workers to attract industries that require a highly trained work force. In such places, structural change is not just a transitional problem but a long-term one. The industrial units located here often have little autonomy of their own and therefore have much less stability in the face of major changes in markets and technologies (Armington and Odle, 1982; Cohen, 1981).

An area's physical conditions—both natural and man-made—and its cultural heritage are also important factors in its adaptability to economic changes. An advanced industrial economy does not use urban space in the same way that the old economy did (Breckenfield, 1977; Hicks, 1982; Perloff, 1981). The redevelopment of older urban areas need not follow the traditional concentric patterns of the past. Where simultaneous abandonment, gentrification, and redevelopment are under way, there are opportunities for new forms, improved urban design, and physical relationships that were not feasible during the first generation of urbanization (Berry, 1982; Thompson, 1977). Given their economic history, the functional centers are likely to follow a more polycentric pattern of redevelopment than the national and regional centers, in part because the former have historically weaker central business districts than the latter (Thompson, 1969:28-31).

Newer urban areas that are just now experiencing their most rapid growth have (at least theoretically) more flexibility in meeting the physical requirements of growth industries than the older metropolitan areas. Transportation, land use, and housing patterns are more fluid and capable of being adjusted in the early stages of growth. There is less old capital stock to work around. In some cases, as in Charlotte and Dallas, it may be possible to capture an early comparative advantage, such as an airport that serves as the hub of a regional air service network or as an international airport and headquarters or corporate service center for transportation industries. Because the opportunities for such activities are limited in number, the centers that capture them tend to preempt that function for a fairly large region.

Institutional factors are easily overlooked in economic analyses of urban areas. They can be critical factors in interarea competition and in local economic development strategies that seek to promote local adaptation. Where political boundaries limit the ability of a central city to tax important metropolitan assets, as in the case of most older northern cities, the revenues needed to support the infrastructure and services essential to adaptation are severely limited. Governmental and fiscal autonomy may be almost as important as the economic autonomy of the firms located in an area. On the other side of the institutional ledger, the existence of high-quality educational, health, cultural, and recreational resources in an area may give it a strong competitive advantage in retaining or attracting firms that employ high-level white-collar workers. The quality of civic and political leadership can determine whether an area even recognizes its problems and takes advantage of its opportunities (Committee for Economic Development, 1982).

The powerful forces shaping the urban system and the urban landscape will not be easy to alter, but they are not unalterable. Studies of the behavior of corporate headquarters functions and of producer and other services, as well as the mounting evidence of continuing and wider dispersion of manufacturing, strongly suggest that the command and control centers will continue to enjoy a strong attraction for the management functions of the economy. Of the components of the urban system, they alone offer easy access to the entire array of services that the modern corporate complex needs to perform its management functions. They also provide advantages in transportation, communications, and cultural resources. While some traditional headquarters activities, such as records centers, can and will be relocated in the suburbs or in subordinate centers, management functions are becoming more heavily concentrated in the major national, regional, and functional centers (Cohen, 1977; Noyelle and Stanback, 1983).

Not many more national and regional centers are likely to arise in the near future, especially if the nation continues to approach zero population growth. But there are still opportunities for a new generation of cities to develop, as Dallas, Orlando, Phoenix, and Denver have in the past two decades. Some regional and subregional centers could gradually expand their spheres of influence and move into the next higher rank of areas. A few places may be able to capitalize on unique advantages and transform themselves into regional rather than subregional centers, particularly in areas of substantial population growth, such as central Florida. Others, such as San Diego or San Antonio, may evolve from industrial-military centers to regional centers (Noyelle and Stanback, 1983).

The future for other parts of the urban system seems to lie in some degree of specialization and in establishing economic ties to the larger and more diversified centers. For some it may involve conversion from one kind of production to another. Some may have potential as centers for innovation, building on linkages among local firms and with firms and markets in other centers (Rees, 1983). There may also be opportunities in some centers, such as those that have specialized in heavy machinery and machine tools, to become centers for manufacturing the "smart" hardware required in more knowledge-intensive jobs. The manufacture of industrial robots requires a skilled work force for their production. For other subordinate areas, back office support services, distributive services, and provision of attractive residential communities or recreational services may fill needed niches in the urban system.

4 Basic Concepts for Urban Economic Strategy

Before examining policy options or strategies in detail, we should examine some basic concepts that might guide their selection. Our analysis of the impact of the changing economic structure on urban areas suggests that there are foreseeable differences in the economic potential of different types of cities in the urban system. Serious mismatches can be anticipated between available jobs and available labor. The most critical problems are in the subordinate centers with historically specialized manufacturing economies and labor forces.

The transformation of urban areas and the emergence of a new urban system raise questions about how policies concerned with the economic change and development of urban areas can be reconciled with policies concerned primarily with the overall national economy. For some urban areas the transition to a new kind of economy is already well advanced; for others it is just beginning. For all urban areas, long-term changes in economic roles seem highly probable.

Development and growth are not synonymous. *Growth* refers to the proportional expansion of area, population, firms, and jobs. *Development* implies structural change and may accompany either growth or decline. It involves adjustment to new economic roles, changes in the capital stock, development of skills in the labor force, and many other activities that change the character, appearance, and economy of a place. Each type of urban area that we have discussed has different kinds of development problems stemming from the historic mix of industries and occupations and the current state of the markets for them. These important differences

59

make it virtually impossible for a uniform policy or economic development strategy to work well in all types of metropolitan areas.

Development strategies will need to be tailored to the resources and potential of different types of urban areas, if not to each specific area. A simple strategy of concentrating on overall national economic growth will not result, even if it is successful, in prosperity for all urban areas. The reason for this is that the growing and declining manufacturing and service sectors of the economy are often located in different places. Some of the sectors that are in decline will not be substantially revived by general economic recovery because structural changes in those sectors will permanently eliminate many jobs that previously existed.

That the conditions of each area are unique does not mean that there is no place for national policy concerned with urban economic development or that all of the problems are entirely local in nature. It means rather that there are national, regional, and local aspects of most urban problems. Accordingly, national policy might concentrate on providing a general framework and kit of tools that can be used, within a wide range of discretion, by regional and local decision makers at each level of the political system to fit their specific needs (Committee for Economic Development, 1977; National Research Council, 1982b).

RECONCILING NATIONAL, URBAN, AND SECTORAL INTERESTS

The national economy is a composite of little economies, functioning largely through the urban system and linked by economic institutions and transactions. For an urban economic development strategy to be effective within such a system, it must operate at both national and subnational levels. While national and urban interests in economic development are not always the same, there are no rigid distinctions based on constitutionally proper functions. Just as national and urban interests differ, the interests of industries may diverge substantially from those of the cities that house them. Understanding these interests and where they converge or diverge is a necessary first step in devising a workable urban economic development strategy.

The Formation and Flow of Capital

Each component of the political economy has an interest in the formation of capital and its investment in activities that contribute to the expansion of the national economy. Making the economic pie larger eases the problem of sharing it among regions and groups, although there is still a distribution problem. Traditionally, the national government has assumed responsibility for policies to promote capital formation. But from the earliest days of the Republic, as exemplified by Alexander Hamilton's *Report on the Subject of Manufactures*, the national government has not been neutral about where the capital that is formed goes. It has regularly (if not consistently) favored investments in some sectors and activities over others.

The chief instruments of national economic policy—tax policy, the federal budget, monetary and credit policies, trade regulations—have each played major roles in the allocation of capital to different sectors of the economy, to regions, and to urban areas (Glickman, 1980; Vaughan, 1977). This effect is now widely acknowledged, but policies primarily concerned with the formation of capital have not been particularly sensitive to their effect on its geographic distribution (Howell, 1981). The results are substantial but often unintended and unanticipated. A recent study by the Rand Corporation (Vaughan, 1977) shows that the effects of many policies are unknown. Some policies, such as those for monetary, fiscal, and defense programs, whether intended or not, have quite different impacts on regions and on central cities than on their suburbs.

The Distribution of Economic Opportunity

Although not all policies reflect it, there has been a long-standing national interest in distributing the nation's economic growth in a manner that reduces the number of places and groups that are left outside the economic mainstream. This important national interest has been reflected in a great variety of policies throughout the nation's history. It includes policies that encouraged settlement of the frontier, developed ports and waterways, provided land grants to canal and railroad companies, regulated interstate transportation rates, and built a national highway system.

Other policies declared the national interest in limiting business concentrations through antitrust legislation, equalizing minimum wages and maximum hours of work, providing for secure retirements through social security, and encouraging employment opportunity for minorities. The Full Employment Act, the Tennessee Valley Authority (TVA), the Area Redevelopment Act, the Appalachian Regional Commission, the antipoverty program, and the Model Cities program were all manifestations expressed through the political system of a national interest in intergroup and interregional equity and widely distributed economic opportunity.

This national interest in the distribution of opportunities and the growth of jobs and incomes for all groups and regions has been an important means of promoting social stability and of reducing the social costs of having a large, dependent population. There has generally been a recognition that not all places in the nation can grow fast, but there has also been a readiness either to shelter troubled areas through devices such as tariffs or to try to stimulate growth in areas that were lagging behind the rest of the economy through more direct programs, such as reclamation projects, the TVA, and the location of federal installations.

The national interest in the distribution of economic activity has sought to avoid the most serious, debilitating, and damaging interregional conflicts and competition.[1] In recent years this interest has involved providing infrastructure, such as the interstate highway system, the urban mass transportation program, capital grants for sewage treatment, and a system of fiscal transfers designed to assist states and localities in maintaining levels of public services for their residents and adequate systems of infrastructure for the growth of local economies.

Although historically the national interest in urban economic development has included a recognition that the aggregate level of growth can be materially retarded if some region or group is left substantially behind others, it has not included a systematic approach to either regional development or the flow of capital to particular sectors of the economy, which may also have important regional implications (Schwartz and Choate, 1980:65-87).

Economic and Social Stability

Given the respect for pluralism that characterizes policy making in the federal system, the national interest recognizes that regional or local interests may at times be in conflict with each other and with national interests. These conflicts are permitted in the interest of diversity and experimentation, so long as there is no direct challenge to a clearly stated federal power.

At the local level, interest in economic development often embodies an intensely parochial concern for economic and social stability that is indifferent or even hostile to the economic fortunes of other areas. From the perspective of overall national interest, it may matter little where new or expanded economic activity occurs, but that issue is central to local interests. They will fight hard to save subsidies that favor them, even if such subsidies can be shown to be counterproductive to national interests in economic growth.

---

[1] To some extent this was the underlying purpose of the commerce clause of the Constitution (*Gibbons* v. *Ogden*, 22 U.S.1 [1824]).

Each jurisdiction tends to maintain a competitive interest in its own economic health relative to other jurisdictions in the vicinity. Each is therefore deeply interested in maintaining and expanding the pool of capital available for investment in local businesses, housing, and consumer credit. The interest in the size of the pool, however, may be secondary to the interest in the geographical flow of capital, whether its source is the local pool or financial institutions in other places within whose sphere of influence the jurisdiction lies. One of the persistent problems for older central cities, in particular, has been the flight of capital from downtown to the suburbs, even though the amount available within city institutions has been growing. The flight of private capital affects the availability of public capital, since most jurisdictions depend heavily on the growth in the assessable base of real property as the principal source of revenues for public capital investments. Thus, where private capital expansion is slow, intergovernmental fiscal transfers become increasingly important as a means of meeting budget needs (U.S. Congress, Joint Economic Committee, 1981a, 1981b).

Expansion of Local Economic Opportunity

While the institutional interest of local jurisdictions in the growth of the revenue base is crucial in the local political economy, there is also a strong urban interest in economic development as a source of opportunity for the upward income and occupational mobility of the local labor force and as a source of prosperity for local businesses. To a considerable extent the growth of the metropolitan or regional economy benefits these interests, wherever it occurs in the area. There are two problems with such a generalization, however. The first has to do with the availability of new jobs generated by growth to the existing work force of the area. Growth in sectors for which the local labor force is not prepared can result in simultaneous increases in the net number of jobs and in the number of unemployed workers or dependent households. There is, of course, an interdependence among job levels. The growth of jobs for highly skilled workers and the filling of them with either local residents or imported labor can generate some jobs in the local economy for less-skilled workers.

The second problem has to do with physical access of the lower strata of the labor force to the new jobs. In many cases neither the public transportation nor the job information network facilitates access to lower-income members of the labor force. In other cases the jobs realistically available to such workers do not make moving to them worth the effort (G. Clark, 1983). Such conditions can frustrate both national interests in labor mobility and economic efficiency and local interests in economic growth and development.

The restructured economy has its most profound effects in those metropolitan areas that have been the centers for manufacturing, although the effects can be felt in almost all areas to some extent. Displaced production workers, who have enjoyed high wages and benefits in unionized industries, often find that new service jobs pay less than their old jobs, and they are often reluctant to accept them. When they do, they often find that they are dead-end jobs, with little opportunity for promotion or increasing levels of pay. Poorly prepared young people and other unskilled workers have difficulty entering or reentering the labor market and in moving up the occupational ladder, either in the places where they currently live or in new places to which they might move. The unemployment and underemployment of both groups of workers could become a substantial social cost for all levels of government, particularly for local governments in the communities where redundant laborers and unemployed or underemployed people are concentrated. The most critical situations will be in those places where the loss of firms and jobs employing manual workers cannot be offset by jobs in services and other manufacturing industries that provide incomes and opportunities for advancement comparable to the jobs that are lost. At the same time, it is possible to foresee critical shortages of workers to fill some kinds of jobs.

The challenge to public policy is to come to grips with the mismatches between the demand for labor in the growing sectors of the economy and the supply of labor that exists among occupational groups and among local or regional labor markets. Responding to this challenge involves developing strategies for the education and training of the current and future labor forces. It also involves developing programs that encourage redundant workers and other unemployed people to redirect their interests and skills to other occupations and, in many cases, to other places. In an age of international competition and rapid technological changes, both with pervasive impacts on American economic structure, strategies seem called for to avoid future high rates of obsolescence for groups of workers by the development of transferable skills and of continuing programs of transitional education and training for much of the labor force.

In thinking about urban economic development, there is a tendency to focus policy on the declining parts of the economy, the most devastated neighborhoods, and the most distressed people. Certainly ameliorative actions are needed for such places and people, but an exclusive emphasis on helping the "worst first" can result in overlooking important opportunities that can ultimately improve the prospects of the most seriously disadvantaged groups (Schwartz, 1983). While attention is focused on the worst, higher-income residents and business firms may slip away.

Urban policy should be concerned simultaneously with two realms: the mainstream and those left outside (National Research Council, 1982a). In a strategy that is concerned with how to channel the mainstream of economic growth and that builds on the strengths of the local economy, a number of factors are important:

- the size of the market and the quality of the producer services;
- the mix of industries and the skills available in the labor force;
- educational, health, and cultural institutions;
- amenities; and
- the quality of public facilities and other capital stock.

Each factor may have comparative advantages for particular types of industries. Each affects the current role of the area in the urban system and the potential that exists for carving out a stronger position.

Careful delineation of the position of an area with respect to the mainstream of economic development involves more than a casual determination to offer itself as a capital for high-technology industry. As the discussion of the new urban system in Chapter 3 points out, some places have a substantial head start toward performance of certain functions in the new economy.

Not every area is destined, even with intense motivation and strong public-private cooperation, to become a national or regional center for high-technology industries, corporate complexes, and producer services. There may be substantial potential, however, for other functions, such as distribution centers or specialized services or goods production. Because it is now possible to disperse parts of a service or manufacturing industry to locations distant from the headquarters, many more cities are candidates for communications, records, or training centers than in the past.

Subordinate centers will need to link their strategies consciously to the economies of command and control centers and to seek activities that broaden the range of economic functions they can perform. In particular, there is a need to identify activities that can operate as accelerators of other kinds of development, such as research and development or other specialized business services (Rees, 1983).

It is important to recognize that, following the best strategies and even with the best of luck, some places will endure further disinvestment, decline in personal income, and some population loss before a long-term role in the new economy is well established. In fact, assuming that role may depend on some reduction in size.

A strategy that seeks to take advantage of mainstream opportunities is incomplete if it fails to address the problems of the least resilient communities and people. The object of such policy is to improve access to the mainstream. Policies concerned with those left outside necessarily include some elements that are primarily designed to ameliorate the impact of structural change. The principal thrust of policy, however, should be to create opportunities for people and their communities to make adjustments to new jobs and new functions. This may be done with measures to stimulate new jobs in existing communities as well as by enhancing the ability of other displaced workers to follow opportunities to other areas. Thus, strategies for those left behind—whether they are workers whose skills are made redundant by changing markets and technology, the unskilled working poor, or members of the emerging underclass— include elements of education, training or retraining, capital investment, local job creation, and mobility assistance.

TRANSITIONAL AND LONG-TERM STRATEGIES

Not all urban areas have reached the same point in their development, and not all are changing at the same pace. Some have already gone through a major transformation in their economic functions and have assumed new roles in the urban system. Others are in the earliest stages of structural change. In light of this, urban economic development policy must be concerned with two different time periods. First, it must be concerned with the period of transition. During this time, old familiar functions may be diminishing, and new areas of strength may be hard to identify. Second, decisions must be made to guide the longer period that follows the transition, a time when a new and fairly stable pattern of economic activity has emerged. The two periods are, of course, related. Actions taken during the transition will affect the long term; choices of long-term strategies will limit options during the transition. The character of federal policy for each time period should also be different.

Transitional Strategy

The transition period is the most difficult, both conceptually and politically, for in one sense urban areas are always in transition. There usually is little hard economic information on which to base decisions. Even when the leaders of an area are aware that major changes are taking place, they often fail to understand the reasons for them. It may be difficult to distinguish between cyclical adjustments by local firms and more fundamental structural shifts that will extend far beyond the end of a business cycle downturn.

Rapid and persistent change, as has occurred in the automobile and steel industries, may place the local economy in shock as firms that historically have been stable sources of income and employment reduce their work forces and permanently close some facilities. The ripple effect of decline in the basic industries of an area tends to induce a self-aggravating process of general urban decline (Bradbury et al., 1980). Disinvestment in some sectors may discourage investment in other, potentially healthy sectors. The loss of income from jobs and sales and the reduction in property values of abandoned plants and slow or negative appreciation of private homes reduce local revenues and services, making the community less attractive for new investment and for higher-income residents. Out-migration of more educated younger workers and higher-income families tends to leave the central city with a smaller population, a higher proportion of which is heavily dependent on a diminishing public treasury (Fossett and Nathan, 1981; Government Finance Research Center, 1982).

One factor that makes the formulation of transition strategies difficult is the reality that a subarea, particularly the older, more central jurisdictions, may lose population and jobs. This often produces stopgap rather than strategic thinking, with a fixation on the parts of the economy that are declining rather than a focus on sectors of the economy that have considerably more potential for expansion. Transitional strategies in particular need to incubate new business and expand those sectors with growth potential. They also must be concerned with stabilizing the local economy and the fiscal system so that change can occur without trauma.

To some degree the transition period can be likened to the triage process in emergency medicine, in which the hopeless cases are separated from those that can be saved, and priorities are assigned on the basis of the seriousness of the cases (Ylvisaker, 1981). The problem for declining urban areas is that the triage process must often be conducted by the wounded themselves.

In rapidly growing urban areas the transition period produces an entirely different impact. Sudden population growth and economic expansion induce a process of growth and development that seems almost self-generating. For these areas the strategic problem is likely to be one of managing development to avoid future social and environmental costs and to provide public facilities and services in reasonable sequence with the development of the private economy. Such areas should try to avoid externalities from one stage of growth that can strangle future development opportunities or impose high social costs.[2]

Long-Term Strategy

Urban development is a drawn-out process. It is never complete because cities continue to change as they mature. Formulating and carrying out a long-term strategy require an enduring consensus among the principal actors in the development process on its broad elements. Long-term thinking is impaired, moreover, by the institutional structure of urban and metropolitan politics. It is particularly difficult for those beset with immediate problems, such as the executives of declining businesses and the leaders of unions whose members face imminent loss of jobs, to think about the long term. Corporate thinking tends to concentrate on short-term profitability. The political system operates with two- to four-year time horizons. At the federal level, urban policy has been inconstant, making it virtually impossible to make long-term plans that rely on federal programs.

Those places that seem to have produced the most successful economic development strategies usually have a stable political regime and an underlying consensus among leadership groups on overall goals. Baltimore, Dallas, Boston, Columbus, Indianapolis, Atlanta, and Pittsburgh are examples of such places. Their political leadership has usually been complemented with a strong and cohesive economic leadership group (Fosler and Berger, 1982).

---

[2] Houston and Phoenix provide examples of alternative development strategies for fast-growing metropolitan areas. Houston, with an aversion to any public development policy, allowed development to proceed to such a point that severe traffic congestion and flash flooding problems have become common. The result is a dampening of the market for further growth. Phoenix, in contrast, has a development strategy, based on the "urban village" concept, to try to produce a more orderly pattern of development, channeling the location of the market but not attempting to reduce its overall volume.

Other fast-growing communities have fashioned more detailed growth-management strategies. Among the most sophisticated are those of San Diego, California; Boulder, Colorado; and Montgomery County, Maryland. For examples of some (mostly restrictive) growth-control strategies and their consequences, see Scott and Brower (1976). Growth management produces its own costs. In general, restrictions on development add to the cost of housing and other construction. Unless operated on a fairly large geographic scale, they also tend to cause the growth in a rising regional market simply to spill over into nearby areas under less restrictive control (Frieden, 1979).

Long-term strategy involves some notion, however vaguely formed, of the future role of the area in the national economy and the urban system. This notion, or image, need not be expressed graphically, as in an end-state master plan; it can be fairly general, such as an intention to become a center for energy industries, robotics, or recreation, or some combination of objectives. Such idealized statements should change as experience is gained, the competition assayed, and assets counted. The value of objectives or goals is that they raise the more important questions of how to reach them, which are at the heart of making long-term strategy. If there is no reasonable prospect of achieving them, more realistic goals should be developed.

What must be done may involve fundamental pieces of urban engineering, such as the provision of reliable water supplies or a workable transportation system. An urban area has little prospect of performing a role as a regional center, for example, if it cannot provide good air transportation to other regional and national centers.

Essentially, long-term strategy involves the conscious creation of comparative advantages. In an age in which capital is highly mobile, several places can be equally suitable, from an objective view, for many economic activities. Thus, the qualitative aspects of the urban environment are becoming more important factors in economic development strategy—physical appearance, public and commercial services, the cultural atmosphere, the quality of the educational system, the proximity of research institutions, and parks and recreation resources. As employment gravitates toward service occupations, a community's success in urban development will depend on its ability to provide the kind of labor force and environment that are attractive to specific types of firms. Most of these things involve more than policy that drifts behind pure market choices. They often require market-forcing decisions.

The growth of Dallas, for example, was stimulated by the creation of a major international airport and the location of a branch of the state university. Both were critical pieces of its long-term economic development strategy. Pittsburgh has begun consciously to develop capability as a center for robotics, fusing the interests of some of its industries, such as Westinghouse and Unimation, with its universities. In the Detroit area the automobile companies are engaging in joint ventures with the University of Michigan to develop new manufacturing technologies.

The point is that urban development can no longer be taken for granted. Public policy plays an important role in the process of transition and long-term reorientation and adjustment. At the local level, strategic policy making is the process through which a community goes as it learns about itself and the new economic environment within which it lives and as it redefines its intentions and the steps that public and private institutions will have to take to realize them.

While it is unlikely that national or local policy can change the direction of the international economic forces transforming urban areas, it can influence the rate at which trends move and can affect how readily many areas anticipate and adjust to change.

CONCLUSION

In light of these basic concepts, a framework for urban economic development strategy seems to require, first, policies that accelerate the process of transformation, concentrating on the flow of capital to those activities on which the future of urban economies ultimately depends. By themselves, however, such policies could exacerbate disparities in the performance of cities with growing and declining economies and could destabilize both in the short term. To facilitate adjustment of urban areas to new, long-term economic roles and to smooth the transition, it would be prudent to balance actions that accelerate change in the aggregate national economy with policies that help stabilize communities as they undergo substantial change. In this context, communities and their residents should be encouraged and enabled to rethink their roles and to identify and pursue appropriate functions in the urban system.

5 Investing Private and Public Capital in the Urban Future

Just as today's urban areas reflect past patterns of capital investment, those of tomorrow will reflect the flow of capital that is occurring now. Private capital flows to economic activities and, incidentally, to the places where those activities occur. The activities that attract private capital and the speed with which they attract it can have a profound impact on patterns of development and, as we have seen, on how areas evolve in the urban system.

Because they rarely reach major money and stock markets, local and state policies appear to have relatively little effect on the flows of private capital to firms; the market and federal policies are far more influential. State and local policies are, however, far more important factors in the location of firms. Public investment in urban infrastructure, environmental regulations, and economic development policies can influence where firms are able to locate. Federal policy also substantially affects the level of state and local public investment and the kinds of facilities that are provided.

This chapter discusses the implications for urban areas of policies that would stimulate the flow of capital to those sectors of the economy that show promise of strong performance in international markets and others that need modernization or are important to national interests. Such policies are significant for urban policy because they could accelerate the transformation of urban areas; they raise significant issues about the use of capital resources in urban economic development. The level and quality of public investments are other aspects of national urban policy that can

71

affect how well, and how fast, urban areas are able to adjust to a major shift in economic structure. We thus consider the need to make sufficient capital available for infrastructure to support economic development. We conclude the chapter by discussing a framework for urban economic development strategy.

INVESTMENT IN PRODUCTIVE SECTORS

When we talk about the flow of capital to particular sectors of the economy, we do so with considerable modesty. The state of knowledge of capital markets and how they work is still rudimentary. What causes investors to move their money from one sector to another and especially from one region to another is not always clear. Classes of investors seek different objectives: some are content with secure, long-term low yields; others take high risks in hope of quick, high returns. The sources of capital are diverse. Financial institutions, businesses, pension funds, and individuals make millions of calculated or impulsive decisions every day. They consider factors ranging from exhaustive studies by market and industrial analysts to their horoscopes. Net flows of capital reflect the cumulative result of those decisions. In this context one factor that influences investor choice is public policy.

Whether it is deliberately interventionist or passive toward capital markets, public policy affects levels of risk and rates of return on investments. It also influences how investors perceive certain sectors of the economy. For example, monetary and fiscal policies affect how much capital is available to the private sector for investment and its cost to borrowers. Credit and tax policies may encourage investments in industries such as housing or energy development. Direct subsidies may improve yields from investments in agriculture or defense industries. Indirect subsidies such as tax credits or loan guarantees can reduce risks for activities such as research and development or new enterprises.

Although they do not fully determine the direction of capital flows, the effect of national economic policies on the flow of capital to different sectors of the economy is increasingly recognized as a serious national problem (Schwartz and Choate, 1980:65-88; U.S. Congress, Joint Economic Committee, 1974). In spite of gaps in our understanding of just how or to what extent policy affects capital flows, some sectors have been consciously subsidized over a long period of time—housing, agriculture, defense, and transportation are examples. An estimated 13.9 percent of the GNP in 1980 was consumed in subsidies to various industries, exclusive of the costs to consumers of various special barriers to international competition, such as tariffs, market quotas, cartelization (Reich, 1982).

Whatever the original reasons for these subsidies, they have often continued, almost as entitlements, without serious assessment of their impact on the flow of capital to other sectors that might improve both national economic efficiency and interregional or intergroup equity (Schwartz, 1983). The lack of any coherent strategy results in part from the fact that most subsidies arose initially more from the success of specific industries in legislative lobbying than from a careful determination that their net effect assisted the economy in meeting international competition, increased productivity, or provided for real growth in the GNP.[1]

Once established, such subsidies are extremely difficult to terminate because they produce an organized constituency that represents both labor and management; it often spans the ideological spectrum from right to left. The withdrawal of subsidies, whether direct or indirect, can create genuine economic dislocation. Adjustment problems are no less severe than those created by technological change or foreign competition. Financial institutions, for example, have undergone major restructuring in the wake of changes in monetary and credit policies and as a result of changes in federal regulations. Similarly, the sectoral consequences of the 1981 Economic Recovery Tax Act are substantial, but many of them were both unanticipated and unintended (Palmer and Sawhill, 1982).

In the absence of any conscious sectoral perspective, national macroeconomic policies are highly susceptible to political pressure and panicked governmental responses to industrial crises, as in the cases of Lockheed, Chrysler, Wisconsin Steel, or the thrift industry. While all or any of the actions taken to rescue these industries or firms might be defended from a rational economic policy perspective, they offer no suggestion of what U.S. policy might be toward the next crisis. Moreover, the ad hoc approach to sectoral policy that they illustrate tends to focus on the most troubled among specific industrial sectors, leaving the growth sectors of the economy to chance.

Sectoral Policy and Its Critics

This lack of coherence has led a growing number of economists and business interests to propose that the United States establish an industrial or sectoral policy aimed at strengthening the international competitive

---

[1] Reich (1982) points out that in 1980 five times as much was being spent on research and development in the commercial fisheries industry as in the steel industry and that while the timber industry received tax breaks of $455 million, the semiconductor industry received none (also see Schwartz and Choate, 1980).

position of U.S. industries and at facilitating the adjustment of the economy to structural changes (Bell and Lande, 1982; *Business Week,* June
30, 1981; Leone and Bradley, 1981; Reich, 1982; Schwartz and Choate,
1980).

The advocates of this position argue that national economic policy has
been concerned primarily with the aggregate growth of capital and that,
while this is necessary, it is not sufficient when the overall restructuring
of the national economy is occurring simultaneously with the internal
restructuring of many sectors and industries. Thus in contrast with the
thrust of traditional national economic policy, sectoral policy would be
more concerned with capital allocation than with aggregate capital formation. It would focus on the most productive pattern of investment,[2]
favoring those linked industries that show strong promise as international
competitors and as sources of economic growth as well as other industrial
groups that are important to national interests. At the same time, sectoral
policies would seek to develop the industrial infrastructure and the skilled
work force that is needed to support those linked industries. They would
also recognize the need to balance the growth of regions, to maintain a
strong productive capacity in certain industries, and to assist workers
forced to retrain or relocate in order to defuse the resistance to economic
change likely to come from those who would be hardest hit (Reich, 1982:75).[3]

The critics of sectoral policy contend that it would involve the government in planning the economy and in the selection of industrial winners
and losers through a political process rather than through the market.
National economic policy, they argue, should concentrate instead on capital formation, letting the market determine where capital should flow.
The basic concern of the national government should, therefore, be on
the aggregate growth of the economy, without regard to where that growth
occurs regionally or in which sectors of the economy.

While advocates of sectoral policy point to the success of other countries, particularly Japan, in promoting the growth of some industries and
facilitating the shrinkage of others that were less competitive, the critics
remain skeptical of the actual effect of public policy on national economic

---

[2] The evidence is weak that the restructuring of the economy that has occurred, as such, has
increased productivity—at least as productivity is usually measured. Since 1973 the effect on
productivity has been slightly negative (Jorgenson, 1980). A more recent study concludes,
however, that the shift to services has had a negligible effect on productivity decline, a fact that
is attributable mainly to shifts in goods-producing industries (Kutscher and Mark, 1982).

[3] Such authors as Reich (1982) and Schwartz (1983) distinguish their proposals from "reindus-
trialization," which implies an effort to revitalize industries with a declining share of world
markets or those that make products that have little growth in demand.

performance. They see government intervention primarily as a ratification of market or industry choices rather than as a decisive factor in them. They point to failures in decisions or refusals of industries to follow policy and to great differences in national attitudes toward monopolies, labor relations, and banking systems as constraints on transferring cooperative approaches to industrial policy, such as those in Japan, to the United States (Eads, 1981).

Critics also argue that the market, with all its faults, is still far better at selecting competitive industries than a bureaucracy or the Congress. The market provides a reliable feedback mechanism that tests the soundness of investment. Because government-induced investments generate constituencies devoted to the perpetuation of the intervention—even if it is unsuccessful from the point of view of the overall economy—any industrial policy would lack the self-correcting discipline of the market. The result would be unnecessary overinvestment in some sectors and underinvestment in others because of political choices (Eads, 1981).

A Strategy for Sectoral Policy

As we have discussed in Chapter 4, macroeconomic policy makes choices that may favor some industries or sectors over others. The result is an implicit industrial policy. The decision-making process is not structured in a manner that requires the consequences of those choices to be weighed against each other. In many cases, subsidies are not identified and their costs are not even acknowledged (Eads and Graham, 1982).

Political choices about the economy tend to be made largely in terms of anticipated first-order consequences, that is, will they stimulate or dampen the growth of the GNP? In an increasingly interdependent economy, second-order consequences—effects on specific sectors of the economy or on economic regions—though often unintended, may be more significant. These consequences are also harder to foresee or forecast. There is a need for a more sophisticated understanding of these second-order consequences and for consideration of alternative policies that might have more salutary effects or fewer adverse impacts. Just as the Full Employment Act and the creation of the Council of Economic Advisers and the Joint Economic Committee have made the President and the Congress more sensitive to the first-order consequences of their economic decisions, it is now desirable to require wider understanding of second-order consequences for particular sectors of the economy and for urban areas.

Given the pluralism of our political economy, it may not be possible, even if it were deemed desirable, to produce an internally consistent, comprehensive, and explicit sectoral policy. In that light the task is to understand the policy system well enough to obtain a better result from the implicit policies. This suggests a conscious strategy as distinguished from a specific policy or comprehensive law on the subject. It also allows for a more experimental approach in an area in which too little is known to justify a doctrinaire program.

Such an approach recognizes that some sectors and activities may indeed be more promising than others for improving the competitiveness of U.S. industries in the world economy; to the extent that our competitiveness is enhanced, the number of jobs and the levels of income would be increased. In this approach, economic policies should be examined to see whether they are likely to reduce friction that impedes the development of those sectors that are growing in response to market forces (Schwartz and Choate, 1980:109ff.). This approach to sectoral strategy is concerned with accelerating or at least not impeding the shift of capital and workers from declining to more promising sectors, as they are defined by the market. It is also concerned with revitalizing and modernizing those sectors that are important to national security, such as energy, machine tools, and basic metals (National Academy of Engineering, 1983), and to other national interests, such as public health and agriculture.

Sectoral strategy is concerned not only with the traditional or troubled industries, such as the automotive sector, in which new capital is needed for modernization, but also with emerging industries, such as genetic engineering and international health services, and with sectors in which the United States may already be dominant but could maintain or expand its market position, such as computer technology. This strategy assumes that some sectors can be expected to shrink and others to grow as they adapt to new technologies, new markets, and new relationships within the economy (Schwartz, 1983).

In addition to marginally influencing the flow of capital to those sectors with strong market potential, sectoral strategy should support investment in the development of the resources and systems they need to thrive. This includes support for research and development, either directly or indirectly through incentives built into macroeconomic policies (Mansfield, 1982).[4] It also includes support for infrastructure (both public and private), training the labor force, and improving management and productivity systems.

---

[4] See Landau (1982) for a discussion of the importance of research and development to the national economy and the relationship of tax policies to research and development. The delay between invention and innovation and the discontinuity between old and new technologies appear to be serious issues in need of policy attention (see Girifalco, 1981).

Different sectors require different treatment during their growth cycles. While price deregulation may be sufficient to reinforce enormous flows of capital to energy-related industries, a quite different, more detailed approach is required to speed modernization of the automobile, steel, and machine tool industries. For them it is important not only to introduce new technology, such as robotics, but also to bring about major institutional changes in research and development, to change the locations of some parts of the production process, to change management and labor relations processes, and to improve international trade and marketing conditions (National Research Council, 1983). Public policy can affect the degree and timing of these changes. Tax credits for plant modernization or research and development, trade agreements, and the regulatory climate all affect investment decisions.

Strategies appropriate to growth in high technology may also require more than general tax credits for investments. Special incentives or programs for high-risk ventures seem required, particularly since one of the principal forms of capital in new small enterprises is the talent of a few scientists, engineers, and managers (Landau, 1982). Front-end venture capital for such enterprises may often be far more crucial than tax abatement or tax credits. It may also be important to consider changes in supporting institutional systems, such as small-business development corporations, patent law reform, university-corporate relationships (Giamatti, 1982), and university-government relationships (National Academy of Sciences, 1983). In this sector and others, such as health services, the supply of trained workers is a basic requirement for growth. The availability of business services can also be critical to high-risk, small-scale enterprises. This is suggested by the high survival rate of firms assisted by Control Data Corporation's Business Technology Centers (Norris, 1982).

Considerations such as these argue that the principal instruments of macroeconomic policy could, at a minimum, be better informed and sharpened by a conscious identification of those sectors that show considerable promise for growth, those that are in trouble, and how each is likely to be affected by existing or proposed policies (Eads and Graham, 1982). Macroeconomic policies could also benefit from an effort to identify their intended (or at least their anticipated and probable) consequences for flows of capital to particular sectors of the economy and how they might, correspondingly, affect the structure of the labor market. Although economic theory has not reconciled the conflicts in perspective between macroeconomic and microeconomic thought, a unified theory does not seem necessary in order to establish a regularized feedback process to allow these two perspectives to confront and be informed by each other (Landau, 1982; Michalski, 1982).

The admonition of critics of industrial policy that it would be unwise for government to try to choose specific winners and losers is sound. Experience with government support of research and development in seven different industries suggests that the support was most successful when it was associated with government procurement or a well-defined public objective, when the expenditures were guided by the scientific community, and when potential users guided fund allocations. Programs in which government officials tried to identify projects that would be commercial winners were the least successful (Nelson, 1982).

It should be possible, however, to do a better job of coordinating national economic policies to complement or reinforce the strategies of industrial sectors as they seek to strengthen their positions in the market. It should also be possible to reinforce the ability of market participants to plan ahead more confidently but still leave private investors free to evaluate business opportunities and to make decisions (Michalski, 1982). In this sense, sectoral strategy is not national planning but an attempt to make the economy more adaptable and dynamic. Its objectives are to smooth the movement of capital and labor out of declining industries and to ensure that capital, labor, and other support is available to the more promising and essential sectors. It aims to "accelerate and smooth the adjustments that capital and labor markets would otherwise achieve more slowly on their own" (Reich, 1982).

Implications of Sectoral Policy for Urban Areas

Policies that prop up industries with poor futures on an equal basis with industries that have promising futures ultimately waste resources and do not really improve the long-run economic prospects of the urban areas in which the troubled industries are located. The capacity of urban areas to adjust to the new roles they must play depends heavily on the performance of those sectors that are central to their economies and on their ability to attract and nurture new kinds of economic activity. From an urban perspective, a sectoral strategy at the national level would help urban areas understand better where the economy is headed and how their communities and labor forces may be affected. It would help them identify the parts of their local economies that have the most potential for growth in market shares and jobs as well as those that have less, even though they may continue to be viable enterprises.

Neither a general recovery of the national economy nor a more coordinated approach to policies affecting the flow of capital to particular sectors will result in an even distribution of economic opportunity and wealth among regions and urban areas. The introduction of a sectoral perspective into the shaping of national economic policies would alter some of the urban effects of macroeconomic policies, but it would not confront many of the most difficult issues of urban economic adjustment. The phenomenon of simultaneous growth and decline within many urban areas will continue. So will the concentration of services in the national and regional centers and the decline of some of the older manufacturing centers as capital flows are directed to higher-yielding investments that, incidentally, are located elsewhere.

Some areas will get richer while others become poorer. There will still be substantial labor redundancy in places where old industrial and labor markets are contracting and changing structurally, even while some local industry is being revitalized. The rate of job creation will diverge on the basis of the economic function each metropolitan area performs. There will still be serious institutional barriers to the mobility of workers from one industry or occupation to another and from one metropolitan area or region to another.

Sectoral strategies are concerned primarily with the mainstream of the economy. This means that in all likelihood the reinforcement of capital would flow to high-technology enterprises, producer services, and some nonprofit services such as health and education. Substantial and accelerated growth would be expected in those places that have the natural resources, labor forces, or other established growing industries on which these activities depend and the institutional base, external economies, and environment conducive to their needs. Similarly, the higher-level workers—professionals, technicians, and managers—could expect greater gains from national economic growth than could service, clerical, and blue-collar workers. Within individual areas and within the urban system, there will be firms, places, and people that lose and gain.

A change in national tax policy, for example, that provides increased incentives for research and development could provide some advantages to cities in which research institutions associated with growing industries are located. Policies that make it easier to sell services abroad would help urban economies in which large-scale business service firms are concentrated, chiefly the diversified and specialized service centers.

Large-scale military expenditures are most helpful to the military-industrial centers and to those diversified or specialized centers that contain substantial suppliers of military hardware or services. Some defense expenditures, especially for research and development, and set-asides for procurement from depressed areas are important tools for urban economic development when they are consciously used to complement market forces in the diffusion of innovation to other industries and to different urban areas (Rees, 1983).

It is important to recognize that modernizing an industry does not necessarily mean restoring the same jobs in the same places. The urban areas that could be most affected by sectoral policies aimed at modernizing the automobile industry can be easily identified. But modernization may in fact entail closing inefficient plants, mechanizing much of the work, and relocating some operations in other regions or countries.

Two hard-to-swallow realities should be acknowledged: (1) greater competitive advantage in any single set of linked industries does not necessarily lead to more jobs in all of the industries in that sector, and (2) all places do not stand to benefit equally from structural adjustments (Schwartz, in press). There are, in fact, substantial conflicts between sectoral and regional or urban policies (Garn and Ledebur, 1982).

INVESTMENT IN PLACES

Shifting From Distress to Opportunity

In a perfect world no policy would be necessary for those left behind. They would adjust to the emerging economy, and a new market equilibrium would be established. In the real political economies of advanced nations, however, friction impedes adjustment and prolongs it because the economic system is not pure and because its parts—places, people, and firms—are not interchangeable and have considerable inertia. Some places and people have less resilience, less capacity for positive adjustment to different long-term economic roles, than others. Because the growing and declining sectors are not evenly distributed among the regions of the country and among the different types of areas within the urban system, there is a need for a spatial as well as a sectoral perspective on national economic strategy.

What happens at the level of the urban area is important to the national economic system. When local unemployment is prolonged, some of the unemployed become unemployable. The decline of local industry can lead to a shrinkage of resources available for maintaining infrastructure and services. A change that may appear minor from the national perspective can be calamitous in the communities in which it is concentrated. Because of the preexisting mix of industries and occupations in specific communities and because of enormous investment in capital stock, there are far more rigidities to overcome at the local level than free market theory acknowledges. What appears as a national equilibrium can be composed of offsetting conditions of disequilibrium among urban areas, in which capacities for adjustment vary widely.

Historically, national urban policy has consisted primarily of place-oriented policies. These have included local planning assistance, urban redevelopment programs, employment training programs,[5] and a variety of income and fiscal transfer programs (Hanson, 1982; President's Commission for a National Agenda for the Eighties, 1980). Although these programs were substantial in number and have involved billions of dollars over the past two decades in direct grants, fiscal and income transfers, and tax expenditures or credits, they have been marginal to national economic policy. Like sector-related policies, urban policy often has been made as if national economic policy did not exist (Howell, 1981:346-347). There has been a tendency among national policy makers to think of distressed cities and urban neighborhoods as backwaters rather than as parts of the mainstream of policy.

Criticism of place-oriented policies by the President's Commission on the Eighties and the Reagan administration is valid to the extent that these policies were often designed to delay economic changes through subsidies to obsolete enterprises, skills, or settlements (U.S. Department of Housing and Urban Development, 1982). But such criticism is too sweeping. While some place-oriented policies have probably been counterproductive to constructive economic change and some have simply been ineffective, others have materially assisted cities, industries, and workers in making a transition to new functions and in generating better long-range local economic opportunities.[6] In general, however, program evaluations are so fragmentary that conclusions about whether programs have worked belong more to the realm of political than empirical judgment. About all that can safely be said is that place-oriented programs have had a minor if not negligible effect on the primary forces at work on the urban and national economy (Vaughan, 1977:132-137). But most of these policies were not intended as measures to alter primary economic forces. They were conceived instead to address specific local conditions, such as physical deterioration, lack of job skills, or poor public services.

Place-oriented policies have typically been targeted on the basis of indices of "distress." Because of the politics involved in developing statutory formulas for the distribution of funds, some have argued that

---

[5] The Comprehensive Employment and Training Act, however, was not strictly a place-oriented policy.

[6] For example, see evaluations of the Urban Development Action Grants program conducted by the Reagan administration (*Housing and Development Reporter*, February 1, 1982:687) and the Comprehensive Employment and Training Act (Mirengoff et al., 1980a, 1980b; also see Glickman, 1980).

there is almost an iron law of political dispersion that produces formulas allowing some money to be spent in almost all congressional districts (Dommel et al., 1978, 1980).[7]

These observations about place-oriented programs suggest that greater attention should be given to the role an area might play in the restructured economy and in the urban system, its current stage of economic transformation, and how local institutional capacity for transition and adjustment can be enhanced (Rasmussen, 1981:316-329,339). Urban development policy that works in concert with sectoral strategy and is aimed at improving the overall competitive position of the nation must recognize that for some places to grow stronger in their most promising new functions, they may have to lose some jobs from obsolete functions. This means not just retraining some of the labor force but relocating it (Schwartz, 1983). It also means that such localities may need to shift substantially their course of development.

Leverage Capital

For an urban area to capitalize on its opportunities, it must first have capital. Private capital flows to those firms and activities for which returns are expected to be highest. As a general proposition, return from investment in older, distressed areas is lower than for similar firms in other areas because the costs of doing business are greater. Crime, transportation costs, regulations, and other factors external to the business influence such costs and, consequently, the level of risk for investors. In addition, some urban areas are capital-short, especially for higher-risk ventures. This shortage may result from lack of strong local banking institutions or simply from local banking policies that restrict investments to more conservative and conventional enterprises (Rees, 1983). It may also stem from decisions of resident corporations to invest their retained earnings in facilities located elsewhere. For slowly growing or declining areas to attract capital, it is often necessary to "leverage" private investments to make the return on them competitive with more robust locations.

Federal policy has long been an important factor in influencing the location of private investment in urban areas by offering investors realistic advantages instead of letting the private market take its course. Those advantages have consisted largely of access, available only through par-

---

[7] The law is perhaps illustrated by the Urban Enterprise Zone Bill reported in both 1982 and 1983 by the Senate Finance Committee. Because of concerns by rural state senators, it was amended to require that 8 of the 25 zones chosen each year be in rural areas.

ticular kinds of investments or in particular areas, to federal programs that increase the financial yield from those investments. This leverage may take the form of direct subsidies (urban development action grants), a "write down" of land costs (urban renewal), low-interest or guaranteed loans from the Federal Housing Administration or the Small Business Administration, supporting or complementary public facilities (interstate highways, urban mass transit), tax credits, and other incentives.

While state and local governments have powers such as land acquisition and clearance, they cannot be exercised without funding. The funding source has frequently been federal. Although the amount of federal funds involved may be only a small percentage of a project total, the funds have often been critical to the financial success or failure of a project because they represent the leverage needed to obtain the commitment of private funds, often at favorable rates of interest, from private lenders.

How critical federal leverage capital often has been to an entire development package is illustrated by a recent $40 million joint development project in Buffalo. The city acquired the land, using in part funds available for joint development from the federal Urban Mass Transportation Administration. It combined some of its unused Community Development Block Grant (CDBG) money with an Urban Development Action Grant (UDAG) to reduce developer borrowing costs and to provide low-interest mortgages. This leverage allowed a consortium of local banks and a union pension fund to provide the bulk of the financing at low interest rates (*Housing and Development Reporter*, September 27, 1982:360-361).

The effectiveness of federal leverage programs, particularly UDAG, has been widely accepted.[8] The critical question is therefore not whether to maintain federal leverage programs but what form they should take.

In addition to UDAG, two other approaches to providing leverage capital have been widely discussed in recent years: a national urban development bank and a new version of the Reconstruction Finance Corporation (RFC). Both would provide mechanisms for direct federal financial participation in loans, grants, and guarantees to firms or local governments (Sternlieb and Listokin, 1981). Aspects of both proposals were fused in legislation introduced in the 98th Congress (H.R. 638).

Neither proposal fits well into a framework that emphasizes tailoring strategies to local conditions or the development of strong local institu-

---

[8] The Reagan administration, for example, has reversed its initial inclination to terminate the program after a study commissioned by the U.S. Department of Housing and Urban Development confirmed its effectiveness. A separate study by the General Accounting Office reached similar conclusions. The administration has, however, reduced requests for funding leverage programs and continues to advocate elimination of the Economic Development Administration.

tions. Both the bank and a revived RFC would be capital retailers. As banker, the federal government would judge each project application independently and directly negotiate the loan. A funding mechanism that bypasses the local and state governments neither strengthens the continuing local institutional capacity nor provides strong incentives for public-private leadership and cooperation. While UDAG is also a retail capital program, it overcomes the second problem by making a partnership a sine qua non for grant eligibility.

Rather than establish new federal institutions to retail capital, it would seem more consistent with the concept of flexibility advanced in this report to conceive of the future federal role in urban economic development financing as that of a capital wholesaler. One way of performing such a role would be to consolidate various capital leverage funds that now exist into a single national fund. Such programs as Economic Development Administration loans and grants, Small Business Administration loan and loan guarantee programs, and various other general financing programs (possibly including UDAG) could be combined. Capital from the fund could be made available under UDAG-type rules to state, regional, and local development corporations that include both public and private leadership and that can produce a well-developed strategy for economic development.[9] Under this approach, the actual decisions on where to use the funds (so long as loans meet criteria for financing projects that facilitate economic transitions) would be left to the discretion of the state or local lending arm of the development corporation. The difficulty in establishing such a fund should not be underestimated. The Carter administration proposed an urban development bank with some of these characteristics, but the proposal ran afoul of competing congressional committee jurisdictions.

Another current proposal for stimulating urban economic development by attracting businesses and jobs to chronically distressed areas is the enterprise zone. As proposed by the administration, the federal government would approve 25 zones a year for 3 years. Businesses locating in the zones, which would be in distressed areas of cities or rural communities, would be eligible for tax credits and regulatory relief. Local governments would compete for the zone designations with a package of incentives and inducements of their own. No new federal leverage capital would be provided (U.S. Congress, Joint Committee on Taxation, 1982).[10]

---

[9] A limited version of this idea was embodied in H.R. 6100, the reauthorization act for the Economic Development Administration. In 1982 the bill passed the House but not the Senate.
[10] The Reagan administration's budgets have in fact reduced the amount of such capital available to urban areas.

While it is attractive, the concept of enterprise zones presents a number of difficulties. First, tax incentives do not appear to be nearly as effective as the provision of front-end capital in stimulating the formation of new firms, especially small ones (Carlton, 1975). Second, the pressure exerted on the cities in which the zones are located to reduce local taxes or to provide tax abatements to match the federal tax credits may actually work against the fiscal interests of the cities, particularly when one of the primary interests in economic development is to generate a stronger tax base. Such reductions are actually counterproductive if the city needs to enrich its services and improve its facilities as part of its package of inducements for industry to locate in the zone.[11]

In addition to these factors, there are doubts about the ability of a zone to attract net new jobs instead of simply to induce some businesses to move from their present locations into the zone to avoid taxes and regulations.[12] Finally, the wisdom of establishing a geographically confined zone in a distressed area of a city is highly questionable. In some respects it throws good money after bad. It can work only if other conditions are favorable; and if the conditions—e.g., land prices, market access, labor availability, services—are favorable, then the investments will probably occur without the tax breaks.

It may well be that a more reasonable strategy for economic development and for providing more and better jobs for a city would include promoting other locations that already have reasonably good public services. In many cities, stimulation of residential development may be a more important aspect of overall strategy than programs that directly create only a few jobs. The most critical factor in economic development is the multiplier effect of each increment of development on the rest of the economy. For some cities the projects of choice may well be firms that cannot operate efficiently in an enterprise zone but could operate successfully in other locations. It might thus make more sense to extend tax credits to any firm that locates or expands in an economically distressed city *and*, in doing so, hires a significant number of local lower-income or structurally displaced workers and strengthens the local tax base. This modification would give both local governments and the market greater flexibility in tailoring programs to meet local needs and in using the enterprise tax provisions

---

[11] The British central government has recognized this problem in its enterprise zone program. It replaces local revenues lost through tax concessions.

[12] These doubts would seem borne out by experience in Britain. *The Economist* (November 20, 1982) reported that in the Swansea zone, almost 46 percent of the firms had relocated from nearby. The land value of nearby industrial sites had fallen by 10 percent.

in tandem with other strategic tools, such as leveraged loans and infrastructure improvements.

DEVELOPING A NATIONAL SYSTEM OF INFRASTRUCTURE

No national or local economy can prosper without an adequate system of facilities to support trade and commerce, to ease the travel of workers, and to dispose of waste generated by urban life and industrial production. There has long been a consensus that the federal government has a responsibility for promoting the development of a national system of infrastructure that can attract, support, and serve economic growth in all regions of the country.[13] This has meant, historically, a major contribution by the federal government to sharing the cost of the necessary facilities with state and local governments.

A national system of infrastructure includes the international and interregional transportation system, advanced communications capability, an energy supply and distribution system that is reasonably stable and serves all regions of the country, adequate regional water supplies, and waste disposal facilities that do not endanger the public health or safety. A national system also involves adequate systems of urban facilities that make it possible for the economy to function efficiently.

While all of these are components of a national system, the same level of federal participation is not required for each. Electric power and energy pipelines and most industrial waste disposal or reclamation systems can be provided primarily by private industries. Federal involvement can be limited primarily to tax policies that encourage business investment in the facilities providing the necesary service and to regulations that deal with fair pricing and environmental protection. Most urban infrastructure is provided by state and local governments through their own capital financing systems, primarily general obligation and revenue bonds. When facilities are financed through revenue bonds, users pay fees that retire the debt. Federal assistance has been crucial to the ability of state and local governments to finance some public works, however. If substantial federal financing of facilities is available, limited state and local funds can sometimes be devoted to other projects.

Some parts of the national system are financed primarily by the federal government, either directly, as in the case of water reclamation and water-

---

[13] Both the Reagan and Carter administrations, for example, identified urban infrastructure as a major concern of national policy (U.S. Department of Housing and Urban Development, 1980, 1982). Major business groups have also strongly encouraged federal support of urban public works (Committee for Economic Development, 1977).

ways projects, or indirectly, as in the case of the interstate highway program. Except when it retains operating jurisdiction, the federal government provides little in the way of operating support for the capital projects it helps finance. The urban mass transportation program has been an exception to this generalization, but the Reagan administration has proposed that the operating subsidies for public transportation be terminated.

While a direct and substantial financial role for the federal government in every aspect of the country's infrastructure is unnecessary and undesirable, there is a national interest in ensuring that the infrastructure is provided, that it adds up to a national system, and that it is kept in good operating condition. Despite the broad consensus that the quality of infrastructure is important to the national interest, the nation as a whole in recent years has fallen behind in maintaining existing systems and constructing new facilities.[14] The causes are complex. Many of the public facilities built during the depression and the early post-World War II period now need replacement or major repair. Systematic maintenance programs have rarely been as attractive as new construction. Public expectations have risen for the performance and quality of facilities. The costs of debt service have risen, and repairs and new construction have been postponed. The growth of urban social programs has competed with maintenance and debt service for local budget priority.

The Need to Assess Need

The federal government is, and is likely to continue to be, a major source of funding for key elements of urban infrastructure that are directly related to economic development, particularly transportation and urban sanitary systems. In addition to specific facility grant programs, a substantial amount of the money made available to localities through the Community Development Block Grant program is used for local public works projects.[15] Aside from the issue of the adequacy of funding for these programs, there is a fundamental problem that should be promptly addressed because its resolution will affect the future levels of expenditure

---

[14] The exact level of need is in considerable doubt, but there is agreement that it is substantial. Estimates of need range from less than $1 trillion (Peterson et al., in press) to $3 trillion (Choate and Walters, 1981). The problem is complicated by the absence of reliable data on existing conditions in many cities and by the use of standards that often exceed possible funding levels (National Research Council, 1982a; O'Day and Neumann, 1984).

[15] Since 1975, when the program began, 30 percent of all Community Development Block Grant funds available have been used for public works.

at all levels of government as well as the costs to users of the system. That is the problem of assessing need and establishing priorities for expenditures. To a considerable degree, federal standards for construction or performance of these systems drive estimates of need. Since all estimates of need are far higher than any foreseeable level of combined federal, state, and local expenditures for public works, the cost-effectiveness as well as the scientific or engineering basis for some of the standards that are currently used should be closely reexamined (Hatry, 1981; O'Day and Neumann, 1984; Public Technology, Inc., 1980).

The federal government should sponsor research on cost-effective standards and techniques for needs assessment and disseminate the results. It should promote the development of guidelines for use by local governments and states in assessing the condition of their infrastructure and in setting priorities and creating funding mechanisms for both construction and maintenance programs.

Financing Urban Capital Improvements

Even if savings are possible through adopting more cost-effective standards for performance and through developing better techniques for extending the life of existing facilities and for replacing them, a major new investment in public facilities in a number of urban areas clearly is needed. Given the level of investment that will be required to provide, repair, replace, maintain, and operate urban infrastructure, many state and local governments will not be able to achieve acceptable levels of service without some form of federal assistance.

One critical contribution of the federal government to urban infrastructure has been the income tax exemption for interest from state and local bonds, although it is debatable whether it would be more equitable and less costly to subsidize local capital programs directly than to take the loss in taxes. This policy, however, has made possible the financing of public works at relatively low rates of interest until recently, when bond rates soared into double digits, effectively doubling the cost of debt service in the course of a few years. High interest rates on general obligation bonds have forced postponement of bond issues and deferral of construction and major renovation or replacement projects by many governments. Continued deferral leads to even greater deterioration of facilities, resulting in higher operating costs for governments and lost productivity for the private sector and contributing to a jurisdiction's overall economic problems. Even in more favorable markets, cities and states with weak credit ratings have an extremely difficult time marketing their bonds at reasonable rates of interest. The bond rating of cities varies considerably, and in recent years more major cities have lost ground in the bond market ratings than have gained (Government Finance Research Center, 1982).

The cost of money for capital improvements is only one aspect of the problem. For many decades, municipal bond markets were remarkably stable, with interest rates hardly fluctuating from year to year. Long-term capital improvement and debt retirement programs were possible. In recent years, however, the bond market has become volatile, with greater fluctuations occurring over a month than used to occur over several years. This has made long-term financial planning extremely difficult for many governments. These uncertainties have been compounded by fluctuating funding levels for intergovernmental capital programs and changes in direction or emphasis in the kinds of facilities eligible for federal assistance. It is not of much value to a city if funds are available for bridge repair when its most pressing need is for a new water system.

Other institutional problems abound at local and state levels. Only a few jurisdictions have strong capital planning, budgeting, and management systems. Consequently, needs are often inadequately measured, and priorities are established more often on a political basis than in a framework of effective investment in a jurisdiction's capital plant.

Many of these problems should be addressed by state and local governments, regardless of federal infrastructure policy. Their resolution could be facilitated, however, and the uncertainties of the bond market and of federal assistance, which are well beyond state and local control, could be ameliorated by establishing a national infrastructure bank linked to similar banks at the state level (Peterson, 1984).[16]

An infrastructure bank could be capitalized by consolidating current capital grant programs and issuing Treasury bonds. Such an approach should be preferred over a new block grant because it offers a long-term commitment to a long-term problem. Instead of making direct grants to jurisdictions, it could lend, refinance, or guarantee loans from the state infrastructure banks for part of the cost of projects. Loans tend to impose a tighter discipline than grants; since they must be repaid, they require more careful attention to such matters as maintenance and user-fee financing, when that is feasible. This approach would reintroduce long-term stability to the financing of public facilities and permit better long-term capital planning. The bank could provide, first, a source of capital that could enable urban areas to catch up with their backlog of facility needs. Second, the bank could use its considerable leverage as a lender and its technical expertise to bring about needed institutional reforms,

---

[16] Governor Thomas Kean of New Jersey has proposed such a state infrastructure bank.

such as restructuring financial management systems, requiring loan recipients to develop programs for regularly assessing the condition of their facilities, developing long-range capital programs, and improving and adequately funding facility operations. The latter could include requirements that appropriate revenue-producing facilities recover full user costs and that loan recipients establish depreciation accounts sufficient to meet or at least substantially offset the eventual replacement costs incurred when a facility wears out. Such accounts could help prevent future crises in facility financing. In many respects, leverage for strengthening state and local institutional capacity for financing and managing public facilities is more important to the long-term quality of infrastructure, and to urban economic development, than any one-time infusion of capital (Peterson, 1984).

Setting Priorities for Investment in Public Facilities

One of the recurring criticisms of federal programs in support of urban public works is that they distort local priorities because of the varying amounts of money available for different programs and because some programs have more favorable ratios of federal-to-local support than others. Consequently, it is argued, local and state governments tend to "need" what the federal government will finance with the least local matching contribution. In addition, there are few federal programs that provide any support for the operation and maintenance of the highly sophisticated facilities that are built with federal funds. Thus a bargain in facility construction often becomes a burden to operate for the jurisdiction or for its users.

The consolidation of all urban public facilities grants programs into a single national infrastructure bank would permit state and local governments to draw on it to help support their own capital improvements programs to aid the economic transformation of a community. Loans could encompass major maintenance and replacement programs that properly should be financed through long-term debt. Before grants or loans from the fund are approved, there should be assurances that a jurisdiction has a long-range capital budget and a plan for financing the operation of the facility. The proportion of the program financed by the federal bank could be related to the fiscal capacity of the jurisdiction to finance its capital debt in the context of its overall fiscal condition.

Peterson (1984) has estimated that a national infrastructure bank capitalized initially at $20 billion could provide the leverage and stability needed to help the nation's urban areas catch up with their public facility investments. The determination of how much capital to make available can be made only in the context of all other federal budget commitments. It seems clear, however, that there is a growing perception of a crisis in urban infrastructure and that existing levels of expenditure by all levels of government will need to be increased.

One important reason for increasing the level of national financing for urban public facilities is to accelerate the process of economic transition and to help cities equip themselves with the basic public systems appropriate for their functions. In a number of older cities where the economy is contracting, this may mean closing down rather than replacing obsolete parts of their infrastructure, mothballing excess capacity, and enhancing the capacity and performance of parts of the system that support growing and developing sectors and neighborhoods. Growing urban areas may need to create new systems or enhance existing facilities. In newly developing urban areas, the economic functions being performed may not require total re-creation of all the large-scale integrated systems that have characterized municipal engineering for the last 90 to 100 years. Smaller systems may be more appropriate for some new patterns of urban settlement and development. In other cases it may be possible to substitute management strategies for new capital improvements.

A FRAMEWORK FOR URBAN ECONOMIC DEVELOPMENT STRATEGY

Using Economic Leverage

The objective of urban economic development policy is to strengthen the local economy, which usually means diversification and adjustment toward more economically competitive activities. The basic technique for achieving that objective is leverage—using available resources and policies to facilitate higher levels of private investment in those activities than would otherwise occur. The federal government can exercise some of this leverage through more careful formulation of its economic policies and through the creation of banks that wholesale leverage capital for public and private investments in urban areas. The ultimate effectiveness of such leverage, however, depends on how state and local governments use the leverage capital available to them.

Using Capital and Maintenance Budgets

Both state and local governments should recognize the importance of their capital and maintenance budgets to their economic strategies. It is their transportation systems, water and sewerage systems, parks, and other amenities that influence the specific location of private capital investments.

Public facilities can be used to influence the location of employment centers. A few states and localities have begun to make deliberate use of them in this manner, both to encourage economic development in places where it can best assist in meeting economic development objectives and as a means of containing public costs.[17] A number of states—notably California, Florida, and Oregon—as well as many local governments have used public facilities as a major growth management tool that favored urban over rural areas by denying urban infrastructure to the latter. A jurisdiction may stage the development process by scheduling the extension of facilities to particular areas. Not only is the presence of facilities important, but the level of service is also critical to future investment decisions by private business (Federal Reserve Bank of New York, 1981).[18]

Using Joint Development Techniques

Infrastructure can be used as part of a package in joint development projects to improve an area's attractiveness to investors. This strategy is particularly appropriate for transit and parking facilities that are integrated into a project but financed with public bonds rather than at commercial interest rates. In addition, such facilities may qualify for federal grants or may involve land or air rights that can be used to reduce private front-end costs. In such cases the land and facilities may be used as investments, the government retaining an equity interest through a limited partnership; the land may be leased to the developer, cutting development costs and providing larger future revenues than would be obtained through taxation of the project; or the land may be sold below market price, recovering the revenue conceded in the sale through later appreciation in the value of the property (Gladstone Associates, 1978).

For these kinds of leveraging arrangements to be possible, the states' basic enabling laws governing capital programming, condemnation powers, and land management must be flexible enough to permit state and local governments to select the most workable techniques for a particular activity. State law should permit and encourage joint ventures without specifying the form they must take. This should include authorizing local

---

[17] For example, the governor of Maryland issued an executive order in June 1982 requiring all state agencies to relate their facilities programs to support economic development considerations and to reinforce local development plans (also see Schwartz, 1982).

[18] For example, the Houston Chamber of Commerce estimates that traffic tieups cost Houstonians $1.9 billion a year. One major company, Diamond-Shamrock Oil, relocated to Dallas, reportedly because of traffic problems (*New York Times*, September 28, 1982:A16).

governments to enter joint ventures as equity partners with private corporations.

Land assembly is often essential to successful development, particularly in the older parts of cities in which ownership has been fragmented, preventing industrial expansion and the development of attractive designs for reuse. Some states have broadened their eminent domain doctrines to include public benefits as well as public purposes, allowing condemnation of land for resale to private entities for industrial development even though urban renewal powers are not used. It should also be possible for local governments to lease publicly owned land or to use their interests in the land as equity. Either action can have substantial leverage on the profitability of a project that has several options for location in a given metropolitan area.

Avoiding Ineffective Incentives

While greater flexibility is needed in the ability of government to fashion institutional arrangements to meet the needs of specific projects in order to carry out overall development strategies, there are disadvantages to indiscriminate subsidizing of private economic development. Local tax abatement schemes, for example, have been shown to have little leverage in actually attracting investment, compared with such other measures as venture capital, high-quality services, and public facilities. Industrial revenue bonds can provide leverage capital, as can the use of tax increment financing districts to support service and facility improvements for an industrial park or business district, but these devices should be used only when the private investments they supplement or subsidize are likely to achieve local goals for jobs, tax base growth, and adjustment to new economic functions.

Indiscriminate use of industrial revenue bonds can put local jurisdictions into a subsidy-bidding war with each other for investments. Such competition often wastes tax capacity and does not add to the total metropolitan economy. If industrial revenue bonds can be used to secure investments that would not otherwise be made, they are valuable tools in economic development strategy. If they merely work to displace development from one community to a neighboring one or shift activity from one local business to another, there is little justification for the federal subsidy of such bonds.

Careful consideration should be given to limiting the use of all leveraging mechanisms to activities that meet the criteria discussed above. This can avoid their use as props for dying industries or as weapons in interjurisdictional competition for tax base. Such an approach also emphasizes the urgent need for states to institute fiscal equalization programs (which are discussed in Chapter 7) and not only help meet fiscal problems but also make possible more rational policies with regard to the development of infrastructure and the location of employment centers in metropolitan markets.

Using Regulations

Reform of development regulations is another aspect of regional and local policy that deserves some attention. Most systems of regulation have grown up in response to perceived abuses of public interests by developers. They are not, therefore, designed to facilitate development or to increase its economic value but to prevent or ameliorate egregious externalities. In many communities, investors have come to regard the regulatory process as capricious, uncertain, and costly.

In reforming the regulatory system, we should remember that major urban projects increasingly are negotiated between public planning and development agencies and private developers, rather than approved through the rigid application of rules. This requires that broad authority be delegated to talented negotiators for both the public and private participants. It also requires considerable procedural skill in the public review aspects of the process and an aptitude for balancing conflicting financial, community, and other interests. There are no formulas for a successful regulatory system, but there are reasonably clear policy objectives: regularity in the basis for decisions, a fair process, substantial reductions in the amount of time it takes to obtain final approval, and opportunity for high-quality design. Reform of the regulatory process need not mean a lowering of standards of design or performance. There is now extensive experience with planned development regulations and performance or incentive zoning demonstrating that a better built environment is possible through a more flexible regulatory system.

Using Urban Design

Finally, an urban economic development strategy should include a strong urban design element. While it need not be provided in great detail, a design concept that establishes an image, theme, or strong idea for future development can guide and stimulate both public agencies and private investors to provide the overall scale, amenities, sense of place, linkages, and sorts of activities that make a place function well as a center of economic and social life rather than as a sterile collection of buildings and facilities. Such concepts may need amendment as experience is gathered, so that there is plenty of room for alternative designs and ability to meet changing market conditions.

Design is not only a way of identifying the character of a neighborhood, a district, or a whole city; it is also an important tool for a realistic leadership statement on the future of the area or some part of it. Every major privately initiated urban revitalization effort has worked from a design concept.

Imaginative and sensitive design can provide the symbolism that is often needed to mobilize public and financial support. It need not be grand or costly to have a strong effect on the quality of the environment and hence its attractiveness to other investors. The innovative reuse of old buildings, as in Ghirardelli Square or Faneuil Hall, can do a great deal to change the character of a much larger area. A new project, such as Baltimore's Harbor Place or Nicolet Mall in Minneapolis, illustrates how good design can play a critical role in reorienting the city's self-image and can contribute to its economic transformation. Attention to neighborhood design, the streetscape, pedestrian spaces, and the linkages between business districts, cultural facilities, and other features of a city or region can make a difference in the kind of investment climate that is created.

Good urban design is functional. It is not abstract but practical and facilitates the functions that the city intends to perform. As we know more about modern services, for example, it should be possible to design places in which they can operate efficiently and comfortably. As capital becomes less constrained, convenience and amenity can be powerful competitive advantages.

The design process is an exercise in policy informed by technology and art. It is important to develop urban design ideas through a process of consultation and legitimization so that they reflect values important to the community. And it is also important to leave room in designs for adjustments the market may find it necessary to make.

CONCLUSION

The framework that we have outlined for capital investment in the urban future is flexible. It does not depend on any given level of federal, state, or local spending or other activity. It seeks only to identify basic considerations that could help urban areas make the transition from old economic patterns to the assumption of new roles in an advanced economy. Clearly the level of resources devoted to urban development is important. The less there is, the more important it is to have a clear strategy for using what is available as effectively as possible. For some things, of course, there must be sufficient resources or the job should not even be undertaken.

Stripped to its essentials, this framework suggests that public policies be aware of their effects on the sectors of the economy. National economic policy should consciously encourage those sectors that the market has shown a tendency to favor or that have prospects of being strong competitors. A more competitive national economy should result. Successful sectoral policy, however, could have serious adverse effects in some urban areas because of the way in which our economic activities and labor force are geographically distributed. We therefore need parallel policies that encourage a flow of capital to urban areas for investment in their more promising sectors and to help them attract such activities. By acting as a wholesaler rather than a retailer of such capital, the federal government can avoid the rigidities of past urban capital programs and leave enough flexibility for local leadership to tailor investment strategies to its special needs.

Finally, an important element of capital investment strategy is a policy to ensure the development of a *national* system of infrastructure that can attract, support, and serve an advanced economy. This does not demand that the federal government directly finance all of the needed improvements in national and nationally related urban public facilities. It does mean that the federal government must pursue policies that ensure that someone builds and maintains them. State and local decision makers should devise means of using the resources and powers at their disposal, from whatever source, in a manner that gives them as much leverage as possible on private capital investment.

These policies, pursued alone, would seldom neutralize and would often accelerate the trend toward a sharp division between rich towns and poor towns. In an economically advanced nation, it is neither equitable, efficient, nor politically prudent to pursue polices that leave some areas lagging so far behind that they operate as a drag on the whole economy. In later chapters we discuss options for stabilization policies, actions to foster the development of strong local institutions to manage the transition of local economies, equalization of fiscal capacities among state and local governments, and other strategies to help the less resilient areas and their people adjust to an advanced economy in a positive way and to accelerate that transition.

Thus far we have dealt primarily with investments in physical capital. As our discussion of what is happening to our cities strongly suggests, investment in human capital is of equal if not more importance for the future of America's urban economy. We turn in Chapter 6 to strategies for addressing that issue.

6 Investing in the Future of the Urban Labor Force

NEW JOBS, MORE JOBS, DIFFERENT JOBS
IN DIFFERENT PLACES

A substantial investment in human resources will be required if the nation is to take advantage of the opportunities offered by the structural changes that are transforming the economy and the urban system and by the growth in demand for occupations that require information, communications, and interpersonal skills. As the mechanization of work in both manufacturing and services continues and accelerates, all types of urban areas, including those with strong service sectors, will need resilient labor forces if they are to take new economic roles. While the importation of labor for the new jobs and the out-migration of workers who lose "old" jobs are always possibilities, the slower national rate of growth for traditional manufacturing means that the redundant blue-collar workers will not have the same opportunities for migration that once were commonplace.

The recent recession has had a powerful reinforcing effect on structural change. It has accelerated the decline of the weaker industries and those most vulnerable to international competition. When the upswing of the business cycle occurs, there will be greater growth in the newer industries and occupations—particularly those offering new products and services—relative to expansion in the older industries and occupations (Bureau of Industrial Economics, 1982). Many of the jobs that have disappeared

97

during the recession, particularly in manufacturing, mining, and distributive services, will not reappear when it is over. The new jobs that are created will be predominantly in service occupations. And in manufacturing, the number and proportion of service jobs will increase, although the absolute number as well as the proportion of traditional production jobs could decline. Many service enterprises, particularly those based on office work, will increase their level of mechanization (Ginzberg, 1982). There will be new jobs, perhaps more jobs,[1] but they will be different, many of them demanding new skills and higher levels of education and training. Many workers will have to acquire new skills continuously to retain their jobs. Unskilled jobs are likely to pay less in relation to other work than similar jobs in the past. Many of the new jobs will not be located in the same places as the old jobs. They will be in different parts of the metropolitan area and distributed in a different pattern throughout the country.

Table 7 shows growth rates for selected industries during the last decade and projections to 1990. Because the figures for 1990 are based on past trends, they probably overstate growth in traditional manufacturing and understate growth in electronic technology and services. Major changes in such basic industries as metals and automobiles suggest that there is likely to be more permanent displacement of workers in these industries than is projected, even in an economy that is on the whole resurgent.[2]

The Geography of Cyclical and Structural Unemployment

The geography of the recession is an important factor in restructuring urban economies. Because of the regional concentration of particular industries, the recession has had uneven consequences for local economies. In September 1982, when the nationwide unemployment rate reached 10.1 percent, it was over 20 percent for workers in the steel industry and other primary metals and over 15 percent in the automobile, textile, and lumber industries. No service industry had experienced unemployment rates of over 14 percent, and the rates in communications; finance, insurance, and real estate services; and government were all under 5 percent (*New York Times*, October 10, 1982:A1). In fact, while employment in all goods-producing industries declined by 5.8 percent between July 1981 and April

---

[1] There is some evidence that technological advances could destroy more jobs than they create (Schwartz, in press). This view is disputed by Levitan and Johnson (1982).

[2] From 1979 to 1982, employment in traditional manufacturing industries fell by 11 percent (650,000 jobs) (Congressional Budget Office, 1982a:8).

TABLE 7   Percentage Distribution of Actual and Projected Annual Growth Rates for Employment in Selected Industries

		1979–1990	
Sectors and Industries	1969–1979	High Trend	Low Trend
Traditional manufacturing			
Motor vehicles	0.9	0.5	−0.7
Textiles	−1.2	0.6	0.2
Rubber[a]	0.3	0.6	0.5
Iron and steel[b]	−0.7	0.8	0.6
Energy-related			
Crude petroleum and natural gas extraction	3.0	4.0	3.6
Coal mining	6.7	5.4	4.1
Construction, mining, and oil field machinery	3.4	4.8	2.4
Electronic technology			
Computers and peripheral equipment	4.6	5.2	4.2
Electronic components	2.9	2.2	2.2
Services			
Miscellaneous business services	6.4	3.8	2.9
Health services[c]	5.2	4.8	4.1
Professional services	5.1	3.1	2.2
Finance, insurance, and real estate	3.6	2.8	2.2
Total employment	1.9	2.1	1.4

NOTE: The projected low trend assumes a decline in the expansion rate of the labor force, continued high inflation, moderate gains in productivity, and modest increases in real output and employment. The high trend assumes a larger labor force, higher production and productivity, and lower unemployment rates.

[a]Includes tires, inner tubes, and miscellaneous rubber and plastics products industries.
[b]Includes blast furnaces, basic iron and steel, and steel foundries and forgings industries.
[c]Includes doctors' and dentists' services, hospitals, and other health-service industries.

SOURCE: Congressional Budget Office (1982a).

1982, service employment actually rose slightly, by 0.3 percent (*New York Times*, May 18, 1982:D1).

Tables 8 and 9 illustrate how these extreme variations in sectoral unemployment have affected particular urban areas. Most of the 20 SMSAs in which unemployment exceeded 12 percent contained high concentrations of the industries in the lagging sectors (Table 8). Of these 20 SMSAs, 8 are classified as manufacturing centers in the urban system. Only 3 are regional (diversified service) centers: Mobile, Birmingham, and Spokane. Of the four functional (specialized service) centers, Detroit and Peoria are centers of the automotive and heavy equipment industries.

TABLE 8   Metropolitan Areas With the Highest Unemployment Rates,
July 1982

SMSA	Unemployment Rate	Classification
Rockford	19.1	Manufacturing
Flint	18.6	Manufacturing
Youngstown	18.3	Manufacturing
Peoria	15.9	Functional
Gary	15.6	Manufacturing
Lakeland	15.4	Mining-Industrial
Northeast Pennsylvania	15.1	Manufacturing
Johnstown	15.1	Mining-Industrial
Duluth	14.7	Mining-Industrial
Detroit	14.4	Functional
Mobile	13.6	Subregional
Jersey City	13.3	Functional
Canton	13.1	Manufacturing
Birmingham	13.0	Subregional
Huntsville	12.8	Industrial-Military
Tacoma	12.8	Educational-Manufacturing
Spokane	12.4	Subregional
Fresno	12.2	Government-Education
Knoxville	12.1	Functional
Chattanooga	12.1	Manufacturing
York	12.0	Manufacturing
U.S. average	9.8	

SOURCE: Bureau of Labor Statistics (1982:Table D-1).

The effect of cyclical factors on different types of cities is further illustrated by Table 9. Of the 22 SMSAs with rates of unemployment well below the national average (9.8 percent) only 1, Lancaster, is a manufacturing center. The 3 functional (specialized service) centers, Tulsa, Hartford, and Rochester, are centers for energy, insurance (a major service industry), and advanced instruments, respectively.

Even with the end of the recession, many cities where declining industries are concentrated will continue to face long-term structural unemployment. Even in areas in which a major restructuring of the economy is well advanced, as in New York City, the introduction of new service jobs does not mean that those who have been laid off from the disappearing manufacturing jobs will find work. Workers for many of the new jobs will be imported from other regions. Skilled and semiskilled workers in areas with concentrations of old-line industries will, in many cases, transfer to consumer service occupations, usually at lower pay and with fewer benefits (*New York Times*, May 11, 1982:A1, A7).

TABLE 9   Metropolitan Areas With the Lowest Unemployment Rates, July 1982

SMSA	Unemployment Rate	Classification
Raleigh-Durham	4.4	Government-Education
Oklahoma City	4.5	Subregional
Harrisburg	5.5	Government-Education
Lancaster	5.5	Manufacturing
Washington	6.3	Government-Education
Minneapolis	6.3	Regional
Tulsa	6.3	Functional
Denver	6.3	Regional
Nassau	6.3	Residential
Orlando	6.4	Resort-Retirement
Hartford	6.4	Functional
Ft. Lauderdale	6.5	Resort-Retirement
Newport News	6.6	Industrial-Military
Atlanta	6.6	Regional
Philadelphia	6.8	Regional
Madison	6.8	Government-Education
Albany	6.9	Government-Education
Pensacola	6.9	Industrial-Military
Anaheim	7.0	Residential
Rochester	7.0	Functional
U.S. average	9.8	

SOURCE: Bureau of Labor Statistics (1982:Table D-1).

Some workers whose jobs have been terminated will seek to move to areas where they think their skills may be marketable. If those skills are limited to industries or occupations that are declining, relocation is likely to change only the site of their unemployment or underemployment. The American economy may have reached the end of an era in which there was always a good job somewhere for a skilled blue-collar craftsman. Clearly, however, new skills in a wide range of occupations are needed. For example, projections estimate that while demand for machine assemblers will increase only 27 percent by 1990, demand for data processing machine mechanics will increase by over 157 percent (Carey, 1981).

Redundant Labor

Estimates of the size of the structural unemployment problem (Table 10) suggest that as of January 1983, depending on the definition used, the number of dislocated workers could vary from 100,000—1 percent of the unemployed—to over 2 million—about 20 percent of the unemployed (Congressional Budget Office, 1982a). Probably a practical estimate for policy-making purposes is 800,000-1,000,000, accounting for most of the workers affected by mass layoffs and plant closings (Congressional Budget Office, 1982a:41).

These estimates describe only the immediate problem. They do not account for continuing worker dislocation from further changes in the economy and within specific industries over the next decade or so.

The problem of redundant labor differs from the problems of temporary unemployment that the nation has faced in the past. First, it is a continuing problem and will exist in periods of prosperity (although it will not be as severe) as well as in periods of economic recession. Second, structural change compounds the impact of cyclical unemployment on skilled workers and older workers. In 1982, for the first time in recent history, the rate of unemployment in the skilled trades exceeded the average unemployment rate (*New York Times*, August 8, 1982). Certainly this situation was exacerbated by a prolonged recession that hit construction industries especially hard. Many skilled workers are older. Table 10 shows that 845,000-1,050,000 workers currently affected by structural unemployment are in their mid-forties or older. Some of these workers have skills that are unsuited to the kinds of new jobs that are being created in the growing sectors of the economy. Thus they may have a difficult time finding replacement jobs either in their existing communities or in places to which they might move if their old jobs are not restored as the recession ends.

The problem is further complicated by the large concentrations of redundant manufacturing workers in middle-sized urban areas with specialized economies. Thus, structural change in a single plant can affect a large percentage of the total local labor force. Even if it is assumed that relocation to another area would increase chances of reemployment, the age of such workers makes migration a difficult option to pursue. Community and family ties, mortgages on existing homes at rates that cannot be duplicated in a new location, and supporting institutions and services in existing communities, unions, and industries tend to inhibit migration.

The redundant labor problem in declining industries has both short- and long-term aspects. In a number of areas there is a short-term problem of finding jobs for those who are unemployed, whose unemployment benefits have been exhausted, and whose prospects for being called back to their old jobs or to work in the same firms are at best remote. They may need retraining, relocation, or both. For the long term, there is a need to devise methods of anticipating declining employment or occupational restructuring in some industries and to institute programs to retrain and relocate workers whose jobs will be eliminated. In the absence of such programs,

TABLE 10 Estimated Numbers of Dislocated Workers in January 1983 Under Alternative Criteria and Economic Assumptions

Criteria	Number of Workers (in thousands)		
	High Trend[a]	Middle Trend[b]	Low Trend[c]
Single criteria	1,065	880	835
Declining industry[d]			1,700
Declining industry and other	2,165	1,785	1,095
unemployed in declining area[e]	1,360	1,150	675
Declining occupation[f]	835	710	845
10 years or more of job tenure	1,050	890	535
More than 45 years of age	760	560	
More than 26 weeks of unemployment			
Multiple criteria			
Declining industry[d] and			
10 years of job tenure	275	225	215
45 or more years of age	250	205	195
26 weeks of unemployment	145	110	100
Declining industry including other unemployed in declining areas[e] and			
10 years of job tenure	430	355	340
45 or more years of age	490	395	375
26 weeks of unemployment	330	255	245
Declining occupation[f] and			
10 years of job tenure	235	195	185
45 or more years of age	335	280	265
26 weeks of unemployment	165	120	105

[a]High trend assumes continuation of March 1980–December 1982 growth rates in the number of unemployed workers in each category. Specifically, the number of workers unemployed from declining industries increased by 32 percent in this period—a monthly average of 1.4 percent.
[b]The middle trend assumes that the number of dislocated workers will remain constant from December 1981 to January 1983. The number of dislocated workers in December 1981 is estimated by adjusting March 1980 Current Population Survey totals for changes in the level and composition of unemployment through December 1981.
[c]The low trend assumes that the number of dislocated workers in each category decreases proportionately with the projected change in the aggregate number of unemployed workers between the first quarter of 1982 and the first quarter of 1983, a reduction of nearly 5 percent.
[d]The declining industry category includes all job losers from industries with declining employment levels from 1978 to 1980 (see Bendick and Devine, 1981).
[e]If a declining industry was located in an area defined as declining, all other job losers in the area were included. Declining areas are defined as those experiencing declines in population from 1970 to 1980 or with an unemployment rate of 8.5 percent or higher in March 1980.
[f]The declining occupation category includes all job losers from occupations with declining employment levels from 1977 to 1980.

SOURCE: Congressional Budget Office (1982a).

structural unemployment is likely to reach beyond the blue-collar ranks into the middle technical and professional levels of many industries, particularly manufacturing, mining, and some services (Ernst, 1982; Gunn, 1982).

The New Worker

A serious, broad policy issue arising from the restructuring of national and urban economies is the inadequate preparation of those who will enter the labor force in the future. More than in the past, the international competitiveness of the American economy will depend on the quality of its labor force, including its flexibility in shifting to new kinds of work and to new ways of working. The increasing knowledge required by many old and new occupations suggests the need to invest in the education of the present and future labor force. Higher- and middle-level occupations will require advanced scientific and mathematical education, computer competence, and strong verbal skills. Lower-level occupations will require literacy, usually more advanced verbal skills, basic mechanical skills, and some introduction to the use of computers. The information content of many service jobs is increasing as the proportion of unskilled private sector jobs shrinks (Mare and Winship, 1979).

Certainly one aspect of this problem involves education in science and mathematics, especially at the secondary-school level. In particular, there is a need for computer literacy, a basic understanding of how to use computers, across the whole population (National Academy of Sciences-National Academy of Engineering, 1982). The problem is, however, far broader and more complex than the education of a new generation of scientists and engineers. It includes the education and training of young people, particularly disadvantaged urban minorities and the poor, for entrance into and advancement in the economic mainstream.[3]

The shift in the economy toward service jobs should signal a need for a reorientation of the local educational system to equip more students for entry into that market. Even in such blue-collar industries as transportation and distribution, traditional manual jobs are being replaced by mechanization and computer-assisted systems. For a wide variety of nonprofessional and nontechnical office and manufacturing jobs ranging from secretarial positions to machinists, some training in computer-assisted work is necessary (Guiliano, 1982:148ff.; Gunn, 1982:114ff.).

---

[3] Less than 2 percent of the nation's scientists and engineers are black, indicating a serious problem of underdevelopment of a potential source of talent.

Because of the ways in which work is being reorganized, career advancement may require a worker to change occupations and firms more frequently than in the past. Without better preparation, many workers will be confined to low-level service occupations that suffer not only from low wages but also from rapid turnover and little or no job security. An alternative for some has been participation in the underground economy.

Both the occupational and geographic mobility of young workers are restricted by the lack of basic skills and work habits that are needed in a wide variety of jobs. The absence of these transferable skills makes workers less marketable and inhibits full or rapid adjustment of regional and national economies. It also often retards the introduction of new technology that can increase productivity and even improve the work environment. The effect tends to be magnified at the local level, particularly in highly specialized manufacturing economies, which tend to be the smaller urban areas.

The problems of redundant older workers and the inadequate preparation of younger workers for the kinds of jobs and work environment that will increasingly characterize a more service-oriented and knowledge-based labor market make the quality of the labor force a matter for urgent national attention. Ways are needed to improve the ease with which workers and jobs can be matched, whether by facilitating migration to places where the jobs are or by attracting jobs to where the workers are. Ways are also needed to facilitate the transition of workers from one job or occupation to another, both within firms and between firms,[4] to constantly improve the skills of those already working, and to improve and broaden education and training for new entrants into the labor market.

LABOR MARKET POLICY OPTIONS

The National Market Approach

There are strong differences of opinion about the way labor markets work and how policy should address their imperfections. One view tends to rely on the "natural" operation of the economy to produce, over time, the adjustments that will be needed in the labor forces of metropolitan areas. This is essentially the strategy advocated by the President's Commission on an Agenda for the Eighties (1980) and the *President's Urban Policy Report* (U.S. Department of Housing and Urban Development, 1982). Both assume that the labor market works spatially through the

---

[4] To some extent this will require the cooperation of unions and management in redefining jobs and job security arrangements within industries (Piore, 1981).

migration of industries and workers to locations that are the most economically advantageous to each. They also assume that these patterns of migration are the consequences of long-term trends that are, for all practical purposes, irreversible, or at least not subject to substantial influence by public policy. The President's commission, for example, argues that "recognition should be made of the near immutability of the technological, economic, social, and demographic trends that herald the emergence of a post-industrial society" (p. 100). In a similar vein, the 1982 President's commission asserts that "the variety of urban conditions is ultimately traceable to natural geographic features and to decisions and preferences of individuals and firms as they respond to innovations in technology, transportation, and communications, and to changing life-style preferences" (pp. 2-30).

Both reports assume that no form of government intervention will result in as efficient an allocation of labor to jobs as the unfettered operation of the market (U.S. Department of Housing and Urban Development, 1982:2-16). They also assume that allowing the market free rein will maximize national wealth, which ultimately will result in a higher degree of individual and urban welfare than any strategy that attempts to redistribute wealth among people or areas on principles of equity (President's Commission on an Agenda for the Eighties, 1980:Chapter 5). This approach relies on the idea that, in the long run, market operation will produce a state of equilibrium in terms of both economic sectors and geographical regions. Finally, they assume that in reaching equilibrium, the various market prices—whether for products or factors such as land, capital, and labor—will reflect all social as well as private costs.

The Local Market Approach

Appealing as national market theory is, we feel it overlooks some important aspects of labor market operation and is therefore not a fully satisfactory basis for policy. First, the labor market is not a completely integrated national market but a series of related, but also segmented, urban labor markets (Berry, 1964). There is not one market but many, and they are not equally competitive; they are sometimes referred to as a dual labor market. Workers in one market may have highly imperfect information about other markets and only approximate knowledge of their own.

Second, one of the most basic assumptions of simplistic approaches to free market strategy—that the forces governing labor mobility are virtually immutable—appears erroneous. There seem to be few immutable forces governing geographic patterns of labor mobility. The decline of a particular region and the growth of another are not inevitable, nor are these occurrences necessarily reciprocals of each other. A short time ago the Frostbelt metropolitan areas were scenes of rapid urban growth, presumably at the expense of the less urbanized South. More recently, many perceived the reverse to be the case as the southern and western states experienced rapid job and population growth. Yet there has been a remarkable revitalization of the New England economy, and although the Midwest has experienced job declines, a continuation of such trends does not appear to be inevitable. A recent study by the staff of the Joint Economic Committee, for instance, found that the Midwest was the region expected to receive the largest percentage increase in new plants and permanent offices of high-technology firms (U.S. Congress, Joint Economic Committee, 1982).

Empirical studies of labor markets demonstrate that the most important single factor in labor migration for rapidly growing and rapidly declining areas is the growth or decline of jobs. The location of investment is the critical driving force of regional growth as well as regional differentiation (G. Clark, 1983). Employment opportunity, or at least the perception of opportunity, is a critical factor in urban growth. The flexibility of the local labor market may also be an important factor because the turnover in jobs may increase the number of chances a worker has of being hired or moving up the career ladder in a particular local market. Turnover also seems to explain continued in-migration of workers to declining areas (G. Clark, 1983:Chapter 3).

National migration trends seem to be second in importance and to respond to the growth in job opportunities. Thus general background conditions influence the flows of workers between local labor markets. The important consideration seems to be how well the national economy is doing compared with the local economy (G. Clark, 1983:Chapter 3). In times of general unemployment and slow economic growth, labor migration slows. The national trends operate to encourage migration when workers perceive not only that their local economy is stagnant or in decline but also that this condition is sharply at variance with other local economies (G. Clark, 1983:Chapter 3). They are willing to take the risk that moving entails when they see their local economy as weak in comparison with the nation's economy and other local economies. When they see things as bad all over, however, they are more likely to stay put.

Third, any interpretation of the operation of local labor markets must be especially cautious in using net migration figures. Such data often obscure more than they explain. The gross flows of workers into and out of an urban area or region provide a far more accurate and useful picture of what is actually happening (G. Clark, 1982a, 1983:Chapter 3; National Research Council, 1982a). Even declining areas continue to have a steady stream of in-migrants. In fact, in both declining and growing markets, the differences between arrivals and departures may be quite small. Net migration is almost always the result of a small imbalance between much larger gross flows and therefore is subject to rapid reversal in response to changes in the external environment.

Two observations are important to our understanding of the dynamics of labor migration. First, there is a relationship between in- and out-migration. Some observers argue that the best indicator or predictor of out-migration is in-migration (Alonso, 1980). It may be that after a certain urban size has been reached, the cumulative inconveniences of dense urban life induce out-migration. It is useful to remember, at any rate, that fast-growing states like Texas and Arizona have rates of out-migration that are almost as high as their rates of in-migration (G. Clark, 1983).[5] These data also help remind us that urban areas rarely grow or decline across the board in all sectors of their economies; in fact, some sectors are growing rapidly while others are declining. Thus we note that the Frostbelt cities have captured more of the growth in producer and headquarters-related services in the last decade than the Sunbelt cities have. The latter, however, have exhibited more growth in manufacturing and consumer services.

Rates of in- and out-migration to individual states and urban areas have fluctuated over time. This suggests that workers are adaptable to local and national economic conditions. Matched against the business cycles of the period they cover, these trends show that workers are more likely to migrate in good times than in bad times. Corporate policy is an important factor in migration because corporations are less likely to transfer large numbers of employees during periods of recession. Migration thus does not seem to follow any inevitable pattern or represent responses to long gestation periods.

Fourth, for the market approach to work fully, not only must it result in people moving to where the jobs are relocating or being created, but people must also move from the declining areas in which there is surplus labor. That is far from the necessary cumulative outcome of the individual decisions of those who move. Workers appear to end up in places where the jobs are, but they do not necessarily come from places with the highest unemployment rates. There is no symmetry between those who migrate to growing areas and those who migrate from declining areas (G. Clark,

---

[5] On the whole, the population of the Sunbelt states is younger and the fertility ratios are higher than in the Frostbelt states. Combined with higher net migration rates, this produces more rapid population growth. Even if net migration rates were the same, the Sunbelt would still be growing faster because of other demographic reasons (Jackson et al., 1981).

1983). Migrants to Texas, for example, are more likely to come from other growing Sunbelt states (including California) than from declining Frostbelt states.[6] This appears to result in part from the regionalization and segmentation of labor markets; states contain markets that are more integrated with each other than they are with other regional markets (G. Clark, 1983). The distance a worker must travel to find a new job has a significant bearing on the propensity to migrate. Migration is also sensitive to cyclical conditions. During periods of economic prosperity, the range of migrants tends to increase; during recessions, workers willing to move at all are likely to follow conventional and narrow patterns of interstate migration (G. Clark, 1983).

All of this suggests that the market alone is unlikely to solve problems of unemployment that are related to the distribution of workers in the spatial economy, at least within some moderate period of time.

Fifth, the assumptions that labor migrates from low-wage to high-wage areas and that the result of such migration is the interregional equalization of incomes are not reliable ones. Empirical research shows mixed results. In some states, average wages fell relative to the nation, while in other states wages rose. The level of unemployment in most states does not appear to affect wage levels significantly. While equilibrium theory cannot be totally rejected, it has not been proved (Ballard and Clark, 1981). In some of the growing states, in-migration did not decrease relative wage rates. In other states, out-migration did not lead to an increase in wages, as theory would predict; rather, the reverse occurred. What is clear from the empirical tests of market theory is that we cannot reliably forecast the results of policy essentially based on it.

This brief discussion of the contrast between theories of how labor markets function and the empirical evidence of how they actually seem to function underscores the difficulty of devising policies to deal with the problem in simple terms, such as placing the principal emphasis in urban policy on worker mobility as proposed by the President's Commission for a National Agenda for the Eighties (1980) or as epitomized in the remark that people in declining areas should "vote with their feet."

The Places and People Left Behind

The most likely out-migrants are middle- to upper-income workers in professional and technical occupations. The higher a worker's occupa-

---

[6] Some migrants move twice (or more), first from areas of high unemployment to moderate-growth areas, then on to high-growth areas.

tional status, the more likely that employment opportunities are national as opposed to regional or only local (G. Clark, 1983). Job information is better, and the ability to estimate the personal risk involved in migrating is greater for higher occupational groups. In many cases the move is made by professionals to a specific job, not merely to a new region in the hope of finding a job. In other words, the move follows the search for a job rather than being a part of the job search itself. Census Bureau studies of geographic mobility during the last decade show that when an area has a net loss in population, the movers tend to be younger and better educated than those left behind (Bureau of the Census, 1980). The poor are the least likely to move from one metropolitan area to another. When they move, they are the least likely to improve their status and income (Salinas, 1980).

Employment opportunities are more geographically restricted for low-income workers and potential workers. The market for the labor of the urban poor covers a relatively small segment of an SMSA, let alone an entire region or the nation. This restricted market is a function of workers' lack of information, the cost of searching for jobs over a broad geographic area, the low value of jobs for which such workers are qualified, and racial isolation (Bederman and Abrams, 1974; G. Clark, 1983; Hutchinson, 1978).

The reluctance of low-income workers to search widely for work can be seen as a rational response to the market choices available to them. The risk of layoffs from low-paid jobs is greater than that for other jobs. Wage differences from changing jobs rarely cover the costs of the searches. Such jobs are also least likely to be unionized or subject to other forms of employment security. This suggests that a submarket for the poor operates in urban areas. It is a market that can operate on an assumption of a surplus of workers with sharply limited mobility (G. Clark, 1983; Clark and Gertler, in press).

Although the shutting down of firms and the migration of workers from an area may leave it worse off in economic and fiscal terms, such places continue to function; they depend increasingly on transfers of revenue and income from the more prosperous parts of the state and the nation. Even places that suffer no net loss of jobs, such as New York City or Boston, both of which have had a net gain in jobs in the past five years, can have substantial problems in adjusting to changes in their economic structures. The people whose jobs have disappeared—largely manufacturing jobs—often are not qualified to take the new jobs in services that have been created. Moreover, many of the lost jobs have simply been terminated; they cannot be followed to some new location. The result is that such places experience a period of dual development in their labor markets:

rapid expansion of one segment and rapid decline in another, a need to attract in-migrants to fill jobs, while the unemployed or underemployed population grows at the same time (Prial, 1982).

Declining Mobility

Finally, any discussion of labor mobility must consider that, for the nation as a whole, mobility rates have been declining slightly (Bureau of the Census, 1982), for a number of reasons. First, the average age of the population is rising, and the baby boom generation is reaching an age at which mobility tends to decline. There is now a smaller number of young people in the most mobile age groups. Second, there are barriers to migration. Housing costs in growing communities are usually higher than those in declining or stable communities, and selling a home in a declining area is increasingly a problem. The number of two-earner households has greatly increased in the past decade, which tends to make job searching in a new community more complex. The second earner also alleviates the impact of unemployment on the household and probably prolongs a decision whether to move. Finally, the differences among areas in worker support systems, ranging from unemployment insurance, union contracts containing callback provisions for senior workers, and differences in state welfare benefits, to local schools, churches, and other community groups and affiliations, tend to reduce the propensity of workers to strike out for a new community and an uncertain future (G. Clark, 1983).

Taking into account the structural changes in the economy of the nation and its urban areas and the realities of the labor market that we have summarized, there appears to be a need for labor market strategies that can deal with both nationwide and local concerns. One of these concerns is with the ability of workers who are structurally unemployed to move to other jobs, whether in the communities in which they now live or elsewhere in the country. Another is the ability of urban areas to develop, retain, or attract the kind of labor forces they need to perform their economic functions in the urban system. In this light, urban labor market strategies can be grouped under two headings: mobility strategies and human investment strategies. These strategies are not mutually exclusive; they reinforce each other. They are also related to urban stabilization strategies, which we discuss in Chapter 7.

STRATEGIES FOR INCREASING WORKER MOBILITY

While there are hazards in expecting any demographic trend to continue, much less be immutable, these trends must be considered in developing policies that rely on mobility for their fulfillment. Policy concerned with geographic mobility should focus, particularly for the transitional period, on skilled and semiskilled workers who are most vulnerable to job loss and who have larger investments in skill to protect. The job market for these workers is growing very slowly; in some occupations it is actually shrinking. Craft-centered skills often are not readily transferable to new occupations. Information about job availability is not well developed for use by workers. Skilled and semiskilled workers who are unemployed as the result of structural changes have less likelihood than professional and technical workers of improving their incomes or status by moving to a new community. The likelihood of improving the prospects of unskilled workers is even lower.

The Problem of Choice

In developing a mobility strategy, it is important to keep in mind that, given a choice, many people prefer not to move, and resistance to moving may be high even among the unemployed. Therefore any mobility strategy is unlikely to cause everyone who theoretically should benefit financially from moving to do so. What can be done is to improve the access to employment opportunities of those who choose to move and to help make mobility a realistic option for workers who might otherwise not move at all or might not move wisely. The central objectives of a mobility strategy should be to increase the freedom of choice for workers and to help match jobs with the people who can fill them.

Mobility for workers requires several related elements: reliable information about available jobs, including levels of pay and the kinds of skills needed to fill them; assistance, ranging from counseling to travel costs, in arranging employment interviews; and assistance in relocating to a new community, including moving costs and some services to help the worker and his or her family adjust to their new surroundings. In addition, workers may need counseling and retraining to enable them to use basic skills or abilities in a related but different occupation and a new work or community environment.

Intermarket Job Information

Since we already have a sizable redundant labor force that has little prospect of returning to jobs held before the recession, a first step in a worker mobility strategy might be to establish a national job information and displaced worker relocation program. No such service now exists in the United States; in fact, there is no effective interstate or intermarket listing service. The U.S. Employment Service (USES) does list jobs available in each state as they are submitted by employers and provides some job counseling. Generally the listings tend to be for lower-paying jobs.

The U.S. Department of Labor did conduct a pilot program—the Job Search Relocation Assistance Project—from 1976 to 1980, which, although it involved only 20 states, had a fairly good rate of success in relocating workers (G. Clark, 1983; Westat, 1981). It provided interarea job information, job search grants, and financial assistance to cover moving expenses to take a new job. The program also succeeded in substantially increasing the number of moves made by some groups, such as less educated, blue-collar workers who normally do not migrate as readily as professional and technical or managerial workers (Westat, 1981).

This experience contrasts sharply with efforts at job search assistance made by USES under the Trade Adjustment Act program. The program made little difference in the success of its participants (Corson et al., 1979; Newman, 1978). The Congressional Budget Office suggests that this failure may be attributable to limitations in USES staffing. It concludes, however, that even the limited job referral service provided by USES shortened the unemployment period for both men and women (Congressional Budget Office, 1982a:45).

Job clubs—groups of job seekers who meet regularly to aid each other in searching for work—have had uniformly high placement rates. More than half the displaced steelworkers in Ohio, for example, have found new jobs through this method (Bruml, 1981). This experience suggests the value of industry, union, and public support for job clubs.

Given the diversity in urban labor markets, intermarket information clearly is needed if a higher rate of geographic mobility among structurally unemployed workers is to be achieved. Job market information for the unemployed average-wage and low-wage worker is normally very poor and highly restricted in its geographic extent (G. Clark, 1983). In this light, a disinclination to move is quite rational, even if it results in continued unemployment. Searching for work is costly, and the farther one travels to do it, the more costly it becomes. When the risk of coming up empty handed is high, it makes sense to conserve resources rather than spend them on a fruitless effort (G. Clark, 1983). When relocation costs are considered, unemployment benefits—even given their temporary nature—are a lower-risk option than moving for many unemployed workers.

The Canadian Job Bank System

The experience of job clubs and the USES job relocation assistance program suggests that a well-designed mobility assistance program could substantially broaden opportunities for the structurally displaced worker and perhaps for other unemployed people as well. An analogue for such a system can be found in Canada.[7]

Canadian unemployed workers must register at the local office of the Canadian Manpower Council (CMC) to collect unemployment insurance. As a condition for unemployment benefits, they must look for work in the local labor market. Available to both counselors and registrants are lists of job vacancies in the local area as well as those outside the local labor market. Clients can ask to see the lists of outside job vacancies, which are available on computer throughout the national CMC system in over 500 offices across Canada. Workers who find a job that matches their skills and experience are eligible for a travel grant for an interview. If they are subsequently hired, they can receive a grant covering relocation expenses. For a number of maritime provinces (Newfoundland, for example) this system has been well used by individuals to find and take jobs in the west.

Inevitably, however, the jobs listed with the CMC are relatively difficult to fill. Employers use the CMC when they have trouble filling a job through ordinary channels or when the skills needed are so specific as to require expert screening of qualified applicants. Typically the jobs listed are in semiskilled, craft-oriented trades, but more skilled jobs in most occupational categories are also listed. The CMC system also provides job training, if appropriate, and job counseling, which includes job search skills, aptitude testing, screening applicants with respect to specific skill demands, and even attitude screening. For an individual client the local CMC is a resource for unemployment insurance and a place to search for both local and out-of-town jobs. For employers the local CMC is a means of finding qualified employees without having to advertise either locally or outside the area, to screen potential employees, or even to provide relocation expenses if the best employee comes from outside the local area.

The CMC recently placed computer terminals in shopping centers throughout Canada to allow individuals, whether clients or nonclients, to use them at their discretion. Job bank searches with these terminals have been very popular; queues of at least two hours in some localities have been observed.

There are two guiding principles behind the Canadian system. The primary principle is that workers should choose whether to relocate. Local

---

[7] Our discussion of the Canadian program relies on G. Clark (1983). In preparing his study, Clark interviewed a number of Canadian officials and observed the operation of the program.

CMC offices are reluctant to encourage clients to consider outside listings and will only provide that information on request. Of course in the maritime provinces, which have very high levels of unemployment, this notion of choice may be illusory. Although unemployment insurance, with extended benefits associated with the level of local unemployment, and welfare are provided, in many situations in those areas there are few jobs available locally. While the Canadian government has attempted a program of job creation, many of the unemployed in those areas, like their American counterparts, face the prospect of unemployment for long periods of time. By force of circumstances many have to look elsewhere for jobs, and the CMC has played an important role in helping these individuals once the decision has been made to relocate (even if temporarily). As in the United States, relocation expenses incurred by individuals can be claimed on federal taxes. Thus the Canadian government facilitates relocation decisions directly and indirectly at levels unknown in the United States.

The second organizing principle of this system is distinctly market-oriented in that it seeks to improve the efficiency of labor market transactions and thereby to reduce the social costs of potential market misallocations. By improving the match between employees and employers, the market for both is enlarged and made more responsive.

Fortunately, the costs of shifting a worker across the country to a new job are very small compared with the costs to the public of supporting the same worker and family on unemployment. The CMC's key function is to minimize the costs of matching employers and workers from dispersed and heterogeneous local labor markets. The costs of searching and finding jobs have been minimized through the use of computer technology. A second important aspect of CMC policy involves the costs of the organization of production. Mining towns located away from centers of industry and trade have been integrated into the national labor market network through both the listing of job vacancies and the use of relocation grants. Plant closings have also been considered an integral responsibility of the CMC system; cooperative tripartite agreements have been made between companies, unions, and the government, facilitating the transition from employment to unemployment to reemployment.

Most important, the CMC system directly addresses the costs of uncertainty in labor market transactions. Search and information costs have been reduced. The job bank finds workers and employers and transmits the terms of employment. The costs of negotiation and contracting have also been reduced. The job bank allows comparisons among job offers, terms, and conditions. Interview travel grants speed face-to-face contracting. Through screening the CMC is able to reduce potential problems of employee compliance (for example, absenteeism).

Since unemployment is high in most local labor markets in Canada, transactions that match workers with jobs requiring specific skills related either to a particular industry or to particular modes of operation are represented in high numbers in the CMC system. Opportunities exist for unemployed workers to cross the nation, assisted by the federal government, to take new jobs and hence reduce their dependence on welfare. By linking mobility assistance to the unemployed, the Canadian government is able to speed the efficiency of market allocations by linking excess supplies of labor to firms and places with labor shortages. The policy assumes that the initiative must, however, come from the individual worker. It is choice-oriented, unconditional, and seeks to be noncoercive.

A National Job Information and Mobility System

The Canadian policy may suggest to American policy makers an important way of both facilitating individual choice and reducing the social costs of prolonged unemployment. Modifications to the Canadian system, however, would undoubtedly be desirable in adapting it to the United States. The computer technology is now available to operate it; the most difficult problems would be in setting up and administering such a system. Given the problems in past efforts made through the USES and its often unfavorable perception in the business community, one option would be to design a system through a cooperative process that involves business, labor, and state and local governments as well as the federal government, since all must use it for the system to succeed. A national job information system might operate more effectively if it were established as an autonomous quasi-private corporation receiving some of its funding from its industrial users. It seems wise to consider integrating the information/ relocation system with the unemployment compensation system, making it a service automatically available to any worker covered by unemployment compensation. Whatever the administrative structure, the important elements are a nationwide information system combined with screening, counseling, travel grants for interviews, and moving expenses.

Such a program should be cost-effective. The Congressional Budget Office has estimated that weekly unemployment benefits average $160, while a combination of job search assistance and relocation subsidies cost less than $100 per dislocated worker in most situations (Table 11). Thus, if the program shortens a worker's unemployment period as little as 1.7-3.8 weeks, as preliminary evidence suggests it would, substantial savings in direct federal outlays for unemployment insurance payments could be achieved (Congressional Budget Office, 1982a:45). By putting people

TABLE 11   Federal Costs of Providing Readjustment Services to Dislocated Workers Defined by Selected Criteria, FY 1983 (in millions)

Criteria	Expand Job Search Assistance	Expand Use of Job Clubs	Subsidize Relocation Expenses[a]	Expand Job Training[a,b]
Declining industry	79	352	26	549
Declining industry and				
More than 10 years of job tenure	20	90	10	210
45 years of age or older	18	82	9	192
26 weeks unemployment or more	10	44	5	103
Declining industry including secondary losers	161	714	54	1,113
Declining industry including secondary losers and				
More than 10 years of job tenure	32	142	16	332
45 years of age or older	36	158	18	369
26 weeks unemployment or more	23	102	11	239
Declining occupation	104	460	35	717
Declining occupation and				
More than 10 years of job tenure	18	78	9	182
45 years of age or older	25	112	13	262
26 weeks unemployment or more	11	48	5	112
Plant closings and mass layoffs	68	304	23	474

[a]Assumes that 50 percent of workers under single eligibility criteria and 75 percent of workers under multiple criteria would remain unemployed after the initial period of job search.
[b]Assumes 10 percent of trainees in community colleges, 45 percent in vocational education, and 45 percent in subsidized on-the-job training.

SOURCE: Congressional Budget Office (1982a).

back to work in productive industries, the benefits to the national economy should also be positive.

From the point of view of local governments and their economies, the movement of workers from areas in which their prospects for continued unemployment are high to places in which they can go to work should be beneficial at both ends. The adjustment of new urban areas to new economic roles should be accelerated, and the fiscal stress of economically distressed areas caused by high levels of long-term unemployment should be reduced.

National Assumption of Welfare Costs

In developing a mobility strategy, national assumption of standards and costs for income and health maintenance programs could be very useful. Standards of eligibility for these programs and levels of payment vary from state to state. They are widely regarded as impediments to mobility of the labor force. Only in a national system in which benefits are reasonably equalized for local living costs and available throughout the country are people free to choose to migrate and accept the risks of unemployment that such movements often entail. Otherwise, it is not irrational for a worker to refuse to move for an insecure job in a state with a lower level of welfare support and a higher threshold of eligibility than in his or her home state.

A second reason for federal assumption of responsibility for welfare is that welfare loads are largely a function of national economic conditions and policies, the costs rising with accelerated unemployment. States and localities have few policy options available to them as means of influencing that load. Since the effects of national recession and prosperity are not evenly distributed among the states, those with the weakest economies are presented with the heaviest burdens at times when their budgets are most vulnerable to other demands (Storey, 1982).

National assumption of welfare financing has been recommended for many years (Hansen and Perloff, 1944). Both Presidents Nixon and Carter sought substantial reforms in the welfare system that would have reallocated more of the cost to the federal government. The Reagan administration, by contrast, has sought devolution of primary responsibility for welfare to the states. The states have, understandably, declined the honor. The current stalemate should be resolved, perhaps in the context of renegotiating national and state responsibilities under the rubric of the New Federalism. States might well accept devolution of other programs in return for national responsibility for the welfare program. The benefits to the nation in income gains from increased mobility could conceivably offset some of the cost. Federal assumption of full welfare costs would place responsibility with the level of government with most power to cope with the basic economic forces that affect those costs, freeing the resources of state and local governments for more basic and traditional services, such as education.

STRATEGIES FOR INVESTMENT IN HUMAN RESOURCES

The quality and resilience of an urban area's labor force are essential to its ability to compete with other areas and to adjust to structural change within its own economy.[8] Many would agree with Mills (1981:259) that "a skilled and competent work force is as important to economic growth and well-being as is physical capital."

No area can expect to function without some exchange of labor with other areas. But since most workers should not be expected to move except under extreme circumstances, it is highly desirable that both those who stay and those who move be fit for the jobs that exist and that they possess skills or potential that is attractive to productive enterprises. Advancement beyond the most menial jobs requires education and training beyond what can be gained through experience in lower ranks. Workers in industries that are being phased out, even if they possess basic skills and good work habits, need retraining, whether they migrate in search of work or seek other local employment. Retraining and adult education programs are also needed, particularly if current tendencies toward a dual labor market persist, so that workers can gain the knowledge and credentials necessary to enter more rewarding careers and to move from the secondary to the primary market.

Another problem surfaces as levels of educational attainment rise in the work force at large. Fewer workers will be satisfied with routine, tedious jobs that require little individual initiative, autonomy, or control over the work. We can foresee a major transformation in the nature of work itself, spurred on one hand by the increased skills and training that go into the making of products and services and by better-educated workers with higher expectations for more personally satisfying work on the other. Given the demography of the American work force, with a smaller number of workers entering it in the next two decades than in the last two,[9] most firms must become less labor-intensive (Marshall, 1982).[10]

Even if we assume that the least personally satisfying and financially attractive jobs could be filled with marginally trained American workers or with untrained immigrant labor, such a wide-open immigration policy

[8] Regional recognition of the importance of the quality of the work force is illustrated by a recent report of the Twin Cities Metropolitan Council, which concluded that a well-educated labor force and good training institutions gave the Minneapolis-St. Paul area an advantage over others in attracting industry (Metropolitan Council, 1982).

[9] The proportion of people ages 16-24 will decline from 24 percent in the 1970s to 19 percent in the 1980s, a drop of approximately 20 percent (Congressional Budget Office, 1982b; also see Drucker, 1981; Marshall, 1982:20-22).

[10] An illustration of this can be seen in the difference between U.S. and Japanese fast-food firms. The former are labor-intensive, low-wage, high-turnover enterprises. The latter are more capital-intensive, with higher wages and more job security for workers. Each reflects the current conditions of its labor market.

seems unlikely to be acceptable except for a relatively short period of time. Moreover, a labor policy that would depend on the persistence of an underclass is highly questionable on both moral and practical grounds. It seems more likely that the practice of exporting labor-intensive parts of industries and the more undesirable jobs to less developed countries will continue (Drucker, 1981).[11] In addition, there are often strong business as well as social reasons for automating the most dangerous, dirty, and boring jobs to eliminate inefficient performance and employer liability for worker injury and disease. Both business and government thus can justify investment in the quality of the American labor force.

Another aspect of this problem is the way work is organized in firms or industries. Reducing the skills required to perform certain jobs by introducing new technology may produce short-term gains in productivity at the expense of serious long-term competitive advantages for both the firm and its employees. To the firm it can mean a loss in the adaptability of its work force and greater vulnerability to changes in the external environment—the labor market, product changes, technological advances. To the workers it means a loss in their employability in other occupations and firms. By contrast, work organization that broadens workers' skills makes them more employable and enhances their mobility.

From a community perspective a competitive labor force includes more than a supply of cheap labor ready to work in almost any enterprise that can be induced to locate in the vicinity. The "new" manufacturing plants in southern cities that have closed offer many examples of how insecure an employment base such firms provide (Armington and Odle, 1982). Except for labor-intensive businesses such as food services, the growing sectors of the economy and those with the best prospects for future growth tend to require higher skills. They are attracted to areas with a well-trained labor force or with amenities that can help attract one. Because many modern industries need an environment that fosters knowledge in their line of commerce, the presence of education and research institutions that can ensure a high-quality labor force are themselves important factors in the location of such firms.

A human resources investment strategy for an urban area, then, requires at least three kinds of investment: (1) investment in the development of basic, transferable knowledge and skills for those entering the labor force; (2) investment in programs to improve opportunities for occupational mobility and personal growth for those already in the labor force, including programs that improve the quality of working life and the workplace; and

---

[11] For an estimate of the extent of such exports to date, see Bluestone and Harrison (1982).

(3) investment in higher education to prepare professionals and managers for employment in national and international markets and to maintain a mutually supportive role with respect to local and regional educational institutions. The remainder of this section deals with these three kinds of investment.

Preparing People for Work

The urban educational system is the foundation for any strategy of human resources development. In almost all cities, high priority should be given to the education of the minority poor (Anderson and Sawhill, 1980; National Commission for Employment Policy, 1979). The youth employment rate is alarming, particularly among black men ages 16-24; in September 1982 it was over 40 percent (Bureau of Labor Statistics, 1982). The employability of young people is encumbered by a 12 percent rate of functional illiteracy for high school graduates. A 1975 study found that 42 percent of black high school students, in contrast with 8 percent of white students, could be considered functionally illiterate (Gadway and Wilson, 1979:15). At least while there is a high rate of unemployment, employers are unwilling to hire functional illiterates or school dropouts (Prial, 1982).[12] Even when they are hired, job retention rates are particularly low for untrained young minority workers (Congressional Budget Office, 1982). This ultimately results in high rates of welfare dependency, low rates of participation in the labor market, and participation in the underground economy (K. Clark, 1982).[13]

Problems of this magnitude and persistence clearly signal a need for revisions in urban education systems. The major efforts of the last 15 years in compensatory and remedial education have produced mixed results and a realization of the difficulties that confront even the most imaginative and resourceful educators and school systems. Given the institutional inertia resisting changes in education systems, interim measures designed to improve the preparation of young people for the labor market are needed, as are some alternatives to traditional education and training approaches. It is beyond the scope of this report to deal with such educational issues

---

[12] For example, over 40 percent of New York City's high school students drop out. Even fast-food outlets will not hire them when there are high school graduates in the job market (Prial, 1982).

[13] Clark (1982) points out that persistent racial segregation in public school systems is at the core of inferior education for blacks.

in detail.[14] Our inquiry is therefore limited to discussing how educational and training policies may fit into urban labor and economic development policies.

Studies of education and training programs for the unemployed and disadvantaged agree on the primary necessity of developing basic skills that can be transferred from job to job. These must be combined with disciplined work habits and clear rewards for performance (Congressional Budget Office, 1982b).

Training and education alone are not enough, as a variety of earlier programs demonstrate (Wurzburg, 1978). Many disadvantaged people need help in entering the labor market and in staying in it. Programs that integrate formal education for the disadvantaged with labor force entry programs appear to be more effective than those that leave people to their own devices to find jobs (Congressional Budget Office, 1982a). The school-to-work transition is difficult for the young, low-skilled worker who has little if any experience in searching for a job or in working. Part-time employment of high school students has proved an effective device for keeping students in school until they graduate, thereby raising their level of basic verbal and mathematical literacy (Mangum, 1982). Work-study programs can also be effective when they are combined with close supervision and regular counseling. In all such programs, placement is an important part of the process. Job search counseling has also proved to be a relatively inexpensive way of increasing the chances that a young worker will be employed and retained (Congressional Budget Office, 1982a; Farkas et al., 1980). And if initial employment has been conditioned on enrollment in adult education or special training programs, success for the worker has tended to increase (Congressional Budget Office, 1982a).

The primary burden for basic education and training will continue to fall on the public education system. Private employers have generally not provided basic skills training, although they do provide specific job training. Private and public employers can be effectively involved in public education, however, and several approaches seem to be producing useful results. In the adopt-a-school program, for example, corporations or other institutions participate directly in a school's education program through part-time instruction, visits for students, summer or part-time jobs, job counseling, curriculum development, and donation of instructional ma-

---

[14] See the report from the National Research Council's Committee on Vocational Education and Economic Development in Depressed Areas (Sherman, 1983), which deals with the role of vocational education in distressed urban and rural areas and related issues.

terial, such as computers. While the level and quality of participation vary widely and there are problems of maintaining initial enthusiasm and commitments after the first year or two, the basic idea of an employer's sharing responsibility for the education and the introduction of a student to the labor force is one that can be built on.

Other forms of business involvement with schools are being tried in a number of cities. These include on-site training involving the use of corporate classrooms for study of "nonschool" subjects, working with educators to establish career high schools, and establishing summer youth employment programs, academic and work-based scholarships, career workshops and seminars, and private industry councils to operate federally funded training programs.[15] A more systematic approach in school-business relations is being tried in Boston. A formal compact developed among the school system, the city government, and the business community sets measurable goals for the schools in improving reading and math skills. Businesses, in turn, agree to provide tutors, counseling, school partnerships, and, most important, jobs for graduates (Anonymous, *The Boston Compact*, 1982).

Even with substantial help from the private sector, any strategy designed to improve the quality of public education for the disadvantaged will require strong state and federal government financial support targeted sharply on inner-city and other disadvantaged schools. Because enrollments are often declining due to lower birth rates during the 1970s, there is a greater opportunity to increase the effectiveness of these schools. There is also a need to make that generation more productive to offset its smaller size. The effective schools movement, which has aimed at reform in individual schools, has demonstrated that it is possible to improve substantially the performance of disadvantaged students in schools with meager resources if improvements are made in administration, teaching, counseling, and community support (Rutter et al., 1979). So far, however, it has been difficult to duplicate these successes, particularly if they have been based on a strong, charismatic educator.

Alternatives to traditional public education may also prove effective in some circumstances. Some schools or programs might be operated better under contract to private firms. In such arrangements the public role would change from actually providing the service to ensuring that it is provided. Educational vouchers might also be used by some disadvantaged students to obtain specialized education not offered in the public system or to

---

[15] There is some question of whether training operated by private industry councils is more effective than programs in which the government is the prime sponsor (Bendick, 1982:262).

supplement that of the system. The education might include tutoring in basic subjects, such as mathematics, or various kinds of vocational training.[16] Finally, consideration might be given to creating a few selected residential or specialized schools offering advanced high school programs as a means of developing the potential of exceptional young people when the regular public schools cannot provide an environment that supports their intellectual growth. North Carolina's School of Science and Mathematics is one example. Created by the state legislature, it draws students from the entire state, reflecting the racial, sex, and income distribution of the whole population. It has produced a high percentage of merit scholars while serving as a seedbed for educational techniques that can be used by the regular public schools (Dymally, 1982).

Clearly, the public schools will not be able to serve everyone. Seriously disadvantaged young people will continue to need special programs such as the Job Corps. Despite its relatively high cost per enrollee, the success of that program appears to have built a bipartisan consensus in favor of maintaining it as an important direct federal responsibility for training disadvantaged people and placing them in jobs (Congressional Budget Office, 1982b). Military service also remains an important source of basic skill and job training for some young people. Additional attention might be given to the quality of both regular and reserve training as an integral part of the nation's training strategy.

A great deal of experimentation is now going on in education and training programs, much of it in response to the financial distress of school budgets and the simultaneous public demand for improved performance by schools. While much of this activity has been highly creative, and room for experimentation is always desirable in education, one of the tasks of state and local leadership is to begin to use this experience to help organize investments in education and training in ways that contribute to an overall strategy of urban economic adjustment and stabilization. State involvement can be particularly crucial, because no matter how well some communities educate their children, there still may not be enough jobs in a particular local market. If part of the process is conceived as job placement for the young worker, the placement program has to be integrated with state, regional, and national systems. New entrants are among the most mobile members of the labor force, and programs should recognize that it is often easier for them to move than it is for older workers.

---

[16] A paid tutoring program could have multiple benefits—e.g., making use of temporarily redundant baby-boom college graduates and developing new skills among undereducated 25-year-olds.

The educational system should also be seen as a critical part of the economic development strategy of an urban area. Recent initiatives by Massachusetts and other states to establish stronger vocational education programs illustrate the importance that states are placing on training their labor forces as an integral part of efforts to attract and keep industries (Magarell, 1983). Since industry tends to be reluctant to provide basic skill training but has increasingly recognized the need for it, the creation of an industry-supported fund, perhaps channeled through a community foundation, might be an effective device for developing industry financial support for the better preparation of young workers and for concentrating those resources where they are most likely to be effective. In addition to support for basic education, such a fund might assist in supporting, jointly with public funds, a system of postsecondary training vouchers. These vouchers could be issued to high school graduates for training or retraining at a time of their choice, provided that they are not eligible for other public subsidies of educational expenses, such as tax deductions or credits. The vouchers could be used immediately after graduation for specialized training or to offset college costs, or they could be banked with interest for training at a later stage of a person's career when a job change was necessary or desirable.

One way of looking at this proposal is as an extension of public responsibility for the education process by one year—but not necessarily a consecutive year—on the theory that the returns to society through greater productivity and earning power will more than repay the cost. Many self-employed professionals are able to deduct their continuing educational costs from their income taxes, thus shifting part of such costs to the public at large. Ordinary workers who are less able to bear the cost, however, have no such opportunity. For most American workers, a tax deduction or credit would have little dollar value, whereas a voucher would allow them to discount the out-of-pocket cost of retraining or a special course to an affordable level. With a long-term decline in the proportion (and in many states the absolute number) of students in regular kindergarten through 12th grade, a postsecondary voucher program would result in a less rapid decline in the proportion of the public budget devoted to education, but would not axiomatically increase education outlays. A supplemental source of funding for postsecondary training might be tax credits for corporations that provide training vouchers to their employees for use in cooperatively funded institutes operated by an industry, a regional association of firms, or a government-industry partnership. Like credits for research and development, employee training provides a substantial long-term benefit for a small, early cost.

While the proposal at this stage is conceptual, the basic idea is to provide, much as the G.I. Bill did, a flexible opportunity for education that fits individual need and produces a national social benefit. Postsecondary vouchers could be used, for example, for regular public vocational training, privately provided training, union programs, and, conceivably, for self-teaching programs such as computer courseware that have been accredited by the appropriate educational or training authorities.

Such a program would be to the advantage of industry as well as workers, since it is increasingly obvious that all the jobs that will be created cannot be filled by new recruitment alone. Retraining the existing work force will be a continuing necessity for any industry that hopes to keep abreast of new technology and remain competitive (Mills, 1981:267). Moreover, as an increasingly important objective of collective bargaining agreements, labor organizations are considering the rights of employees to retraining and to participate in judgments about the introduction of mechanized systems (Levitan and Johnson, 1982).

Keeping the Skills and Knowledge of Workers Up to Date

We can no longer assume that a high school graduate who does not go to college or some other postsecondary educational program will need no further basic or special training apart from that received on the job. Success in the labor markets of an advanced economy will increasingly entail continuous education as part of a worker's life. It is conceivable that in the 1990s some urban school systems will enroll more adults than children. This suggests a restructuring of urban education, with more attention to adult and continuing educational programs, to adult vocational education, and to expanding the role of community colleges. It also suggests changes in the basic social contract involving labor, industry, government, and educational institutions.

Redundancy planning should become a normal function of industries and communities.[17] Essentially, redundancy planning means anticipating changes in the economy, markets, and technology and the ways they will affect patterns of employment in the industries located in a community.

Such a program would attempt to identify those industries and firms that can be expected to experience substantial changes in their labor requirements as a result of shifts in markets or technology, giving emphasis to urban areas in which there are heavy concentrations of such firms. By

---

[17] Our discussion of redundancy planning is based on Drucker (1981:249-251); also see Oreskes (1982:5).

anticipating and preparing for transitions, it may be possible to smooth the process for firms, workers, and their communities. Firms that operate in changing markets are often under great pressure from their unions and local communities to maintain practices that may even speed their demise. Workers are understandably anxious about the prospect of losing a job when they have skills but no known prospects of continued employment in their trade and no sense that they may have skills that are transferable to other jobs in the same firm, in another firm in the same community, or to another firm in another community.

Redundancy planning also means having preventive unemployment programs available for retraining the dislocated workers and a process set up to place them in new jobs. If established, such a process can ease the transition considerably. Workers can be offered training and new jobs before their present jobs are terminated.

A preventive strategy essentially consists of foreseeing the decline of employment in an industry and preparing workers through retraining programs for other types of jobs, preferably new jobs in the same labor market. Such a program has been used, with some reports of success, in West Germany (National Research Council, 1982b:19; Wolman, 1982:113). Where industries are unionized, contract clauses providing for early warnings of permanent layoffs and for job training may become fairly standard, reflecting both a growing sense of corporate responsibility for the welfare of employees and union realization that their members' interests can be protected best if they are assured of gaining and maintaining marketable skills. In many cases this assurance may consist of training in the general verbal and quantitative skills needed to operate computerized equipment or to compete for the better jobs in service industries.

While it is reasonable to assume that industries will increasingly accept responsibility for retraining workers who face layoffs, communities should also become involved in redundancy planning. Because many workers would probably prefer not to relocate and because substantial relocation of workers can have a serious ripple effect on the local economy and fiscal capacity, the community should also assume some part of the obligation for redundancy planning and for helping to train and place as many workers as possible in new jobs in the community or within commuting distance. From the perspective of industry, if no redundancy planning or retraining programs exist, decisions to change corporate investment patterns or to introduce new technology will be resisted more strenuously by both workers and their community leaders.

Redundancy planning should be aimed primarily at workers who have several years of experience but who are well under retirement age. They are the most vulnerable because they have families to support, children in school or college, mortgages, and usually strong ties to the community. Redundancy planning may be considered an adjunct to unemployment insurance; instead of providing only a temporary stipend to offset cyclical unemployment, it involves an active program of planning for change, retraining, and placement in the event of structural unemployment.

Part of the cost of redundancy planning should be paid by the employer when that is possible. Part may be considered legitimate public investment in the human resources of an area and of the nation. The advantage of such an approach is that it tends to increase the security of workers, allowing technological progress to occur in their industry without unreasonable labor resistance. It gives workers more bargaining power in the labor market and more control over their own careers. It helps a community keep its labor force up to date and in a position to compete for other industries that need the kinds of skills for which the labor force is trained. While retraining will make it easier for some workers to move, it can also make it possible for others to stay and be productive or to move up the local employment ladder. The community can then more readily accept change rather than fear it or find itself reduced to spending its funds to buy out a declining industry. It should not be necessary for a community to hit bottom before it can begin to think about itself as a different kind of place.

While redundancy planning, including education and training programs and the mobility option discussed above, is the most urgent of the transitional problems raised by structural unemployment, attention must also be given to the continuous training of the workers in a community who take jobs that require a high degree of skill and training. This means engaging the resources of a community for adult education, community college, business-based education, and other education and training in a broader and more intensive effort than has been common. It also involves a higher degree of cooperation among private and public institutions.

Computer training and education is clearly a high priority. If computer literacy is to be advanced in the school system, current teachers must themselves become masters of these powerful machines that have become as important to both practical and theoretical thinking as our standard languages and traditional mathematics.[18] Among other groups, office workers are obvious targets for continuing education in computer technology. The scientists and engineers of a community, in particular, must continuously refresh their information and skills with new ideas and technology. In

---

[18] Rader (1982:18) argues that "computer literacy is essential if a person is to participate fully in an information society, and will be as important as reading literacy."

fact, workers of almost all sorts will need to keep abreast of new technology.

One cautionary note is important in designing computer literacy programs. Advances in technology are rapid and computers are increasingly usable by people with minimal training in programming. There is thus risk that some forms of computer training could rapidly become obsolete and virtually worthless. This suggests a tiered approach, with a program for almost everyone that emphasizes basic skills and applications—a sort of driver training for a wide population of potential users. From the basics, other tiers can be added for education in computer applications, mechanics, and theory.

Any effective program in continuous education of a large part of the work force represents a major departure from past practices. We have tended to assume that most of the work force is already adequately educated, so that training efforts represent only a marginal part of the responsibility for the quality of work. Even so, the nation has been spending $40 billion a year on training, and government has been contributing only a little over $9 billion ($4 billion from state and local governments, $5 billion from the federal government) of the total (*New York Times*, October 17, 1982). This is a low level of commitment in comparison with that of other economically advanced countries. If the United States had a retraining program with an effort equivalent to that of Sweden, for example, it would involve a cost of at least $100 billion a year (Haveman, 1982). Some of the added effort may be paid for by those who receive the training. Even if it were entirely paid by employers and government, however, it could be the most important investment made in the future of an area and of the country (Drucker, 1981:251):

There is a need, above all, to realize that the labor force of today—and even more the labor force of tomorrow—represents a tremendous resource of knowledge and experience which has to be continuously tapped and continuously upgraded. We need to shift from the traditional approach of the nineteenth century which saw labor as a "cost," to the approach which so far only the Japanese have taken, the approach of seeing labor as a "resource" and therefore, as a "profit center" rather than a "cost center." There is a need to organize the human resource around continuous learning and continuous training.

The Role of Higher Education

If the public school system is the foundation for human resources investment strategies, the urban universities and community colleges are the capstone. They should be considered as centers for investment in the development of human capital (Rudnick, 1982).

The universities in an urban area are not of a piece. Some are traditional, private institutions; others are truly national or international universities whose mission is scarcely local at all. Perhaps the most important are state or city universities, many of which are part of a multicampus system. The universities of an urban area are internally complex, respond to a variety of external interests, and are often ambivalent about the relationship they should have toward their immediate environment. Notwithstanding the difficulties that they present for participation in an urban strategy, their contribution to such a strategy can be crucial, particularly in the long term. [19]

Taking advantage of the potential of the universities, however, requires a sensitive understanding of their institutional limitations and of their many roles in education, research, and public service, regardless of the fortunes of their locations. Thus, many universities will consider themselves as institutions that coincidentally are located in urban settings, while others will characterize themselves as urban universities with a primary interest in addressing the higher education needs of the local population (Brown, 1982). Community colleges and postsecondary technical schools have generally been more aggressive in relating their programs to local labor markets.

Universities and colleges are important parts of the local service economy. They can also contribute to the fund of intelligence necessary to formulating local and regional economic development strategies. Our chief interest, however, is in the university's role in developing human resources. This involves three functions that are fundamental to the competitive position of an area: (1) the education of minorities, (2) the improvement of the primary and secondary educational system, and (3) the continuing education and retraining of professionals, managers, and technicians.

The higher education of minority and disadvantaged students has become a primary function of publicly supported urban universities and community colleges. These schools enroll large proportions of minority students, many of them graduates of weak secondary schools; low-income students; part-time students; students of older average ages; and a generally high percentage of married and working students (Rudnick, 1982:31). Despite these difficulties for students and for the institutions that such populations pose, there is a need to support and expand such opportunities and to assist students in completing their courses of study. Higher edu-

---

[19] For a discussion of the pitfalls of expecting too much from universities and other think tanks in solving urban problems, see Szanton (1981).

cation is the surest way to break an intergenerational chain of poverty. It is also necessary for entry into most credentialed occupations. At the same time, the rising educational profile of an area increases its attraction for employers in industries that are expanding and need well-trained workers. A strong university in an attractive city provides a significant competitive advantage. Over time it may even operate as a magnet, draining talent from other places in a cumulative, reinforcing process. Inner-city universities and colleges are important stabilizing forces insofar as they help offset the other competitive disadvantages of inner cities by reducing migration flows. In some cases they can do much more, especially when used as a focus for urban conservation and economic development.

In this sense an urban university can do more than almost any other institution to give an area a competitive edge over places that are not mining the potential of their minority populations for entry into jobs that require advanced training and education. This is a costly role, however. It involves costs that are not imposed on institutions that confine themselves to traditional approaches to the education of traditional, full-time students with good academic backgrounds. State funding formulas generally do not recognize the differences. States should revise these formulas to provide priority support for higher education of minorities and the disadvantaged. From a programmatic point of view, there is also a need, both in urban universities and in the traditionally black colleges, to provide and promote educational programs geared to the disadvantaged.

The second crucial role of urban universities in a human resources strategy is fostering change in the urban school system. The universities have a vested interest in the quality of primary and secondary education; if its quality is high, they can dispense with remedial programs. They will also attract more students who can be expected to do well in college, having received a sound primary and secondary education in science, mathematics, computers, and language.

As centers for teacher training and the development of educational theory, universities are beginning to recognize an obligation for direct involvement in local educational systems. For example, a project sponsored by the Ford Foundation currently involves state university presidents and school superintendents in working relationships designed to increase support for primary and secondary educational improvements and better preparation of students for higher education.

Ultimately, universities should be involved in restructuring the entire urban educational system, including approaches to training and retraining the adult work force. While some aspects of the educational system are not directly associated with higher education, creating new techniques to retrain redundant workers or to motivate and prepare new entrants to the labor force requires a strong element of multidisciplinary research and experimentation. Programs created through the association of area schools, businesses, and unions can be major catalysts in the timely reform of both public and corporate training and education.[20]

Urban universities are also a valuable resource for the private sector in terms of training and retraining professionals and other workers. Universities can develop strong relationships with the private sector through the use of industry professionals in their teaching programs; through research and development programs, including industry-sponsored research; and in the analysis of new technologies and related educational needs. Involvement of a university in the economy of its region can be of material assistance in keeping that economy competitive.

The experiences of Silicon Valley, the Boston area, and North Carolina's Research Triangle illustrate how important university-related economic development strategies can be. To be sure, the universities involved— Stanford, Harvard and MIT, and Duke and the University of North Carolina—are unique and strong institutions. But many less prestigious universities have strengths that could be harnessed for economic development. They may not be able to generate a Silicon Valley, but they can support other activities that materially improve an area's economy (Sheridan, 1982).

To some extent, universities are in competition with advanced education programs offered within industry, programs that in part have been developed because of default by institutions of higher education. Many of these programs could be recaptured by educational institutions, which alone are able to offer the credentials often required for professional advancement. To do so, however, urban universities would have to accept the obligation to provide continuing degree and nondegree education for professionals and to ensure that the quality of these programs matches or exceeds that which industry can provide alone. Universities may also have to be more flexible in allowing industry a sufficient say in the content and methods of instruction for special courses and programs. Particular attention might be given to the educational needs of managers and professionals in smaller, growing firms that lack the capacity to provide in-house education on a par with that provided by large international corporations. Universities could provide such programs on a cooperative basis, with smaller firms providing development programs that offer the

---

[20] An illustration of how a university might approach this task can be found in the proposal of Wayne State University to establish a comprehensive education and training program to retool Michigan's automotive work force for new jobs and career mobility (Rudnick, 1982:24).

quality of the large corporate career development programs at relatively modest costs for each firm. In this way, university education could also be directly related to local economic growth.

SUMMARY

The economic fortunes of our urban areas rest on their human capital, which has replaced factors such as natural resources as the major source of comparative advantage among firms and urban areas. That human capital can become as obsolete or inappropriate for competition in an advanced economy as deteriorating infrastructure and antiquated industrial plants and technology. It must be continuously renewed.

Most American cities have a large pool of underdeveloped human capital in their existing labor forces and in those people who could enter the economic mainstream in years to come if they are adequately trained and educated. Well-trained workers are, of course, mobile if they choose to be. But a well-trained labor force is also a major attractor of capital. Since, in most instances, capital is more mobile than labor, the development of a region's human resources is probably the most useful investment that it can make in its own future.

In this chapter we have recommended that in devising a strategy for investment in its human resources, the nation and its urban areas should first invest in developing the basic knowledge and skills without which a worker cannot function in the economic mainstream. These include a working knowledge of science, mathematics, and computers and, above all, a level of literacy that is functional to the type of society and work environment that will exist. Particular attention should be given to educating and training the disadvantaged youth of the inner city. They represent a substantial resource that the nation cannot afford to waste, particularly as the number of new entrants to the labor force declines from rates of the last two decades. Without training they will operate as a brake on the rest of the economy, requiring expenditures on which no return can be expected.

Second, we have recommended that substantial investments be made in maintaining knowledge and skills and in retraining dislocated workers. Redundancy planning should become a regular function of national, state, and urban governments working in combination with industries, universities, and schools. We are particularly concerned with productive older workers who happen to work in industries that must change the nature of the work they offer or even their locations in order to remain competitive or to stay in business at all. Retraining such workers is essential if they are to maintain their incomes and to find new jobs. It is also essential to their communities and to industry itself to reduce resistance to economic change and growth.

Third, we have recommended that special attention be given to the role that universities might play in a strategy of investment in human resources. Urban universities are in a position that allows them to be catalysts in bringing together the public and private parties necessary to make investment strategies work. Urban universities are also in a position to offer both moral and intellectual leadership in restructuring urban educational systems, in rethinking their own role in preparing minority youth for the new world of work, and in continuously refreshing the knowledge of the professional labor force.

As in other topics discussed in this report, these elements are not independent of each other. They are interrelated parts of a strategy of using existing resources to expand economic opportunities and to foster new enterprises and development.

7 Stabilizing Metropolitan Economies

In the two preceding chapters we have examined two major facets of national policy affecting the fortunes of urban areas: capital investments and investments in human capital. The aim of both is to reinforce main currents of the economy and to facilitate the rapid and smooth adjustment of urban economies to new roles. We have commented on the implications of various policy options for urban areas and on how particular policies, such as those that leverage private capital, improve urban infrastructure, increase worker mobility and training, and improve the urban educational system, can be used in local and regional economic development strategies. All of these policies, however, contain elements that are inherently destabilizing to urban areas because they deliberately promote change. In this chapter and the one that follows, we turn more directly to the other realm of policy of concern to us throughout this report: policies for those left behind—places and people who have a hard time making a fast adjustment.

Specifically, this chapter addresses some of the options that are available to help urban areas stabilize their economies during the period of transition when established economic and community relationships are endangered. Three major areas of policy are explored: (1) strategies that promote local employment and development of the local work force; (2) the selective use of public employment to enhance services and to provide work; and (3) policies aimed at equalizing the fiscal capacity of communities, enabling them to maintain a reasonable level of public services when their economies are under stress.

STRATEGIES FOR PRESERVING COMMUNITY INTEGRITY

As we have pointed out, every worker who might benefit economically from moving to a new job in a new location will not do so. Even in communities with substantial unemployment, most workers will not migrate, and other people will arrive. Some new businesses and jobs will be created, and most of the labor force and the existing firms will remain. Efforts will be made by local government and community leaders to stimulate new activities and to improve the quality of neighborhoods, working places, and services. In light of these realities, measures designed to encourage local economic development and employment opportunities and to stabilize the economy and fiscal system are an integral part of any national urban development strategy.

Mobility is not without cost to the individuals, firms, and communities concerned at either end of the migration stream (Bluestone and Harrison, 1982:67-72). We should also remember that the sense of community remains a powerful value in modern society; in many cases it offsets economic values when individual and group choices are made. Many people are less exclusively career-oriented than in the past, even in professional and technical groups. They often seek community values and qualities as well as career and income advancement. This kind of choice is easier, of course, when modern communications makes it possible to change functions without moving to a different place.

Even in declining communities, resistance to moving remains strong. It is not surprising, therefore, to find that local governments in states in which unemployment is high and lost jobs are not likely to be restored are devoting considerable resources to revitalizing the local economy rather than accepting the inevitability of economic decline. This is a natural response of people who value their community and do not wish to leave it. The same resistance to moving can be seen at the neighborhood level.

Mobility works reasonably well for professional and technical workers whose skills are in demand and who are generally the leading edge of migrations, pulling the market for less skilled jobs behind them. It does not work as well for those less skilled, for older workers, for minorities, and for those who must be retrained at the same time they relocate. When other constraints, such as those imposed by housing markets and two-earner households are added, it is clear that mobility and training strategies combined are unlikely to address many of the problems of urban labor markets. There is still a need for strategies that strengthen local communities and their economies by stimulating the creation of jobs.

Labor mobility strategies presuppose capital mobility and assume that there are compelling reasons for capital to locate where it does. In some cases this is of course true. Extractive industries are a good example; they have no choice but to be where the resources they use are found. As we have seen, however, many modern firms are not constrained to locate in specific places, although certain local factors are clearly important in attracting them and in providing benefits from the presence of similar and supporting activities. The industrial parks of Silicon Valley and the converted textile mills of New England both house computer firms, but there is a labor force in each region that can adapt to the needs of the industry, a strong university-related research and development complex, good air transportation, and the presence of related industries and services.

In some cases the decision of a firm to close a facility or to move to a new location can be made without having to take account of the full social costs and benefits involved. Market prices rarely reflect such impacts. In a few cases—mergers, for example—relocation may reflect an administrative more than an economic rationale. In such cases the interests of the firm more clearly conflict with those of its employees and their community. Serious questions can be raised about the responsibility of such firms to the community that has supplied them with infrastructure, services, and labor, in some cases for generations (Bluestone and Harrison, 1982). The host community or nation pays a part of the cost of relocation when, for example, the still-operable capital stock in one community is forsaken only to have to be replaced with a new stock in another. Thus, what appears rational from one firm's calculus may not be so in a larger context.

The point is that capital can locate in many places and, to the extent that it is genuinely free to do so, there may be substantial advantages from both national and regional perspectives in encouraging it to remain or to locate in places where it can strengthen the integrity of existing communities rather than impel the construction of new urban settlements.

We do not urge the propping up of enterprises that are unable to compete because of obsolete products, technology, or management. Rather, we are suggesting that there may be opportunities for both capital and labor to adapt efficiently to changing markets without moving to another area. Where such opportunities are taken, community integrity can be preserved and enhanced. Workers gain a greater range of choices, and communities are stabilized. Substantial waste because of the underuse of existing capital stock in older communities and the duplication of it elsewhere can also be avoided. Some of this waste may be borne by the firm, as when it abandons a factory. Part may be passed on to taxpayers through various tax write-offs for both old and new facilities. Waste may involve homeowners, through depressed property values, and local governments, through underuse of public facilities.

Recognizing the Value of Community in Public Policy

That all communities are not destined to become new centers of high technology and producer services does not mean that many communities cannot retain or develop jobs. In some situations it may be possible—through cooperative work by an endangered firm, its employees, the community, and others—to adjust production processes or enter a new product line. Plant expansion or modernization, with some community assistance, may be a viable approach if the enterprise is basically sound but needs more space, needs to improve its technology and productivity, and needs to lower its operating costs. In the enthusiasm for technological change, it is often easy to forget that there is still a need for many jobs using routine manual skills. These jobs can be important to a community, both in their own right and as essential links in the chain of jobs in a worker's career, particularly if they are viewed as a way for more local workers to enter the mainstream of the economy. A good example of how such jobs serve this function is the Selby Bindery in St. Paul.[1]

The bindery was established in an inner-city neighborhood in 1971. It employed 300 workers in 1979, almost three-fourths of whom were residents of the immediate neighborhood, the result of a deliberate corporate policy to prefer such employees. Two-thirds were women, over 60 percent were less than 21 years old, and a majority were black; 65 percent had not completed high school. Many of the jobs are part-time, reflecting the tedious nature of the work and the fact that many workers, such as young women with children, can more easily work a part-time schedule. An important feature of the plant's operation is that pay is keyed to the productivity and opportunities for upward mobility and out-placement in jobs in the parent company and other industries in the St. Paul metropolitan area. This employment policy includes the opportunity to transfer to full-time jobs and gives special attention to employee training, including work with computers. Special educational programs are also provided, including scholarships for training in skilled occupations. When Bendick and Egan compared the bindery's performance with that of the rest of the industry, they found the company to be financially sound, although it was not as attractive to investors as some other firms because of its relatively low return on investment.

The Selby Bindery and similar inner-city enterprises are not models to be specifically copied, but they demonstrate that careful selection of activities geared to local labor force characteristics, when combined with

---

[1] The discussion of the Selby Bindery is based on Bendick and Egan (1982).

effective management and community relations, can produce profitable enterprises that contribute materially to the economic well-being of the residents of a neighborhood. A substantial underemployed labor force resides in such areas and could be made more productive. The inner city can be competitive with other locations for some kinds of industry. The primary significance of such jobs is that they provide entry into the labor market and access for workers to better opportunities in a wider labor market. Such enterprises are often essential if the labor force is to gain the basic working skills and habits necessary for upward mobility.

The Selby Bindery also illustrates how public policy is important in leveraging private capital to create jobs that otherwise would have located elsewhere at substantial social cost in unemployment in the inner city. Inner-city businesses often are less profitable and take longer to become profitable—as in the case of the bindery—than similar businesses in other locations. Policy needs to recognize these facts. In St. Paul, public powers were used to write down land costs to make the site competitive with suburban sites. While some tax credits were available, they do not seem to have figured in the business decision. Thus, by combining public action with private entrepreneurship, capital located in a distressed area, productively employed local labor, developed human resources, and helped to stabilize a neighborhood while returning a profit to its owners. Although the bindery is to some extent sheltered by its parent company, it is no example of corporate charity. It arguably is an example of corporate advertising, since it has produced substantial favorable publicity for the company.

Development projects in Boston, Baltimore, Toledo, and Norfolk illustrate a somewhat different approach to preserving community integrity. These projects involve revitalization of downtown or waterfront areas of the central city. Each has used a site advantage or a historic association to heighten the city's self-image as a center of culture, variety, and commerce. These new centers of commerce and entertainment generate some employment in themselves, but more important, they tend to have a multiplier effect on other businesses and encourage additional development. They are particularly attractive to both producer and consumer services and help to establish a new economic base for the core area of a city.

Other policies can also strengthen community integrity. There is good reason to require recipients of federal grants for new development, such as those provided in the Urban Development Action Grant or the Urban Mass Transportation programs, to set aside some of the new jobs for local disadvantaged or structurally unemployed workers. Boston and Cambridge have begun to apply this principle at the local level, coordinating their unemployment and economic development programs. Both have enacted first-source agreements as a means of increasing job opportunities for their citizens. These agreements between cities and private companies receiving development assistance from or through the government require the companies to set aside a fixed portion of their jobs for city residents and for disadvantaged groups. These agreements require that both economic development and unemployment programs look beyond the raw numbers of new jobs created to the characteristics of the people who are actually employed (G. Clark, 1983).[2]

The Use of Public Employment

While community integrity strategies emphasize private employment, selective use of public service employment can also play an important role. Historically, public service employment has been used as a countercyclical measure to alleviate short-term unemployment. As an alternative to welfare and extended unemployment benefits, public service employment has the added advantage of maintaining services that otherwise are likely to languish, adding to a city's unattractiveness for new economic growth.

Beyond its use in recessions, public service employment has been an important route to upward mobility for minorities and the urban poor. In part this is because wage levels in the lower ranks of public service are relatively higher than for similar private sector jobs and because of policies that strongly favor promotion from within the ranks. Public service employment also offers higher status or dignity and greater security than many jobs in the private sector. Moving from private to public employment increases the earnings of urban ghetto residents from one to three times (Harrison, 1972:193). In every occupation, blacks, both men and women, earn more working for government than for privately owned firms (Jones, 1979).

The increased number of people displaced from jobs by technological change and structural shifts in the economy raises new questions about the role that public service employment should play in both the transitional period and in the long run, when a larger proportion of the labor force will be employed in service occupations. Many of the dislocated workers will eventually be reemployed in private firms. A large number, however, could be relegated to a persistent underclass because of the mismatch between their abilities and the new skill requirements of the labor market.

---

[2] These agreements were upheld by the U.S. Supreme Court in *White* v. *Massachusetts Council of Construction*, _____U.S. _____ , 103 S.Ct. 1 (1983).

To deal with the relative immobility of such people, the government may have to respond with more than mobility programs, temporary counter-cyclical employment, and retraining opportunities. An expansion of both direct public service employment and indirect creation of private jobs that provide similar services or facilities may be needed. A strong argument can be made for preferring the indirect approach over direct public employment. It would provide jobs in private firms and would encourage some competition in the provision of services.

By whatever means, an expanded public service and public works program could be beneficial in several ways. It could channel the urban poor and the structurally unemployed who do not find new jobs in the private sector into productive activities. It could increase the supply of badly needed public services. And it could help stem the deterioration of the nation's infrastructure and capital plant.

Publicly sponsored employment need not take away from the generation of national wealth. It produces services that are consumed collectively rather than individually. It also recognizes that community services and capital investment by government are often prerequisites to private economic development and growth (Sheppard, 1969). Of course, government services, like any others, can be produced inefficiently, and there are special risks in providing temporary services that do not meet the test of market demand. It is important, therefore, to examine carefully the kind of services to be provided and the effect they may have on other employment and businesses in the community.

After several decades of experience in using public sector employment to achieve social objectives of equalizing opportunity and redistributing income, any recommendations for a public employment strategy must be approached with caution. Clearly, there is room for political abuse. Public jobs can become make-work activities that provide little in the way of tangible services to the community beyond providing taxable income to those who would otherwise be unemployed. Idle or unproductive employees on the public payroll can also undermine respect and support for other important government programs. Care must be taken to ensure that the efficiency of the local public sector is not overly sacrificed to worthwhile complementary social goals.

Fortunately, the science of public management has progressed to a point at which effective incentives and performance standards can be built into a strategy of using public service to achieve upward mobility for minorities and disadvantaged workers and to contribute to economic development. Imposing such standards is no easy task in many localities. The demands on management are enormous when one objective of public service is to employ and develop marginal workers. It is a task we have not been willing to impose on the private sector. For local governments to succeed in such a strategy, they must recruit the most able people to use productively those who are the least able.

The nation has had enough experience with public works employment and countercyclical government employment programs to understand both the benefits and problems associated with such efforts. New Deal public works employment programs produced impressive and lasting achievements: 651,000 miles of roads, 16,000 miles of water and sewer lines, 78,000 bridges, 2,300 stadiums, 35,000 public buildings, and 353 airport landing fields (Levitan, 1975). The economic and social utility of the works themselves and the employment they generated now seem beyond dispute.

In more recent times, smaller and more controversial public employment programs have been carried out. The Public Employment Program (PEP) under the Emergency Employment Act of 1971 spent $2.5 billion to provide 325,000 man years of employment to jobless workers. No public works were constructed, but government service workers were hired through grants to state and local governments. The evaluation of the program found that two of every three PEP workers indicated that their public service work helped them find other employment. Their incidence of unemployment and dependence on public assistance declined and, two years after termination of the program, their annual earnings had increased by 86 percent over their earnings the year before they entered it (Westat, 1981). About a third of the program's cost was recovered in tax receipts from those working in it and from savings in reduced welfare and other program costs (Levitan, 1975:62).

In the mid-1970s, training and employment programs were consolidated in the Comprehensive Employment and Training Act (CETA). By fiscal 1977, 2,361,400 people were enrolled in various CETA programs—34 percent of the unemployed. It has been estimated that, without the CETA program, the unemployment rate would have risen by two to three percentage points (Jones, 1979:90). CETA's Public Service Employment (PSE) program enrolled 750,000 of these people—about 10 percent of the unemployed—in 1978, when the program was at its peak, at a cost of $5.66 billion. The program was viewed as not cost-effective in comparison with other programs, such as classroom and on-the-job training programs, and public employment was perceived as consisting of temporary dead-end jobs that were unproductive.

By 1980 the PSE program had been reduced to 328,000 jobs, and it was abolished by Congress at the request of the administration in the 1982 budget. Disaffection from the program was also based on several administrative scandals associated with it. In addition, as the program had been amended in 1978, PSE participants were restricted to economically dis-advantaged people, ensuring that it enrolled only the most difficult group to develop into effective workers and, correspondingly, reducing the value of the program to the state and local agencies that clearly used it to supplement their ability to provide public services (Palmer and Sawhill, 1982:254-258).[3]

At a time when government spending is being drastically curtailed, expansion of public service and public works programs may be viewed as too expensive. However, the net real social costs of funding a job for a structurally unemployed worker or for a chronically unemployed person is much less than the flat expenditure. Even the CETA-PSE program had a cost-effectiveness ratio of 0.53, which did not take into account the fact that CETA expenditures "substituted" for services that states and local governments would have otherwise provided from their budgets. Had these benefits for local governments been added to the reduction in welfare costs and the gains in wages made by participants after they left the program, the difference betweeen the economic worth of the program and its cost would have been small (Palmer and Sawhill, 1982:257).

For local and state governments the choices are not likely to be between providing public employment for a substantial number of dislocated work-ers and otherwise unemployable people and having them find more eco-nomically beneficial jobs in the private sector. The real choice is between some level of public service employment and the welfare system or the underground economy, both of which sap the public budget and the overall economy. The issue, then, is what kind of public employment program to have, how large it should be, and how long it should last.

From a long-term perspective, direct government employment or private employment that provides public services through contracts or other forms of privatization will surely increase as more and higher-quality services such as education, recreation, and health care are demanded by citizens, although the rate of growth promises to be much lower than in recent decades. The current backlog of demand for infrastructure maintenance and new facilities will also require an expanded public service work force. In addition, there may be new quasi-public employment opportunities in such activities as neighborhood revitalization, special transit programs, and community safety programs. A number of these activities lend them-selves to both part-time and temporary employment, allowing for consid-

---

[3] Clearly, CETA had conceptual and administrative problems, in particular with eligibility stan-dards, training and out-placement of enrollees, decentralized administration, and monitoring (Mirengoff et al., 1980a, 1980b).

erable flexibility in program design and administration. Some have the potential of producing a marketable service in the private economy.

Public service employment, therefore, need not be seen as a make-work program. It can be designed to provide important services and facilities while offering productive work to people who would not readily find other jobs. Public works employment, in particular, adds to the economic attractiveness of a community for private investment. It can also be used to instill productive work habits in entry-level employees. The value of such programs must be graded over the life of the projects and in terms of their multiplier effect on the private sector, not just in terms of the annual cost of the payroll.

One of the virtues of public works employment is that most of it may be done through private firms under contract to the government. There is every reason for state and local governments to require contractors to provide for the employment of local redundant workers and disadvantaged persons in their work forces. While it may be argued that this will add to the cost of projects, it is a social benefit that the government should seek. Its cost needs to be weighed against the social costs of unemployment. Working with contractors, unions, and community groups, government may be able to foster training programs and placement services as a part of its overall public works effort. Employment tax credits, if offered at all, should probably be available to construction firms engaged in local public works programs that require employment of the disadvantaged. Certainly there is now enough experience with minority hiring programs in both public and private construction to develop effective hiring and upward mobility programs.

Public works maintenance programs operated directly by governments or under contract to private firms could follow a similar strategy. In addition, there is an opportunity in such programs to create community service corporations that afford local residents opportunities for labor and experience in jobs at different management levels. Again, many of these jobs may be structured so as to be available to part-time workers and to workers with only the bare minimum of marketable skills. Often they will be supplementary jobs for workers or families, providing a margin of income sufficient to raise a household out of poverty. Decentralizing some service programs to neighborhoods has the additional advantage of increasing participation by residents in governing their community. Experience indicates that this has additional benefits in community maintenance and safety (Downs, 1981). At the same time, it must be recognized that many of the most important investments in infrastructure require highly skilled and highly specialized labor. More attention is needed to requirements for specific skills of different infrastructure tasks, so that jobs and investment priorities can be matched.

Governments should, in their public services and public works programs, accept responsibility for the future welfare of their workers in ways that extend beyond the usual retirement and health benefits. Employee training for advancement, inside or outside government service, should be a primary objective of public personnel policy. Training in basic literacy and the use of machinery and computers and improving behavior and skills are all means of helping the short-term productivity of the public work force and the long-term employability of workers. There is no reason why public employment, at whatever level it exists, should not be as much a seedbed as private employment for a more highly skilled and economically attractive labor force. Far too often governments have not followed enlightened personnel development policies. We have already seen that in a service-oriented economy, public service workers are an important element in both the local economy and the national economy. Governments must therefore accept at least as much responsibility as the private sector for the readiness of their own labor forces for participation in an advanced economy.

The growth of the local public sector in the total economy may provide a necessary transitional cushion for some of the structural dislocation that occurs. For it to be so used, however, substantial state and/or federal assistance will be necessary because of the disparities that exist in the fiscal capacities of local governments and the strain such programs place on jurisdictions that are losing jobs and tax base.

In discussing public service employment, we do not advance it as a panacea. It is one element in the battery of policies that may be necessary in some local circumstances to maintain the degree of community stability required for a reasonably smooth change in the structure of the local economy. Properly used, public employment programs can help a community avoid some of the most serious consequences for dislocated workers who face no realistic choice but unemployment and for those who have no other realistic point of entry into the labor force.

EQUALIZING FISCAL CAPACITY

The Need for Local Capacity

If we take seriously the admonition that no uniform approach to urban economic development is likely to succeed because of the diversity among the different types of urban areas, the national interest would seem best served by seeing to it that state, local, and private institutions have the capacity to initiate and effectively pursue development and employment strategies that facilitate adjustment to the new economic and urban systems. They also need a base for strategic decision making. This cannot be done if there is no assurance that necessary resources can be made available. Thus, one of the most important aspects of local capacity for adjustment is its fiscal capacity—the ability to finance a minimum level of public services and facilities at effective tax rates set near the national average (U.S. Advisory Commission on Intergovernmental Relations, 1982).

A severe erosion of fiscal capacity undermines state and local ability to devise, much less carry out, a positive economic development strategy. As the tax base deteriorates relative to other jurisdictions, or even in absolute terms, services must be cut, taxes raised, or both. Either action can inhibit the ability to retain higher-income residents and employers. Jurisdictions in need of a stronger tax base tend to adopt beggar-thy-neighbor policies (tax abatement for newly locating firms, for instance) that add almost nothing to net economic growth for an area but exacerbate interjurisdictional and regional rivalries. And the benefits are illusory because these competitive tax concessions undermine the yield from revenue sources that locate there while new costs are generated. As fiscal disparities contribute to the migration of firms and workers, other costs are created at both ends of the migration stream. Existing public facilities, private plants and offices, and housing are abandoned or inefficiently used. Much of this capital stock must then be duplicated in the places to which capital and labor move.

Interstate fiscal disparities are widening, even though the average personal income levels of states and regions are converging (U.S. Advisory Commission on Intergovernmental Relations, 1977, 1982a, 1982b). The growing disparity comes about in large part from two sources: (1) structural changes in state and regional economies and the accompanying patterns of job and population migration and demographic change and (2) the fact that a few states have access to revenue sources that are not available to others. The energy-producing states, for example, can tax extraction of resources almost without regard to the levels of personal income in their states. States whose treasuries rely heavily on revenues from tourism may have low personal income levels but high tax capacity. There is an important distinction between the ability of the residents of a jurisdiction to pay taxes and the ability of a jurisdiction to raise revenues.

Within the states, disparities in fiscal capacity among units of local government are often even more severe than those between states and regions. These disparities are largely the result of frozen jurisdictional boundaries that prevent an economically declining central city located in a growing metropolitan area from sharing the revenue available from the net metropolitan growth. Over the past 25 years, city-suburban fiscal disparities have widened rather than converged. Except for the infusion of direct federal assistance to central cities, the disparities would have been even greater (U.S. Advisory Commission on Intergovernmental Relations, 1977).

The states possess the legal power to correct many of the disparities among the local jurisdictions within their own borders through redrawing local government boundaries, sharing state revenues with local governments on the basis of tax capacity and tax effort formulas, requiring neighboring jurisdictions to share regional tax sources such as industry, and relocating functions between the state and local levels of government. It is exceptionally difficult, however, for these legal powers to be translated into political action in the state legislatures, particularly when it comes to realigning boundaries. Consequently, few states have made extensive use of their full range of powers to equalize fiscal capacities or to aid distressed local units (U.S. Advisory Commission on Intergovernmental Relations, 1981).

While the use of state power to equalize fiscal capacity within a state is of great importance, for a state that is itself in serious fiscal distress, no amount of reshuffling of boundaries and responsibilities, revenue sharing, or productivity advance will overcome the basic problem of disparity between its major urban units and those in other, more prosperous states that compete for the same economic activities. Without some substantial changes in national policy, interstate disparities are likely to increase rather than narrow during the next decade. There is also a strong probability of a growing number of urban fiscal crises such as those faced by New York and Cleveland in recent years (Bahl, 1981).

This condition suggests that equalizing fiscal capacity within and among the states should be an important long-term objective of any national strategy for urban economic development. The argument that people should leave distressed areas for more prosperous places overlooks the fact that while some migration is inevitable or even desirable, it can exacerbate local economic and fiscal distress.

The more economically advantaged move; the poor and less skilled workers are left behind. Services cannot be terminated. Old cities may shrink but they rarely disappear. The result of such patterns of moving and staying is an even deeper fiscal crisis caused by the higher proportion of residents who depend on public services and the lower level of taxable resources. In some respects this condition is almost a classic reenactment of Gunnar Myrdal's *An American Dilemma* but in an urban setting. These long-term and deepening disparities, however, could be changed. They are, if not created by public policy, at least greatly affected by it. Policy changes, probably made incrementally over some period of time, could substantially alleviate the problem.

Reallocation of the welfare functions of the federal system, discussed in Chapter 6, is a very important step in strengthening the fiscal capacities of state and local governments, but it does not directly address the equalization issue. It essentially equalizes welfare benefits among individuals. It relieves many governments of a fiscal burden they find difficult to carry, but falls short of ensuring that each unit of government has the fiscal capacity to provide services to its citizens and residents at a level near the national average by applying an average tax rate to the resources available to it.

Strategies for Equalizing Fiscal Capacity

Fiscal equalization does not mean that all units of government will provide the same level of service or even the same package of services. Central cities traditionally spend more for noneducational services than suburbs do because of the different composition of their populations and their interests. Some localities will choose to make a greater or lesser tax effort than others—that is, to tax the resources they have at a higher or lower rate. Tax-rich places will undoubtedly continue to enjoy higher levels of services with less effort than tax-poor places. Fiscal equalization reduces the disparities; it does not eliminate them or homogenize services. It proceeds on the assumption that it is in the national interest for all communities to have the capacity to provide basic services at a minimum level of service that approximates the national average, that the range of service levels should be slight so that access to police protection, educational opportunity, or community sanitation should not vary widely simply because of a change of residence.[4]

A Cost-Effective Approach to Intergovernmental Transfers

Looked at strictly as a budget issue, fiscal equalization has some promise of providing a more effective form of intergovernmental fiscal transfer

---

[4] Within the states, the equalization of some services, such as education, is well rooted. In recent years, the highest courts in a number of states have ruled that their state constitutions require equal education services (*Serrano* v. *Priest* (483 P.2d 1241 (Cal. 1971))). The U.S. Supreme Court has held, however, that fiscal equalization of school districts is not required by the federal Constitution (*Rodriguez* v. *San Antonio Independent School District* (411 U.S. 1 (1973))).

than the current mixed system of revenue sharing and block and categorical grants. Studies by the U.S. Advisory Commission on Intergovernmental Relations show that a direct program of fiscal equalization could be less costly than the traditional system. In fiscal 1980, for example, a $12.2 billion program to bring state revenues closer to the average level would have done more to reduce fiscal disparities than the $90 billion transfer program then in effect (Lucke, 1982). Such a program is not necessarily a substitute for all federal aid to states and local governments, but in an era of shrinking federal grants it could offer a more fruitful approach to issues of equitable treatment of the states and regions than a patchwork system of specific grants. It has the added attraction of enhancing the capacity of state and local governments to perform more effectively those functions for which they assume responsibility.

Fiscal Equalization: The Experiences of Canada and West Germany

Fiscal equalization is used effectively in other federal nations. In Canada, where the national government has traditionally played a far smaller role in local fiscal affairs than in the United States, equalization grants are distributed by the federal government only to those provinces whose fiscal capacity is below the national average. The grants are designed to make it possible for each province to meet the average level of service at the average level of taxation (Lucke, 1982:27).

In West Germany the federal government transfers revenues to the states in order to bring the fiscal capacities of the poorer states up to 92 percent of the national average (Zimmerman, 1981:38). Equalization is mandated by the constitution of the Federal Republic and is considered essential to the idea of local self-determination. States, accordingly, are required to share their revenues with their political subdivisions on an equalized basis.[5] The formula used for distribution of federal grants to the states combines the fiscal capacity of the states with that of their local governments. Adjustments are made for the size and density of cities in the formula, since these factors are highly related to service needs. States then redistribute their revenues, including the federal equalization grants, on a similar basis (Zimmerman, 1981).

The German approach provides some latitude for encouraging states and localities to make an extra effort of their own to raise revenues and to reduce urban-suburban fiscal disparities. The system appears to work

---

[5] The West German system also involves directly negotiated payments by the rich states to the poor states, an element unlikely to take root in the United States.

well in achieving its objectives of dispersing decision making in urban affairs. What to do is left to the local and state governments. The federal government merely sees that they all have a relatively equal minimum capacity to do as they choose. The system seems also to have greatly reduced interjurisdictional fiscal rivalry,[6] epitomized in the United States by the "smokestack-chasing" policies of areas hoping to lure new industry.

Conclusion

The gradual introduction of fiscal equalization could be an important means of strengthening state and local decision-making capacity. Because of the pivotal role of the states in reducing urban-suburban disparities, there would be value in channeling the equalization grants in the form of general revenue sharing through the states, basing the state share on fiscal capacity and requiring only that a substantial percentage be redistributed to equalize local disparities. A state's unrestricted share might also be adjusted according to the degree to which it has independently acted to reduce local fiscal disparities, whether by consolidating local governments, sharing state revenues, or reallocating responsibilities for governmental functions.

Fiscal equalization holds promise of providing a solid and understandable basis for long-term fiscal relationships in the federal system. It can go a long way toward giving state and local governments the stability they need to provide facilities and services. Equalization alone, however, is probably insufficient as the federal response to the transition period between the old and new urban economies. Cities in transition—from either rapid decline or rapid growth—often have little capacity to manage their transition. When major structural change is under way, there is justification for special programs for economic development, infrastructure, technical research, training, or labor mobility programs. Such programs, again coordinated through the states, should not be for the purpose of holding on to an industry but to assist an area in anticipating its gains and losses and in making adjustments to them smoother (Bahl, 1981:122). Such grants could also help in identifying strategic strengths and in building on them to accelerate the emergence of new economic roles and activities.

---

[6] As a result of the intergovernmental fiscal system, German cities are far less obsessed than their American counterparts with the out-migration of people and jobs as a normal consequence of the restructuring of the economy (National Research Council, 1982b:11).

Once again the experience of other federal systems offers useful insight into how such programs might be structured. Canada negotiates general development agreements with each province. These agreements provide planning frameworks to help guide public sector investments, with the objective of influencing private sector growth and development. Germany also has a joint federal-state program designed to promote regional economic development (National Research Council, 1982b:5,36). Whatever form they take, such programs should be clearly transitional in character. If they are to strengthen local capacity for planning and adjustment, they might provide support for improvements of infrastructure on the basis of a shrinkage plan rather than on the basis of an expanding system; concentrate on the reuse of existing capital, such as housing and factories; or provide help in making improvements in the management and the productivity of government.

Stabilizing metropolitan areas during a period of economic transition does not mean that they should not change. The purpose of stabilization policies is to permit change to occur, even to encourage change, but to do so in a way that reduces its shock and the resistance to it. To the extent feasible, these policies seek to replace weak sectors of local economies with stronger sectors and to prepare the existing labor force for movement into new occupations, industries, and, if necessary to maintain their employment, new places.

Capital investment and employment strategies are chiefly concerned with the flow of capital and labor to promising sectors. Regional and metropolitan stabilization strategies are concerned with making enough capital available for investment in urban physical and human development to help make it possible for the changes in economic structure to occur as smoothly as possible and to avoid the inefficient abandonment of capital stock that can serve new as well as old forms of economic activity. These policies, of course, must be supported by national macroeconomic policies that are conscious of their regional and local consequences.

8 Fostering Local Institutions to Manage the Transition

Achieving national interests in the distribution of economic growth requires strategies tailored to specific urban areas. Such strategies require, in turn, institutions capable of carrying them out. Thus a major emphasis of national policy should be to help create and strengthen such institutions.

There seems to be general agreement across the political spectrum that strong leadership at the urban level is essential to successful economic development programs (Committee for Economic Development, 1982; U.S. Department of Housing and Urban Development, 1980, 1982). Research on urban economic development indicates that one of the most important elements in the success of such endeavors is the institutionalization of leadership, so that it has staying power as well as the political and technical capacity to capitalize on the competitive advantages and opportunities of its particular area. This recognizes the fact that urban development is a long, drawn-out process, with long lead times before physical changes can be completed. Even longer periods are needed to bring a broad strategy of economic and community development to the point at which financial and social returns can be seen. In an important sense, urban development has no end (Fosler and Berger, 1982). Institutions are therefore needed that transcend the arrangements required for individual projects.

Although institutions must reflect local conditions, three elements stand out as important for an effective urban development process. The first is development of a strong, independent capacity for urban intelligence. The second is sustained public-private leadership and decision-making institutions that create legitimate processes for making development decisions. Third is a strong and active independent sector. When all three exist, it is much more likely that an urban area can use its land, facilities, capital leverage, and human resources in a manner that advances its development.

BUILDING A CAPACITY FOR URBAN INTELLIGENCE

Given the differences among urban areas described in Chapter 2 and the complexities of urban development in an advanced economy, each area needs its own strong research and information capacity that is linked to its decision-making process. A wide range of information should be available for strategy making, including economic, social, political-governmental, and physical-environmental data (Perloff, 1981). These data should be collected and analyzed over time to provide the basis for an urban intelligence system.

The objective of an information system is widespread self-knowledge of an area by its leaders and its people. Its communities, businesses, and interest groups need to understand the way in which their economy developed, how it functions, how it is changing, and how national and international forces affect its fortunes. From this knowledge an understanding can develop of the area's assets, its comparative advantages, its vulnerabilities, and the opportunities that are most likely to be within reach.

Most areas have some parts of such an intelligence system, but the components are scattered among government agencies, businesses, universities, and nonprofit groups. While the deficiency in strategic information can be ameliorated by a special consultant or a civic task force study, such ad hoc efforts, however thorough, are soon out of date. Developing a solid base of economic, social, and physical information about an urban area is a continuing task.

No major city or region now has an institution to monitor the local economy, to report regularly on its analysis of conditions, to forecast, and to provide advice to policy makers on economic development strategy. As a result, local economic development activity is characterized by many projects but relatively little strategic sense of where the area is headed and whether that is the most desirable direction. To some degree this confusion is illustrated by the major development projects under way in the 10 largest U.S. cities during 1982 (*Venture*, 1982). Some of these projects have obvious strategic importance by strengthening downtown or satellite service centers. What is impossible to assess is the net effect of a single city's projects on the structure of the local economy.

This situation suggests the value of a system to monitor such projects and assess their actual impact on the economy, so that the information gathered could be used in planning future projects. In conjunction with a development program, a few key investments in an intelligence system in strategic locations may help reshape a city's appearance and economy and initiate a process of growth and adjustment.

Good information is more important for sectoral and labor market planning in a time of slow growth or structural transformation than in a period of rapid growth. The great differences among urban areas, based on their roles in the urban system, suggest that they must become more selective in the promotion of economic activities rather than continue traditional boosterism, with its eagerness to accommodate any kind of development. Most cities, even those command and control centers in which services have a strong propensity to concentrate, now need to be concerned with not only how many jobs are created and the number of square feet of commercial space or the number of housing units built, but also what kind of jobs and units are being provided, where they are located, and how they contribute to the long-term future of the city.

Particularly where major shifts in economic functions and structure are occurring, it can no longer be taken for granted that a city will continue its historic role in the urban system. In an important sense, the city itself must be redefined in terms of the functions it can perform best in a restructured economy (Knight, 1982a).

This requires an in-depth understanding of the history and evolution of the region and the metropolis, its businesses, labor force, capital plant, amenities, and cultural and social institutions. Such an inventory of assets and realistic potential provides an essential base for redefining the area's future (Perloff, 1982). It may reveal, for example, that change in the structures of the old-line industries that dominated the employment patterns of the region in the past now makes those industries an insecure base for the future economy. Other parts of the economy, however, such as the area's cultural, health, and educational institutions, may have substantial capacity for growth and for attracting other economic activities. It may also reveal that headquarters and producer services are replacing the production of goods in the older industries, thus shifting the occupational structure without changing the industrial mix significantly. A close examination of the local economy may identify firms that are particularly innovative, and even more important, existing or potential linkages among innovative sectors that can produce demands for other services or manufactured products (Rees, 1983). Such findings would commend the use of local resources in different ways than if the analysis concluded that the same industries and occupations have a bright future if facilities and production processes are simply modernized. This kind of information may also help in making decisions about the need for a different mix of public services, investments in facilities and amenities, and changes in the location of activities or in the transportation and communications systems.

Organizing the Intelligence Function

An Urban Council of Economic Advisers

The experiences of cities and metropolitian areas that have made reasonable progress in developing research and information systems suggest the ingredients of a sound urban intelligence system. At the outset, an assurance of long-term funding that is not restricted to the interests of particular sponsors is important in providing both independence and a consistent effort. A permanent high-quality professional staff with enough independence from political interference to allow it to develop a reputation for objective, thorough, and insightful analysis and good channels of access to government, corporate, and community decision makers can provide a valuable resource that improves with time. It develops a respected institutional memory, deepening its own and the public's cumulative understanding of what is happening to the area, and becomes a valued source of in-depth knowledge and judgment about the area, its economy, and people. Finally, there is a need for a system of publication and wide dissemination of findings and proposals. Groups such as the Regional Plan Association (New York), the Metropolitan Fund (Detroit), and the Greater Washington Research Center suggest different ways of organizing to perform some of the functions outlined here. In a few cities a governmental office, such as the planning agency, may be able to provide a large part of this function. In most cities, however, a government agency will lack the credibility necessary for the private sector to accept its findings.

A public-private or independent, nonprofit endeavor may be a more effective way of organizing the urban intelligence function. Greater cooperation and sharing of information among government, business, universities, and volunteer organizations can mutually benefit each participant.

One model that could be tried is an urban modification of the Council of Economic Advisers. Such a local council, with members appointed by the public, private, and independent sectors (see below), could be made responsible for a regular report on the state of an area's economy. Such a council could make an annual state-of-the-area report. If supplemented by the creation of a forum for discussion of the themes of this report, the council could, over time, have a considerable effect on public and private economic strategy. The report could be institutionalized, for example, by an event in which government and business leaders must respond to its findings. Public-private task forces could be organized to pursue and carry out its recommendations.

While no single model can fit all cities, the objective is to develop and maintain an analytical and information group that can speak with authority on strategic economic development issues and can become a resource on which government and business can rely for unbiased information, thoughtful analyses, and evaluations of public and private activities.

Such organizations need a continuous infusion of new ideas, because what served well in the past may not work under new circumstances. This suggests a need for some kind of national network, linking individual urban information systems and various centers of national and international urban research. One model that might be explored is the Cooperative Highway Research Program of the Transportation Research Board. It is a clearinghouse that provides a network of users with technical information. Reports could be circulated not only to members of the network, but also to executive and legislative leaders at each level of government and to leaders of business and nonprofit orgnizations.

Improving the Quality of Regional and Urban Data

The federal government can assist in the development of the urban intelligence function in several important ways without intruding directly into the often delicate and unique local processes of establishing and maintaining it. The federal government can improve the quality of the information that is available to such groups, in particular, the quality of regional and sectoral statistics. The Bureau of Economic Research, the Census Bureau, the Bureau of Labor Statistics, the Department of Housing and Urban Development, and the Advisory Commission on Intergovernmental Relations, to mention only a few agencies, collect and analyze various kinds of information essential to public and private decisions at the regional and local levels (Davis and Wolman, 1981). These data need to be available for regional analysis in a consolidated and consistent format that helps tell a more detailed and accurate story about what is occurring in urban areas (Garnick, 1982; Ingraham, 1982).

A new breakdown of data on economic sectors, particularly the services, is needed that is relevant to the analysis of urban economies.[1] Within metropolitan areas, there is a considerable need to have data organized by major jurisdiction, including large municipalities. The U.S. Department of Housing and Urban Development has sponsored some useful research on developing a system of urban indicators.[2] Work on an urban indicators series should continue, but it should be guided by an interdisciplinary panel of experts and users. Developing an indicator series will require the involvement of the agencies that collect data of interest to urban policy makers and strategists. Among other things, there is a need for reconciling data bases, improving the definitions used, and developing a common format for reporting urban data. The first task should be to develop a consensus on a few statistical series that could help describe major changes in urban economic conditions. This work should proceed independently of efforts to devise formulas for the distribution of federal grants.

Reorganization of the way in which economic data are reported, for example, could help considerably in understanding changes in local economic structure. Another problem that needs to be addressed is how data are aggregated at jurisdictional and metropolitan levels, keeping in mind that what is adequate for national and state analysis is sometimes virtually useless in local analysis.

A second form of federal support for local information systems is technical assistance. Federal agencies already provide a great deal of direct assistance in interpreting information and establishing local information systems. Over the last three decades, the federal government has directly assisted in establishing many local, state, and regional planning and information agencies and processes.[3] One result of the federal planning requirements and subsidies is the development in many urban areas of sophisticated and well-used policy information systems that use nationally collected data, such as the decennial census data, supplemented with local surveys and other data. The quality of these systems, however, is very uneven.

---

[1] For a survey and analysis of data that are available on the service sectors see Economics Consulting Service (1981).

[2] Much of this work is related to the development of indicators of "distress" for use in targeting federal assistance programs, with a heavy emphasis on fiscal conditions, poverty levels, physical deterioration, etc. A bibliography of urban indicator studies can be found in Government Finance Research Center (1982).

[3] These include state and local planning assistance, economic development agencies, urban development organizations, intergovernmental clearinghouses for federal grant programs, and coordination processes for many specific grant programs, such as those for transportation and sewerage systems.

Support for a National Urban Information Network

Federal comprehensive planning assistance has been terminated. While it may no longer be necessary to provide federal financial support for local planning information systems, there is considerable value in some federal support, in cooperation with private funding sources, for a national network to facilitate the exchange of information and mutual assistance among local information agencies. While a number of options are available for providing a national support institution for local economic information and development activities, the most obvious approach would be to strengthen the existing organizations of governments, professionals, and officials, operating through an existing or new consortium but one expanded to include private sector groups such as the Committee for Economic Development and the Urban Land Institute.

PUBLIC-PRIVATE LEADERSHIP

There is some possibility that public-private partnership will become the nostrum for the 1980s that community participation was for the 1960s. Without claiming too much for it, a close relationship between government and the corporate community is indeed often a critical factor in the success of both individual economic development projects and in the ability of a city or a region to improve its economic position over time (Committee for Economic Development, 1982). Clearly, a substantial economic development effort necessarily requires the use of power and resources by both sides of the political economy.

Some 15,000 local economic development organizations already exist in the United States, including public, private, and mixed groups (Levy, 1981). Very few of these, however, are involved in developing and managing a strategic approach to local economic development. We know relatively little about those that are, how they operate, and their degrees of success or failure. The Commission on Private Initiatives (the Verity Commission), however, has compiled valuable information on partnerships. Some institution should maintain and analyze such information, providing valuable assistance to local efforts.

Strengthening public-private leadership requires two elements: (1) increasing the involvement of private sector leaders in making long-term strategic decisions and (2) involving nongovernmental institutions in carrying out those decisions through specific projects.[4] Involvement of private sector leaders and institutions not only provides more experienced judgment to policy making, but it can also increase the legitimacy of economic development programs and help develop alternative policies and alternative ways of approaching problems.

Public-private cooperation cannot be wished into existence, particularly in making strategic choices. Nor can it be willed into being by legislation. Of two cities in the same state operating with similiar powers and political processes, one may have a flourishing process of public-private strategy making and action, while in the other city the two sectors maintain at best a mutual sullen disrespect. For strategic partnerships to take root, there must be a favorable civic culture (Committee for Economic Development, 1982:11). This usually entails some tradition of civic involvement and responsibility by corporate executives. It often means a political climate in which officials and corporate leaders can openly collaborate. The corporate leaders must view the government as competent and as reasonably honest in its dealings with investors; public officials must see corporate leadership as public spirited and as a potential ally rather than as a dedicated adversary. In short, there must be a climate of continuing trust as opposed to one of transitory need.

Differences in Public and Private Perspectives

Each side must understand that its interest cannot be advanced alone as effectively as it can be with the cooperation or support of the prospective partner. The recent experience of Cleveland illustrates the importance of an understanding of mutual interests. The city was brought to the edge of financial default by open antagonism between the mayor and the corporate community. A new mayor set out to work with the business and financial community to improve the city's fiscal and economic position and the climate for businesses and investment in the city. Both sides found sub-

---

[4] There is not a great deal of systematic analysis of public-private cooperation or of the conditions on which it depends. The existing literature consists largely of anecdotal materials, case studies, and exhortation. The richest examples of cooperation tend to be those involving physical development projects, although there is a growing body of information about social programs, particularly those focused on neighborhoods and employment. Useful case studies are found in Fosler and Berger (1982). Several other examples are summarized in Council for Northeast Economic Action (1980). The development of social action programs through private and nonprofit institutions can be found in Woodson (1981). A wide-ranging discussion of nongovernmental initiatives in community programs may be found in the essays and studies in Meyer (1982).

stantial benefits in the new arrangement, which has produced a new financial plan for the city and a major effort to improve its infrastructure.

A productive relationship also depends on appreciating the substantial differences of interest and of decision-making processes between government and corporate leaders (Fosler and Berger, 1982). Public officials must respond to jurisdictional constituencies and clientele under sanction of both politics and law. Corporations are usually primarily concerned with narrower or more specialized groups—stockholders, employees, customers, and suppliers—in a national or international rather than a local context. These interests are likely to be sharply focused and clearly understood by the corporations's officers.[5] Public officials are less likely to have so clear an impression of their mandates or to find them nearly as stable over time. Government is often encumbered from making quick decisions by constitutional or statutory requirements for public participation, by conflict of interest laws, and by requirements for procedural fairness. Multinational corporations, moreover, have internal strategic concerns that may be clearly at odds with the civic impulses of their executives. Increasingly their executives are not homegrown, they serve relatively short terms of office, and they may spend more time out of town tending to branches and subsidiaries than they spend at headquarters.

These differences in institutional behavior can lead to misunderstanding and mistrust of government by business executives accustomed to making decisions in the corporate context and out of the public eye. The fact that everything the mayor does is everybody's business, especially that of the local media, can also be a problem. Businesses frequently fear that adverse publicity will harm sales. Branch office executives are particularly cautious about activities that might provoke the concern of their corporate superiors.

The Importance of Stability

Not only must the partners be mutually trusting and regarded as reliable, but it is also important that the relationship be perceived as stable and that it directly involve the people who can make binding commitments for both sectors. In this regard the personality and leadership qualities of incumbent officials are important to a successful relationship. It is also useful for each group to be able to endure over time, even though the specific members change. The most effective partnerships—those con-

---

[5] We note, however, the salutary growth of the corporate responsibility movement. An instructive example is the Minnesota 5 Percent Club, sparked by the practice of the Dayton-Hudson Corporation of donating 5 percent of its pretax earnings to charitable activities.

sistently used as shining examples—are in cities such as Baltimore and Pittsburgh, where the same basic business and political leadership structure has been maintained for over two decades. While mayors have changed, as have corporate boardrooms, there has been relatively little change in the composition of the interests represented or in the core group of leaders (Fosler and Berger, 1982).

Finally, it is worth pointing out that it is in such cities that the basic partnerships have survived changes in government administration and periods of great urban crisis, such as the riots of the mid-1960s. Most cities were able to form temporary alliances between public officials and business, such as the Urban Coalitions, in the aftermath of the riots, but those organizations have since dwindled to levels of ineffectiveness; many have disappeared entirely. It takes more than fear to build a lasting strategic relationship.

Much of the recent literature emphasizes the importance of private sector cooperation. That is altogether appropriate, but in the enthusiasm for private sector participation, it is important to remember that public leadership is normally the catalyst for partnership and is indispensable to its success. Public leadership usually focuses on the mayor or manager, but where it has been successful there is a deeper institutional base that includes planning and economic development agencies. These institutions must have the resources and leadership to work with private institutions to offer a vision of a more promising future for the community and the administrative, fiscal, and legal skills to translate concepts and visions into development projects, jobs and education programs, and other facilities or services. In many communities it may be useful to combine planning and economic development efforts to strengthen the ability of both to advise the city's leadership and carry out its decisions.

The federal government has historically been an important force in encouraging the creation of planning and economic development agencies and processes. To a considerable extent, federal planning assistance was the seed corn for these agencies. Direct federal support is no longer a necessity in most large cities, but continued encouragement of well-thought-out development plans as a requirement for federal support of projects remains an important way of encouraging the development of local institutional capacity.

The Autonomy of the Urban Area

Another important ingredient in an effective public-private relationship is the autonomy and power of the city in the urban system. Autonomy involves the ability to make decisions that are binding and the ability to commit resources—whether money, time, or talent—to agreed-on activities. It implies accessibility to other resources and power centers. These include banks, state governments, federal agencies, other firms, the media, and local institutions and organizations such as neighborhood associations. This kind of autonomy for both partners is most likely to be present in the command and control centers.[6]

Other places, however, have made remarkable economic transformations. Lowell, Massachusetts; Stamford, Connecticut; and Akron, Ohio, need careful study to identify the factors and processes that made their changes in function possible. This is particularly important because the urban areas that will have the greatest difficulty in coping with change are not command and control centers.

Autonomy appears most likely to be absent on one or both sides of the potential partnership in subordinate centers, particularly those specializing in manufacturing. Government centers also tend to have a weak and diffused corporate sector because they house few national corporate headquarters and rely more heavily on consumer-oriented smaller businesses and some business services. The more fruitful partnerships appear to be based on a relatively equal division of power, with a strong mayor or manager often a key actor. There do not seem to be many outstanding examples of cooperation in cities with reputations of either business or political machine domination.[7]

Models for Partnership

There is no standard model for the formation of strategic partnerships, only clues in the experiences of a few cities. Pittsburgh, Baltimore, Dallas, and Denver illustrate how such partnerships have evolved and suggest both the range of organizational arrangements and the limitations on policy involvements of such partnerships in the formulation of economic development strategy.

Pittsburgh's Allegheny Conference is one of the oldest corporate community leadership organizations in the country. It developed from the realization by a relatively close-knit group of corporate and banking ex-

---

[6] The case studies of public-private cooperation used by the Committee for Economic Development in its study of partnerships were chosen for their effectiveness. All were command and control centers (Fosler and Berger, 1982).

[7] Strong political machines do not, however, preclude such arrangements. Where the business community is also strong and independent of the machine itself, the ability of the partners to cooperate may actually be enhanced. See the case studies of Pittsburgh and Chicago in Fosler and Berger (1982).

ecutives that major reinvestments by their companies in Pittsburgh were essential to both the city and to the future of their own headquarters functions. The conference developed a plan for the redevelopment of the "Golden Triangle" and participated in rebuilding this important part of the central business district. The combined power of major international corporations, regional banks, foundations, state and local governments, and federal urban renewal and transportation funding set a pattern that many other cities have tried to emulate (Steinman and Tarr, 1982).

Baltimore has followed a similar pattern of cooperation. Although its corporate community is neither as cohesive nor as autonomous as that of Pittsburgh, Baltimore has had strong financial institutions and a large number of community-oriented business leaders. The Greater Baltimore Committee had its origins in the work of a more broadly based civic organization, the Citizens' Planning and Housing Association. Much of its success can be attributed to a talented executive director and a series of mayors with whom excellent working relationships were maintained. It was able to develop a consensus plan for the private development of Charles Center, which has served as the keystone for much of the rest of Baltimore's urban reinvestment program. The city government has taken the principal leadership role in the revitalization of the city, with the Greater Baltimore Committee lending support and some of its members playing key roles, either in government or as developers and financiers of other projects, such as the Inner Harbor (Lyall, 1982).

A quite different model for cooperation in the formulation of long-term strategy is represented by the Goals of Dallas program. Initiated in 1964 by Mayor Erik Jonsson, it has involved over 100,000 people from many parts of the community in identifying problems, issues, and objectives for the development of Dallas. A policies plan as opposed to a land use plan, the goals program has provided a corporate and governmental agenda for developing the infrastructure system, the higher-education system, and other elements (such as the international airport) to help Dallas become a "prototypical post-industrial city" (Claggett, 1982). While Goals of Dallas has been a showcase for partnership, another, less publicized institution has been of great importance in the development of the Dallas economy. The Dallas Citizens Council, consisting of the chief executive officers of the major corporations located in the city, has been a means of reaching consensus within the corporate leadership on major community issues (Claggett, 1982).

In Denver, corporate and development interests formed the Denver Partnership, which has produced a development plan for a major sector of the central business district. The partnership has worked closely with local government and has also developed ties with residential communities that are located adjacent to the commercial development area to ensure that the negative spillover effects of commercial district revitalization are ameliorated or even produce instead beneficial effects. The Denver experience is interesting since it started with a more sophisticated understanding of the need to reach agreement with many groups in producing a successful development program with broad community support. It also shows some promise of being clearly oriented to a vision of the future economy of Denver and the other centers of economic activity in the Denver region, based on the operating characteristics of the economic role of a major regional center.

THE INDEPENDENT SECTOR

In earlier chapters we pointed out that the nonprofit organizations—the so-called independent sector—have been one of the fastest growing parts of urban economies. This is a greatly varied sector, ranging from major educational and health organizations, philanthropic organizations, and research institutes, to storefront service centers, community organizations, and volunteer groups. In many cities the independent sector funds or operates a large share of the complex of libraries, theaters, museums, health facilities, and cultural centers and programs that are increasingly important in the economic development strategies of urban areas as well as in enrichments to community life (Salamon, 1983). In addition, nonprofit institutions often serve as catalysts for bringing public and private sectors together through specially created mediating organizations. They provide a means of conducting experimental, high-risk urban development and service programs that could not be supported by government or operated as profit-making enterprises but are necessary precursors of major changes in other institutions and programs.

Seed Capital for Transition

Our focus is on that part of the independent sector often referred to as philanthropy: foundations and grant-making institutions. These institutions are often significant sources of the capital necessary for many urban projects and for support of the operations of other nonprofit organizations. The central economic advantage of philanthropic investments is that they do not require an economic return to the investor. This allows them to be an almost exclusive source, other than a few government grants, for high-risk activities. Foundation funding can also be blended with private sector capital and government funding to reduce risks.

This seed capital can be especially important in dealing with the economic transformation of communities. Neither government nor employers provide much transitional support for families, as distinguished from support for the worker in the family. While the worker may receive unemployment benefits, counseling, and retraining from government or industry programs, the burden of providing family counseling or crisis centers tends to be left to others, such as churches and organizations supported by individual and institutional philanthropy. Yet these services may be almost as important in overall transition strategy as job retraining and unemployment benefits. Programs to mobilize parents and neighbors can have great impact on programs designed to keep young people in school, to enhance the strength of educational programs, or to revitalize a neighborhood. Particularly in the most deprived areas of our cities, such self-help programs often need some stimulus and some capital. Both are often provided by local or national foundations and corporate gifts. Such initial funding is important even when public funds may be available for the day-to-day operation of such groups.

As important as independent sector capital is, there is no realistic likelihood that it can supplant public support for mediating nonprofit institutions (Salamon and Abramson, 1982). What it can do best is provide a base, in addition to public funds or patronage, for the existence of such groups. Philanthropy also has much greater latitude to experiment and—which is important—to fail. The expectation that philanthropy should replace public funding for many community programs undermines one of the most valuable contributions that philanthropic institutions can make: the ability to experiment, to seed new enterprises and ideas. To the extent that this source of capital is siphoned off to support operating expenses of established day care centers, community improvement organizations, health clinics, and job training programs, less money is available to introduce new ideas or create new ventures that may prove to be more effective ways of tackling urban problems. It is also important to remember that federal funds have been major sources of support for many nonprofit organizations and have in fact helped stimulate the growth of the independent sector as an alternative to the public sector as the sole provider of many urban services (Salamon, 1983).

The Catalytic Role

Not only can nonprofit institutions often provide the neutral ground on which government and corporate leadership can meet and negotiate but private grant makers may also occasionally provide the initial earnest money needed to make the other two sectors take a matter seriously.

Programs such as the Kettering Foundation's Negotiated Investment Strategies suggest one way in which the independent sector can aggressively play a catalytic role in urban economic development. Such programs as the Bedford-Stuyvesant project in New York City, funded by the Ford Foundation, offer other examples of how the investment and catalytic powers of the independent sector can materially affect urban life and economics. There are many less well known and far less expensive examples, such as the Local Incentive Support Corporation, supported by foundations and businesses to fund local development corporations. Another example is the work of the Greater Cleveland Foundation with the Rand Corporation and the Urban Institute to analyze local economic and infrastructure problems. In Washington, D.C., the Greater Washington Research Center was able to assemble a distinguished panel of business and community leaders to examine the long-range fiscal issues of the region's local governments.

The decision of the Kansas City Association of Trusts and Foundations in the late 1960s to concentrate philanthropic resources on the development of medical education and services in the metropolitan area has had an important and lasting effect on the local economy. Several local foundations have been the moving forces behind changes in public school administration, curriculum, and programs. The Mott Foundation in Flint, Michigan, has devoted substantial resources over a long period to the improvement of community services and education, including the development of community schools. Each of these programs has focused attention on an important problem, and the initial foundation investment has had a strong multiplier effect, attracting other funds.

The Need for Cooperation

From the perspective of urban economic development strategy, however, one of the difficulties with private philanthropy is that it often is independent almost to the point of being oblivious to the cumulative and supplementary effect of its investments. In many communities this independence arises from the fragmented nature of philanthropy. Philanthropic resources reside not only in the few large foundations with substantial staffs of specialists who can review programs for their probable effect but also in the trust departments of banks and in the hands of family members administering relatively small charitable trusts within very strict limitations set by their founders. Even relatively unrestricted philanthropic efforts of a community are highly fragmented. Rivalry among the givers is, unfortunately, not infrequent.

Where cooperation has been possible, however, the effectiveness of philanthropy in a community has been considerably enhanced. Community foundations have been established in a large number of cities, making possible the consolidation of the decision-making process for investments, if not the actual funds available for distribution. Particularly during periods of economic hardship or transition, the focusing of philanthropic capital would be desirable. An added advantage of the community foundation is that it provides a legitimate and convenient conduit for corporate donations that protects both the giver and the beneficiary from a variety of problems. Community foundations can often attract strong community leaders to their boards, and they can usually afford permanent professional staff, making their programs less subject to idiosyncratic choice by a single director or trustee. Developing some process for coordinating the activities of the independent sector should be a high priority for urban areas. Whether through a community foundation or some other medium, focusing philanthropic resources can be a powerful tool for a strategy of economic development.

Developing Institutions

In our discussion of managing the transition to a new kind of economy, we have repeatedly stressed the importance of staying power. While trusts are distinguished by their continuity, they are frequently afflicted by an equally distinguishing ingredient—a lack of direction or constancy. A laudable interest in experimentation can sometimes be transmuted into an almost random search for innovation. While a number of foundations have begun to fashion annual or longer-range programs to guide their grant making, these are often stated in such general terms as to be virtually meaningless. Program emphasis changes with fads, in order to stay current. This kind of serendipity often produces start-up grants and no follow-through. There is often too little appreciation of the fragility of many kinds of urban activities and the need to distinguish between programs that are single shots, those that should be expected to generate new sources of support, and those that are worthwhile but require a continuing commitment for support. The proliferation of foundations, exceeded only by the growth in applications for support, understandably makes such institutions cautious in making long-term commitments. It is hard to quarrel with the seed-money thesis in most instances.

There are, however, exceptions that should be recognized, particularly in the development of urban institutions. The urban intelligence system discussed above illustrates the point. Such systems need to be professional, continuing, and independent to play the role suggested for them. But it is almost impossible for an institution to continue if it is independent of its sponsors. If it performs well it is almost certain to alienate some of its public or private sponsors, either in diagnoses of economic problems, evaluations of past policies, or forecasts of future conditions. Both continuity and independence could be enhanced by continued, reliable support from local foundations as the only disinterested source of support. There is, moreover, a value to local philanthropic institutions themselves in the intelligence system because the information and analyses it produces can be employed in making grant policies.

Small business and community development corporations are another example of institutions that may need continuing support for a longer period than some foundations consider. It takes time to be effective, especially when seeking to change deeply ingrained patterns of economic or social behavior. Ineffectiveness is virtually guaranteed when staff and board energy is almost completely devoted to institutional survival. All of this speaks to greater selectivity in the first instance, based on a clearer sense of what is strategically important, then a commitment of sufficient resources to make a difference instead of a splash.

LESSONS FROM EXPERIENCE

The experiences of public-private partnerships, philanthropy, and the independent sector suggest that public-private leadership in devising economic development strategy can be direct or indirect, depending on the civic culture of the city or region. Strategies can be the initiatives of a power elite, if it has a traditional base of legitimacy in the community. Or it may be necessary or desirable to pursue a consensus strategy through a more broadly based process. Elite-centered systems have been effective in dealing with redevelopment of central business districts and thus in moving the diversified service centers in which such partnerships are located toward a more rapid adjustment to a service-centered economy.

The private development organizations that have represented corporate leadership have worked well in tandem with public development agencies. Development, largely that involving land investments, is an area of public policy that is congenial to large corporations, which are concerned often for their own facilities or for other land uses that are of interest to them, such as hotels and convention centers. The use of public condemnation powers and the availability of public financing for infrastructure, land, and leveraged loans provides an atmosphere of clear mutual advantage for both partners.

The advantages of the elite-centered approach to economic development strategy are less clear when neighborhood revitalization or employment issues are involved. While some corporations have been actively involved in neighborhood revitalization and job training programs, specially created hybrid organizations are often needed to actually carry out these programs. This simply reflects the fact that not all corporate interests converge in all areas of public policy. Also, unlike development projects, neighborhood and labor market programs often involve more conflicting interests than are represented in the classic partnerships for downtown development. Unions, community organizations, minority groups, churches, and small businesses must frequently have strong representation. In these areas of public policy, specially tailored groups are often critical to give the program legitimacy as well as the necessary constituencies.

The strategic concern is to equip the state or local government and the catalysts—whether they are foundations, leadership coalitions, or specially created local development corporations—with the ability to foster the appropriate matches. These matches may consist of direct involvement of individual corporations, as in the Jobs for Delaware Youth program, which is developing a secondary education program related to specific jobs in cooperation with the public school system. Such a strategy may mean working with a major corporation, such as the Control Data Corporation subsidiary, City Venture Corporation, which has developed a major emphasis on urban facilities, jobs, and entrepreneurship through its direct activities and its profit-oriented technical assistance to small inner-city businesses.

What is important is a regular process for continuous dialogue between the government, corporate, and independent sectors. This process can be used to develop and test strategies and to undertake or initiate specific tactical actions. These might include setting up and providing seed capital for a community development corporation, creating a capital pool for home or commercial improvement loans, or developing a youth employment program.

Strong consideration should also be given in an overall economic development strategy to the use of the private and independent sectors in improving the delivery of public services. Corporate leadership can be especially useful in advising local government on fiscal issues, in supporting bond issues for the maintenance or construction of facilities, and in providing advice on management systems. The key problem is to involve the corporate community in such issues before they become crises that threaten both the fiscal capacity of local governments and private investments.

At another level it is useful to identify those services that might be provided more economically through contracts with established firms or by encouraging the creation of private and nonprofit neighborhood firms to provide services under contract to the city. The government, in consultation with the private sector and other interests, should identify those functions that could usefully become private ones (Committee for Economic Development, 1982; Savas, 1982).

In addition to simply turning services over to private enterprise, urban areas should examine the possibilities of improving some services through ending public monopolies in such areas as public transportation, hospitals, refuse collection, and even some aspects of public safety. By creating competitive service systems, whether through profit-making firms or competing public or nonprofit entities, people can have more choices, and some market discipline can be introduced into local public services (Kolderie, 1982).

SUMMARY

The creation of local institutions to manage the transition of urban economies can follow no standard format. Local civic cultures, interjurisdictional politics, and the composition of leadership in the private and independent sectors are all important factors. Many of the nation's command and control centers already have well-established, public-private leadership systems. Some have long experience in urban development issues. These need little federal or state support beyond general encouragement and improvements in information systems.

Where a good base for cooperation does not exist, as seems likely in many of the subordinate centers, a more active state or federal role may be appropriate in fostering the formation of public-private partnerships. State government in particular may be helpful in enlisting the cooperation of state-headquartered corporations, banks, and utilities in encouraging branch managers to become involved in urban development strategies. The state also may be helpful through its planning and economic development agencies in providing technical assistance to local governments who may be hard pressed to hold up their half of a partnership or to participate effectively in it. The independent sector can also play a significant role in helping to establish community leadership organizations and acting as a catalyst to bring other sectors together.

Federal support through provisions of leverage capital and infrastructure funds is often the indispensable ingredient in making a partnership possible in resource-scarce communities. Federal encouragement of long-term cooperation as a condition of various funding programs also could be helpful, and active federal participation is needed in the development of better information systems.

9 *Rethinking Urban Policy*

National and urban interests in economic development do not always coincide. When growth rates are high, the tension between these interests is lower because there is more than enough to go around—almost every place can expect to grow a little. When growth rates are low or negative or when some parts of the economy are growing and others are declining, regional and urban interests can conflict sharply with each other as well as with overall national interests. States and urban areas pirate industries and jobs from each other and use their political power to resist shifts of capital and jobs away from them. Such shifts may well produce a net benefit to national accounts (although that is uncertain), but they can also deepen economic hardships for the areas on the losing side of the transfer. National economic development interests may be served best by encouraging fairly rapid adjustments in economic structure. Rapid adjustments, however, can be profoundly destabilizing for the most adversely affected urban economies.

One of the central, difficult tasks for urban policy is to help harmonize these national and urban interests so that they work less at cross-purposes, to help fashion a framework for urban economic development that balances two types of policies: (1) those that encourage acceleration of economic development and (2) those that provide a relatively stable environment for the places and people left behind, so that changes can occur with a minimum of hardship and resistance and so that they can develop new roles in the urban system. We offer no formula for achieving this goal. There is an inherent tension between the two policy realms because mainstream policies are often market-reinforcing if not market-forcing, while policies for those left behind often seek to redirect the market or at least ameliorate its most adverse effects.

In this report we have tried to suggest some directions policy might take to advance toward a better balance between the two realms. Here we summarize the major themes and recommendations of the report and offer some final observations about the process of using an urban perspective in making economic policy. We have not attempted to offer a detailed program. The policy options we have discussed are intended primarily as illustrations of how the major themes could be carried out. They are by no means the only approaches possible. The important issue has to do with the directions that policy should take and the recognition of urban policy as a worthy perspective in making general economic policy.

A POLICY FRAMEWORK

Neither a pure free market nor a central planning model of economic or urban policy holds much attraction in light of the economic and technological transformation that is occurring. The most likely outcome of leaving the futures of America's urban areas entirely to the marketplace is an even sharper distinction between the command and control centers and the subordinate centers. The notion of a centrally planned economy is equally unappealing. A heavily planned economy tends to ignore the discipline of the market as a device for winnowing out those sectors that perform inefficiently. Moreover, the pluralism of the United States and the American antipathy toward a strong, centralized bureaucracy present strong barriers to a well-developed system of national planning.

Instead, policies must be fashioned that are able to provide reasonable options for dealing with economic transformation. Urban policy should leave room for continuing debate and course corrections. Such an approach recognizes that public policy has a marginal influence on market forces but rarely controls the market, at least over a long period. Urban policy should therefore seek to understand and reinforce the market—to train the tiger but not fully tame it. This view accepts much of the market's uncertainty in order to retain its energy, and it tries to channel some of that energy toward achieving limited policy objectives, to give a sense of direction but not a final destination. Making policy judgments of such sensitivity requires close consultation with the private sector and with state and urban leaders. It further requires abjuring quick-fix solutions in favor of a more incremental, long-term approach to strengthening economic institutions and governmental processes at all levels of the system. It is, quite candidly, a compromise position and, like all compromises, subject to criticism of where the balance has been struck.

This approach recognizes that each part of the economic and political system plays an important role in furthering economic development. How each public and private actor plays its role and becomes a more responsible partner in economic restructuring and development is the critical issue.

RETHINKING THE ROLE OF GOVERNMENT

While most economic activity and development is carried out by the private sector, government is a major direct participant in the modern economy. It is one of the largest of the service sectors and, although it is growing more slowly than in the past, some further growth remains likely. Local, state, and federal governments are major investors in defense industries, transportation systems, agriculture, and other sectors. Public procurements make a substantial contribution to aggregate demand. Research and development activity is heavily financed by government, as is most of the educational system. But this direct economic role of government is often virtually ignored in discussions of economic development. Public facilities and services are often thought of only as expenditures for which no return is expected. Rather, they should be seen as investments in economic sectors and in urban areas. As investments, some return should be expected, although it may come in the form of private investments or improvements in the quality of the labor force.

Public actions affect other economic interests, whether the particular consequences were intended or not. National economic policy should be more sensitive to its consequences for different sectors of the economy and for different types of urban areas. Substantively this requires that two basic types of policy—acceleration strategies and stabilization strategies— be closely coordinated.

At the national level, acceleration policy requires a conscious strategy of fashioning tax, credit, trade, monetary, and fiscal policies so that they encourage capital to flow toward promising sectors and contribute to the transition to a more advanced economy. Such a strategy would include making a modest amount of capital available on a wholesale basis to leverage private investments in urban development efforts that promote economic transition. It also would include some mechanism, such as a national infrastructure bank, to provide leadership for institutional reforms and to undergird local and state capacities to finance and manage the urban public facilities needed to support and serve an advanced economy. National action is also needed to revise design or performance standards for infrastructure that are not cost-effective or even within the range of fiscal possibility. These market-reinforcing policies could also be strengthened by establishing a national job information, retraining, and worker relocation system to help reduce barriers to the mobility of the labor force—particularly the structurally unemployed. Finally, because the future of the national economy will depend on the quality of the labor force, there is a substantial need for investments in education and training.

Sectoral investments and labor mobility policies have important urban consequences, and they provide tools that are necessary for effective urban development strategy. If they work properly, they will accelerate a shift toward more modern and competitive industries and more productive jobs. This will strengthen the urban economies in which such industries and jobs are located.

Policies designed to accelerate the restructuring of the economy can result in worsening the short- to mid-term economic conditions of many manufacturing and other subordinate centers as they strengthen the economies of the command and control centers. Even in the latter, where much of the new growth in producer and corporate headquarters services will be located, there can be severe problems for the workers who are displaced from declining local industries and who do not find new jobs in the growing sectors of their local economies. Public policy must understand these impacts; it should be prepared to ameliorate them in the short run and reduce them in the longer run.

To some extent, infrastructure investments have a double aspect. They help build a base for national economic expansion, and they can also provide an important tool for local economic development and employment. Without indiscriminately supporting projects that have little long-term potential for sustaining local employment or making contributions to national growth, investments can be made in the quality of public facilities in ways that materially aid a community in stabilizing its own economy and in providing leverage to build the base required to transform itself. Financing programs can be structured, for example, to favor making full use of the existing capital stock instead of the abandonment of facilities that are still operational and their costly reproduction in new locations. Leverage capital can also be made available in a manner that encourages local initiative, flexibility, and growth in the institutional capacity needed for the long haul.

The national government can make leverage capital, facilities, funds, and job training and mobility programs available, but strong local economic development institutions in individual urban areas are essential to tailor strategies to meet local conditions. In some cases, neighborhood revitalization or historic preservation may be a more salient investment than a large-scale new office complex or industrial park. In others, renovation of old industrial plants or even closed public schools to provide incubator space for new businesses or to provide moderately priced housing may be the most appropriate strategy for developing a new and stable economic role. Leverage capital might be used to augment facilities and amenities and provide an attractive environment for private development, for investment as an equity partner in a project, or for acquiring a land bank for future growth.

It is important that national urban policy recognize that the national interest is less in any one form of development than it is in making sure that funds and programs have high leverage and that those using them have a coherent and realistic strategy for strengthening the local economy rather than no plan beyond an isolated project or an effort to prop up an obsolete activity.

A long-range commitment by the federal government and the states to equalize disparities in state and local fiscal capacity could be a most important means of smoothing the process of change. Fiscal equalization could do a great deal to reduce local and regional political resistance to economic change by making it possible for communities undergoing such changes to maintain the services they provide at reasonable levels, especially at a time when their own taxable resources are in jeopardy. Such communities could then compete with others for new firms and jobs without devoting primary attention to self-aggravating processes of urban decline and to staving off municipal creditors. Fiscal equalization also furthers a national interest in promoting the decentralization of decision making and service delivery and recognizes that community integrity is an important value, deserving of consideration along with national economic efficiency.

While a national job information, retraining, and relocation service can help accelerate economic transitions, many workers will choose not to move. Labor redundancy promises to be a major national problem and a crucial problem for many urban areas as the technological revolution spreads from factory floor to offices, distributive services, and even personal services. A substantial cluster of national, state, and urban policies may be required: tax incentives to industries for retraining workers, legislation to require advance notice of major plant closings and to help support industry-employee-community councils to plan for the transition, and planning grants to communities to help them identify alternative sources of employment and to provide for adult, continuing, and vocational education programs to retrain redundant workers. Advance warning of local structural unemployment could facilitate development of other local strategies, such as the creation of jobs clubs, efforts to attract other employers, and better use of transitional public employment programs. Redundancy planning should reduce the period of unemployment for workers affected by structural change. It should also help the urban area prepare for the closing of an employment center and cushion the impact on the communities, residents, and businesses.

Most of the actual investment in education and training will continue to come from state and local governments, with a growing share being provided by private employers in training and retraining their work forces. National leadership and leverage are important, however, if the quality of urban labor forces is to be improved. Identification of education and training needs, stimulation of better public education in science and mathematics, and the development of computer skills are matters of grave national concern. Seeding local school budgets for the education of disadvantaged children and minorities can affect the overall quality and resilience of the labor force as it tries to adjust to change. The federal government should also continue direct responsibility for special national programs for the severely disadvantaged, such as the Job Corps.

The federal government cannot create local institutions capable of managing transitions to new economic roles, but its policies can have considerable effect on the climate for them. Access to federal capital sources for infrastructure and private development, for example, can reasonably require substantial evidence of public-private cooperation in both long-term plans and specific projects without impairing local flexibility or responsibility in the design and execution of policies and strategies.

RETHINKING HOW URBAN POLICY SHOULD BE MADE

Federal Policy Processes

The federal role can be critical without limiting local or private initiative and strategies. It should, in fact, assist and support them. If federal policy focuses on measures that accelerate economic change and growth and on selective strategies for stabilizing urban areas while they undergo change, it need not make local choices but simply set a clearer policy framework within which they can be made.

Making urban policy an integral part of national economic policy is no easy task. No one bureaucratic formula can be guaranteed to work. Various techniques, in some combination, might be considered. One possibility would be for the President to direct the Council of Economic Advisers to explicitly consider urban and sectoral policies and the consequences of macroeconomic policies on sectors of the economy and on urban areas in their annual report. In addition, or as an alternative, the President's biennial report on urban policy might regularly be used as a vehicle for co-ordinating macroeconomic, sectoral, and urban policy. A more informal approach might also be effective, broadening the executive policy process to involve business, labor, regional, state, and urban perspectives. Other informal devices, such as the National Governors Conference and local government associations, could also be more fruitfully used. We could learn some lessons from other federal systems, such as that of West Germany, where a standing conference of state ministers provides a continuous consultative mechanism with national ministries and the Bundestag for discussion of important economic policies with regional impacts. Whatever devices are used, the objective is to ensure feedback between national economic policy makers and those involved in the development of economic sectors and urban areas. Urban policy should not continue to be made in a virtual vacuum, but should be seen as the spatial component of broader economic strategy.

State and Local Government and Private Sector Processes

Just as the process of making urban policy at the national level must be rethought and adjusted to the new economic realities, so must that of the states, local government, the private sector, and nonprofit institutions. On the supply side, all are involved to some extent in capital investments, the quality of the labor force, and local capability for research, development, and innovation. On the demand side, they purchase products and services produced in the local economy and other areas, and their wages fuel local consumer demand. Together they also create and maintain the public environment, including the quality of services, the physical and social infrastructure, amenities, and the regulatory system.

One of the first tasks of urban area strategists is to develop an intelligence function capable of systematically using information to obtain and keep a grip on local and national economic reality. Independent and reliable information, professional research capability, and linkages to similar institutions in other areas are almost prerequisites for sound planning, necessary course corrections, and effective action.

As the economy becomes more advanced, the comparative advantages of particular urban areas flow less from natural location and resources than from man-made (or enhanced) factors. This gives many urban areas more latitude than they had in the past to create their own comparative advantages. For headquarters and producer services, these advantages include cultural, recreational, and educational opportunities and the quality of public services. For almost all sectors, the quality of the local labor force is a vital consideration. This again suggests a major concentration of local effort on improving education and training systems. Access to national and international transportation systems is also important to many firms, although this advantage may decline in importance as communications technology advances.

State participation in urban strategy is of growing significance. Only states can provide localities with the authority they need to carry out major programs of investment and development in cooperation with the private sector. States are the source of land use and acquisition powers, tax powers, and regulatory policy. They are often the principal source for financing facilities, housing, and other programs. Education, particularly higher education, is a major state responsibility.

The time has come for more states to pursue aggressive urban policies, a role that only a few have thus far taken. Several initiatives seem especially ripe for major state contributions. Perhaps the most obvious and important is to equalize the fiscal capacities of local units of government, whether through the reallocation of functions, revenue sharing, boundary changes, more rational tax structures, or other means. A second major state initiative could be to establish statewide infrastructure banks that could be related to a national infrastructure bank. A third role for the states might be to oversee, provide technical assistance to, and occasionally reconcile conflicts among local economic strategies to avoid unproductive interjurisdictional rivalry. State government can play a special role in smaller urban areas that lack the resources to develop their own intelligence systems and development institutions. In such cases the state may need to become directly involved in providing analysis, technical support, and capital for development.

State leadership could be particularly helpful in those subordinate centers in which the managers of local firms and branch headquarters lack the autonomy to provide effective leadership within the private sector. The state may be able to convince home office executives from other cities in the state to empower their branch managers to play larger roles in community affairs and may also be able to buttress the leadership of local public officials. State involvement is also necessary before there will be broad improvements in public education; the state could provide the resources needed by postsecondary community colleges, training centers, and urban universities to play more effective roles as urban institutions.

The states and the federal government together can provide many of the powers and resources employed in the development process. The heaviest burden for producing specific strategies and carrying them out, however, falls on local government and other local leadership institutions in the private and independent sectors.

Except in the relatively few places where the problem is largely to prevent the destruction of the area's environment and original advantages by the waste products of runaway growth, the would-be local development strategist starts from behind. Pockets of decline or abandonment already exist. In some cases the decline of traditional manufacturing firms may be pervasive. There is already a large number of redundant workers as well as a population of virtually unemployable young people. Substantial parts of the public facilities system have deteriorated. Fiscal resources are scarce and the revenue base is static or in decline due to economic conditions and prior political decisions. Existing patterns of law, behavior, and thought have considerable inertia, creating a civic culture (and sometimes a civic vacuum) that must be changed.

There is a need in every community, to use James Rouse's phrase, for an "entrepreneur in the public interest," a person or group who can visualize a more satisfying future and who serves as a catalyst for mobilizing resources to achieve it. This function can occasionally be performed by an individual, but it needs an institutional base so that a strategy of constructive change can be pursued for a long time. No formula exists for creating and sustaining this role. Persistent, stable, and active official leadership or cooperation is a critical ingredient. Extensive cooperation by corporate and community leaders is also necessary. But leadership cannot be empty of resources; mere boosterism will not suffice when an economy must be transformed in an environment of heightened competition from other places.

Effective leadership, then, requires clear understanding of the background forces at work in the economy. It needs to know how local firms fit into their parent corporations, their industries, and regional, national, and international markets. The leadership needs to know how the area functions in the urban system, its hierarchical relationship to other areas, the reasons for existing relationships, and who its competitors for specific kinds of development may be. Urban strategists must be enabled to think globally so they can act locally. The information and ideas that shape their thinking must then be packaged and disseminated in forms that their constituents and clientele can understand in order to build a new consensus on which to base policy. Finally, the strategic information system should contain a feedback loop that monitors and evaluates the effects of decisions that have been made so that a timely basis for course corrections exists.

Intelligence is not strategy; it is a precondition for it. A mechanism or process is needed for setting goals and priorities and defining the means of achieving them. Whatever form the mechanism takes, the private sector, nonprofit institutions, community groups, and universities should, at a minimum, be part of it. Strategy making involves power, consent, and ideas, and it is a means of building a strong underlying consensus for any plan of action. This makes it easier to mobilize the necessary public and private resources.

Private financial institutions are particularly essential in mobilizing private capital for investment to expand existing businesses and to finance new enterprises. Major industries must be involved in any system of redundancy planning, both in training dislocated workers and as part of the relocation process. Nonprofit institutions can often be used as bridges between the public and private sectors, as a means of financing or managing activities, such as community revitalization efforts, education, and service programs, and as development instruments. Local philanthropy may provide the financial glue needed to maintain an effective strategy-making process.

As to the content of strategies, many urban areas will need to rethink their economic functions in the urban system and identify the functions they might realistically expect to perform in a restructured national economy. This may lead to substantial redesign and rebuilding of some parts of the urban area so that it can attract or accommodate different activities. Design changes may improve access to jobs, services, and cultural or recreational opportunities and may help create centers of interest and activity that in themselves foster economic and social development.

Not all urban areas can or should have single dominant, strong centers. Some functions may be performed better in a polynuclear form. The critical quality in this process is to avoid stereotyped thinking about what an urban area must be and instead to survey the assets and opportunities that are there and build on them.

Nothing that we have discussed is more important to the resilience of an urban area than preparing and maintaining a trained labor force for an increasingly knowledge-centered economy. This demands a heavy concentration of local resources and leadership attention on many aspects of education and training: public schools, technical and vocational training institutions, the transition from school to work, the role of public employment as part of the labor force strategy, retraining programs, the system of higher education available in the area, and the relationship of the higher-education system to the labor force, research, development, and innovation.

CONCENTRATING RESOURCES

The Strongest Sectors

At both the national level and in urban areas, it makes sense to build an economic development strategy around the strongest sectors of the economy, those that seem likely to provide growth in employment and income in the years ahead because of their ability to compete effectively in national and worldwide markets. To be sure, there will be good reasons to support some other activities because of their intrinsic value or their importance to national defense. But in an economy with scarce amounts of private and public capital to invest, the prudent course is to encourage investments to flow toward economic sectors that have some reasonable promise of a strong future.

In this sense, national and local interests converge. Such investments include support of the industrial seedbeds of research and development, new business incubation, and the development of technology and processes that can be expected to generate new products and services or to increase productivity, the quality of goods and services, and the quality of working life. It also means a major investment in the training and education system, because most of these new and promising activities are more knowledge-intensive than traditional industries and occupations have been. Keeping ahead of the competition, developing new products or ways of making them, and servicing an economy dependent on knowledge requires an education system capable of exploiting the nation's intellectual capital.

There seems good reason to suppose that increasing the level of knowledge among the labor force can be part of a self-generating growth curve, because a more competent labor force demands more interesting work and invents more things that require more knowledge to produce. With the revolution in office and factory technology, most gains in value added in products and services will be through their knowledge content rather than the final stages of their manufacture or delivery to ultimate consumers. The value of an organ transplant is not in the number of hours it takes the physician to perform the operation or in the materials used but in the knowledge represented by the technology and training that makes the operation possible. In manufacturing, there is every prospect that the direct costs of production will decline sharply as a result of using industrial robots, but the products themselves may become more valuable because of the knowledge represented in their design and the design of the systems used to make them.

Given all the trends in technology, economic organization, and demography that we have considered, it appears that the growth of the nation's economy and the economic future of American cities and urban areas rest on accelerating the restructuring of the economy and in embracing a role of leadership of an advanced economy. It is in the national interest for our cities to be dominant centers of international corporations and services. Therefore, policies that promote industries, as such, need to be complemented by policies that help produce the urban environments in which the activities of an advanced economy can flourish.

The Least Resilient Areas

This refocusing of urban development and national economic growth strategy on opportunities for market leadership does not in itself solve the problems of the urban areas that are caught in the backwash of this massive structural transformation. It is clear that pockets of severe economic distress can exist in a generally prosperous nation. It is also clear that the complex social, cultural, and economic problems of the urban disadvantaged cannot be overcome in a short time or with few resources. We have therefore suggested that resources also be concentrated on the least resilient urban areas in an effort to improve their capacities for adjustment and to accelerate their progress into the mainstream of an advanced economy.

Those areas that are already considerably advanced and have begun to demonstrate that their growth is somewhat self-propelling already have a head start. In many cases, capital is available to them to help bring about their own transformation. There is less need for public leverage, and its impact is more marginal. They also need less external assistance. Within their own strategies, however, they too should divide their attention between those sectors that are strongest and on which they must build their future economies and the workers and neighborhoods that are least resilient in making the adjustment.

Particularly in the older manufacturing cities, there is a need for external support to help develop a higher degree of economic autonomy, institutional capacity for managing the transition, and bargaining power for investment capital. It is here that redundancy planning is most needed because the economies tend to be so narrowly based. Making it possible for some communities to reduce their size, close down some underused infrastructure, and reorient their resources requires more than exhortation and goodwill. Ultimately, labor forces must be retrained, education systems vastly improved, parts of the capital stock replaced, and sections of the city rebuilt or renovated to perform new functions. The purpose of concentrating resources on such cities is to make the transition they must undergo smoother and to empower them and their residents to have more choice about their future.

CONCLUSION

As powerful as the forces reshaping the economy are, their results for specific urban areas are not predetermined. It is impossible to freeze our urban areas in time, to preserve them as they were, but there is considerable latitude for transforming them into livable places that perform important functions. While natural forces still limit economic choices to some extent, the same forces that have made capital so mobile and have increased the importance of human resources also make it possible for cities to have greater choice in what kinds of places they will become.

Local and national economies are inextricably linked to each other. Consequently, national policy must be much more cognizant of its geographic consequences and national urban policy must be integrated into national economic policy so that it can provide a perspective that is now largely missing. As the service occupations increasingly dominate employment and as the changing nature of work demands that more people be trained better than ever before, the nation can ill afford urban areas that lag far behind others. The idea that one area can benefit only if others suffer should be rejected as a basis for public policy. Such a zero-sum policy contemplates a long period of waste for human and physical resources in competition that does little to support overall national growth.

References

Advisory Commission on Intergovernmental Relations
  1977 *Central City-Suburban Fiscal Disparity and City Distress*. Washington, D.C.
  1981 *The States and Distressed Communities*. Washington, D.C.
  1982a *Tax Capacity of the Fifty States: Methodology and Estimates*. Washington, D.C.
  1982b *Tax Capacity of the Fifty States: Supplement*. 1980 Estimates. Washington, D.C.
Alonso, W.
  1980 Population as a system in regional development. *American Economic Review—Papers and Proceedings* 70:405-409.
Anderson, B., and I. Sawhill
  1980 *Youth Employment and Public Policy*. Englewood Cliffs, N.J.: Prentice-Hall.
Anonymous
  1982 *The Boston Compact: An Operational Plan for Expanded Partnerships with the Boston Public Schools*. Boston, Mass.
Armington, C., and M. Odle
  1982 Small business—how many jobs. *The Brookings Review* 1(2):14-17.
Bahl, R.
  1981 The next decade in state and local finance: a period of adjustment. Pp. 191-217 in R. Bahl, ed., *Urban Government Finance: Emerging Trends*. Beverly Hills, Calif.: Sage.
Ballard, K., and G. Clark
  1981 The short-run dynamics of inter-state migration: a space-time economic adjustment model of in-migration to fast growing states. *Regional Studies* 15:213-228.
Beck, E., P. Horan, and C. Tolbert
  1978 Stratification in a dual economy: a sectoral model of earnings discrimination. *American Sociological Review* 43:704-720.
Bederman, S., and J. Abrams
  1974 Job accessibility and underemployment. *Annals of the Association of American Geographers* 64:378-386.

184

Bell, D.
1973   *The Coming of the Post-Industrial Economy*. New York: Basic Books.
Bell, M., and P. Lande, eds.
1982   *Regional Dimensions of Industrial Policy*. Lexington, Mass.: Lexington Books.
Bendick, M.
1982   Employment, training, and economic development. Pp. 247–270 in J. Palmer and I. Sawhill, eds., *The Reagan Experiment*. Washington, D.C.: The Urban Institute Press.
Bendick, M., and J. Devine
1981   Workers dislocated by economic change: Do they need federal employment and training assistance? Pp. 175–226 in *Seventh Annual Report: The Federal Interest in Employment and Training*. Washington, D.C.: National Commission for Employment Policy.
Bendick, M., and M. Egan
1982   Providing industrial jobs in the inner city. *Business* 32(12):2–9.
Berg, I.
1971   *Education and Jobs: The Great Training Robbery*. New York: Basic Books.
Berger, S., and M. Piore
1980   *Dualism and Discontinuity in Industrial Societies*. New York: Cambridge University Press.
Berry, B.
1964   Cities as systems within systems of cities. In J. Friedmann and W. Alonso, eds., *Regional Development and Planning: A Reader*. Cambridge, Mass.: MIT Press.
1974   *The Human Consequences of Urbanization*. New York: St. Martin's.
1981   Inner-city futures: an American dilemma. Pp. 187-198 in B. Stave, ed., *Modern Industrial Cities: History, Policy, and Survival*. Beverly Hills, Calif.: Sage.
1982   *Islands of Renewal—Seas of Decay: The Evidence of Inner-City Stratification*. Pittsburgh: School of Urban and Public Affairs, Carnegie-Mellon University.
Birch, D.
1981   Who creates new jobs? *The Public Interest* (fall):3–14.
Bluestone, B.
1970   The tripartite economy: labor markets and the working poor. *Poverty and Human Resources Abstracts* (July/August):15–35.
1981   *The Retail Revolution: Market Transformation, Investment, and Labor in the Modern Department Store*. Boston: Auburn House.
Bluestone, B., and B. Harrison
1982   *The Deindustrialization of America: Plant Closings, Community Abandonment and the Dismantling of Basic Industry*. New York: Basic Books.
Bradbury, K., A. Downs, and K. Small
1980   Some dynamics of central city-surburban interactions. *American Economic Review* 70(2):411–414.
1982   *Urban Decline and the Future of American Cities*. Washington, D.C.: The Brookings Institution.
Braverman, H.
1974   *Labor and Monopoly Capital*. New York: Monthly Review Press.
Breckenfield, G.
1977   Refilling the metropolitan doughnut. Pp. 231–258 in D. Perry and A. Watkins, eds., *The Rise of the Sunbelt Cities*. Beverly Hills, Calif.: Sage.
Brown, N.
1982   *Urban Universities and National Urban Policy: Report on a Meeting of Urban University Presidents and Chancellors*. Washington, D.C.: Division of Urban Affairs, National Association of State Universities and Land Grant Colleges.

Browning, H., and J. Singelmann
1975   *The Emergence of a Service Society: Demographic and Sociological Aspects of the Transformation of the Labor Force in the U.S.A.* Springfield, Va.: National Technical Information Service.
Bruml, E.
1981   *Self-Directed Group Job Search: The Results.* Washington, D.C.: U.S. Department of Labor, Office of the Assistant Secretary for Planning, Evaluation, and Research.
Burchell, R., and D. Listokin, eds.
1981   *Cities Under Stress.* New Brunswick, N.J.: Center for Urban Policy Research.
Bureau of the Census
1976   *Survey of Income and Education.* Washington, D.C.: U.S. Department of Commerce.
1978   *Social and Economic Characteristics of Metropolitan and Non-Metropolitan Population: 1977 and 1970.* Current Population Reports, Series P-23, No. 75 (November). Washington, D.C.: U.S. Department of Commerce.
1980   *Geographic Mobility: March 1975 to March 1979.* Current Population Reports, Series P-20, No. 353 (August). Washington, D.C.: U.S. Department of Commerce.
1981   *Money Income and Poverty Status of Families and Persons in the United States.* Current Population Reports, Series P-60, No. 127 (August). Washington, D.C.: U.S. Department of Commerce.
1982   *Geographic Mobility, March 1975-March 1980.* Current Population Survey, Series P-20, No. 368. Washington, D.C.: U.S. Department of Commerce.
Bureau of Economic Analysis
1981   Regional and state projections of income, employment, and population to the year 2000. *Survey of Current Business.* (November).
1982   *1980 OBERS—Regional Projections.* Volume 3, Table 4. Washington, D.C.: U.S. Department of Commerce.
Bureau of Industrial Economics
1982   *1982 U.S. Industrial Outlook for 200 Industries with Projections for 1986.* Washington, D.C.: U.S. Department of Commerce.
Bureau of Labor Statistics
1978   *Geographic Profile of Employment and Unemployment.* Report No. 571. Washington, D.C.: U.S. Department of Labor.
1982   *Earnings and Employment.* (August).
1983   *Earnings and Employment.* (January).
Business Week
1981a America's restructured economy. (June 1):56–95.
1981b Revitalizing the U.S. economy. (June 30).
Cain, G.
1976   The challenge of segmented labor market theories to orthodox theory: a survey. *Journal of Economic Literature* 14:1215–1257.
Carey, M.
1981   Occupational employment through 1990. *Monthly Labor Review* 104(8):42–55.
Carlton, D.
1975   *Why New Firms Locate Where They Do: An Econometric Model.* Working paper no. 57. Cambridge, Mass.: Joint Center for Urban Studies.
Cetron, M., and T. O'Toole
1972   Careers with a future where the jobs will be in the 1990s. *The Futurist* (June):11–19.
Choate, P., and S. Walters
1981   *America in Ruins.* Washington, D.C.: Council of State Planning Agencies.

Claggett, W.
1982 Dallas: the dynamics of public-private cooperation. Pp. 243–292 in R. Foster and R. Berger, eds., *Public-Private Cooperation in American Cities: Seven Case Studies.* Lexington, Mass.: Lexington Books.

Clark, C.
1940 *The Conditions of Economic Progress.* London: Macmillan.

Clark, G.
1982a Dynamics of interstate labor migration. *Annals of the Association of American Geographers* 72(3):297–313.
1982b Volatility in the geographic structure of short-run U.S. interstate migration. *Environment and Planning A* 14:145–167.
1983 *Interregional Migration: National Policy and Social Justice.* Totowa, N.J.: Rowman and Allanheld.

Clark, G., and M. Gertler
in   Local labor markets: theories and policies in the United States during the
press 1970s. *The Professional Geographer.*

Clark, K.
1982 Blacks' S.A.T. scores. *The New York Times* (October 12):A1.

Cohen, R.
1977 Multinational corporations, international finance, and the sunbelt. Pp. 211–226 in D. Perry and A. Watkins, eds., *The Rise of the Sunbelt Cities.* Beverly Hills, Calif.: Sage.
1979a The Impact of Foreign Direct Investment on U.S. Cities and Regions. Prepared for the U.S. Department of Housing and Urban Development, Washington, D.C.
1979b The Internationalization of Capital and U.S. Cities. Ph.D. dissertation, New School for Social Research.
1981 Employment Consequences of Structural Changes in the Auto Industry. Cambridge, Mass.: Center for Transportation, Massachusetts Institute of Technology.

Collins, P., and D. Horowitz
1981 *The Rockefellers.* New York: Holt, Rinehart & Winston.

Committee for Economic Development
1977 *An Approach to Federal Urban Policy.* Washington, D.C.
1982 *Public-Private Partnership: An Opportunity for Urban Communities.* Washington, D.C.

Congressional Budget Office
1982a *Dislocated Workers: Issues and Federal Options.* Washington, D.C.
1982b *Improving Youth Unemployment Prospects: Issues and Options.* Washington, D.C.

Conservation of Human Resources
1977 *The Corporate Headquarters Complex in New York City.* New York: Conservation of Human Resources, Columbia University.

Corson, W., et al.
1979 *Final Report: Survey of Trade Adjustment Assistance Recipients.* Washington, D.C.: Mathematica Policy Research, Inc.

Council for Northeast Economic Development
1980 *Local Economic Development: Public Leveraging of Private Capital.* Boston, Mass.: Council for Northeast Economic Development.

Davis, B., and H. Wolman
1981 *Local Economic Development Data Inventory.* Washington, D.C.: National League of Cities.

Dommel, P., R. Nathan, S. Liebshutz, M. Wrightson, and associates
  1978   *Decentralizing Community Development.* Washington, D.C.: U.S. Department of Housing
         and Urban Development.
Dommel, P., V. Back, S. Liebshutz, L. Rubinowitz, and associates
  1980   *Targeting Community Development.* Washington, D.C.: U.S. Department of Housing
         and Urban Development.
Doolittle, F.
  1982   *The Boston Labor Market: A Problem of Mismatch.* Cambridge, Mass.: Harvard-MIT
         Joint Center for Urban Studies.
Downs, A.
  1981   *Neighborhoods and Urban Development.* Washington, D.C.: The Brookings Institu-
         tion.
Drucker, P.
  1981   Demographics and American economic policy. Chapter 11 in M. Wachter and S.
         Wachter, eds., *Toward a New U.S. Industrial Policy?* Philadelphia: University of
         Pennsylvania Press.
Dunn, E.
  1980   *The Development of the U.S. Urban System.* Baltimore: The Johns Hopkins University
         Press.
Dymally, M.
  1982   Expanding the Scientific and Engineering Resource Base. Address to the National
         Convocation of Pre-College Education in Mathematics and Science, National Academy
         of Sciences, Washington, D.C.
Eads, G.
  1981   The political experience in allocating investments: lessons from the United States and
         elsewhere. Ch. 18 in M. Wachter and S. Wachter, eds., *Toward a New U.S. Industrial
         Policy?* Philadelphia: University of Pennsylvania Press.
Eads, G., and E. Graham
  1982   Transparency: a prerequisite for positive adjustment. *The OECD Observer* (119):8–
         11.
Eberhard, J.
  1966   Technology for the city. *Science and Technology* (September).
Economics Consulting Service
  1981   *The International Operation of U.S. Service Industries: Current Collection and Anal-
         ysis.* Washington, D.C.: Office of the U.S. Trade Representative.
The Economist
  1982   Enterprise zones: Hong Kong in Wales? 285(November 20):61.
Ellerman, D.
  1982   *The Socialization of Entrepreneurship: The Empresarial Division of the Caja Laboral
         Popular.* Somerville, Mass.: Industrial Cooperative Association.
Ernst, M.
  1982   The mechanization of commerce. *Scientific American* 247(3):132–145.
Farkas, G., D. Smith, E. Stromsdorfer, and C. Bottom
  1980   *Early Impacts from the Youth Entitlement Demonstration: Participation, Work, and
         Schooling.* New York: Manpower Demonstration Research Corporation.
Federal Reserve Bank of New York
  1981   The economic costs of subway deterioration. *Quarterly Review* 6:8–14.
Fisher, A.
  1935   *The Clash of Progress and Security.* London: Macmillan.

Fortune
1982   The Fortune directory of the largest non-industrial companies. (July 12):130–147.

Fosler, R., and R. Berger
1982   *Public-Private Partnerships in American Cities: Seven Case Studies.* Lexington, Mass.: Lexington Books.

Fossett, J., and R. Nathan
1981   The prospects for urban revival. Pp. 71–84 in R. Bahl, ed., *Urban Government Finance.* Beverly Hills, Calif.: Sage.

Frankena, M.
1981   Intrametropolitan location of employment. *Journal of Urban Economics* 10(2):256–269.

Frieden, B.
1979   *The Environmental Protection Hustle.* Cambridge, Mass.: MIT Press.

Fullerton, H.
1980   The 1995 labor force: a first look. *Monthly Labor Review* 103(12):11–21.

Gadway, C., and H. Wilson
1979   *Functional Illiteracy: A Brief Summary and Highlights of an Assessment of 17-Year-Old High School Students in 1974 and 1975.* Washington, D.C.: National Assessment of Educational Progress.

Garn, H., and L. Ledebur
1982   Congruencies and conflicts in regional and industrial policies. Pp. 47–80 in M. Bell and P. Lande, eds., *Regional Dimensions of Industrial Policy.* Lexington, Mass.: Lexington Books.

Garnick, D.
1978   *Reappraising the Outlook for Northern States and Cities in the Context of U.S. Economic History.* Working paper no. 51. Cambridge, Mass.: Harvard-MIT Joint Center for Urban Studies.
1982   Integration of Federal Regional Information and Development of Modeling Systems in the U.S.A. Paper presented at the Conference on Information Systems for Integrated Regional Development, Institute for Applied Systems Analysis, Laxenburg, Austria.

Giamatti, A.
1982   The university, industry, and cooperative research. *Science* 218(December 24):1278–1280.

Ginzberg, E.
1982   The mechanization of work. *Scientific American* 247(3):67–75.

Ginzberg, E., and G. Vojta
1981   The service sector of the U.S. economy. *Scientific American* 244(3):48–55.

Girifalco, L.
1981   The Dynamics of Technological Change. Herbert Spenser Lecture, University of Pennsylvania.

Gladstone Associates
1978   *Innovative Financing Techniques: A Catalog and Annotated Bibliography.* Washington, D.C.: U.S. Department of Transportation.

Glickman, N., ed.
1980   *The Urban Impacts of Federal Policies.* Baltimore: The Johns Hopkins University Press.

Gottman, J.
1961   *Megalopolis.* New York: Twentieth Century Fund.

Government Finance Research Center
1982 *Indicators of Urban Condition.* Washington, D.C.: Municipal Finance Officers Association.

Greenwood, M.
1980 Population redistribution and employment policy. In B. Berry and L. Silverman, eds., *Population Redistribution and Public Policy.* Washington, D.C.: National Academy Press.

Greer, S.
1965 *Emerging City.* Glencoe, Ill.: Free Press.

Guiliano, V.
1982 The mechanization of office work. *Scientific American* 247(3):148–164.

Gunn, T.
1982 The mechanization of design and manufacturing. *Scientific American.* 247(3):114–130.

Gurwitz, A., and T. Kingsley
1982 *The Cleveland Metropolitan Economy: An Initial Assessment.* Santa Monica, Calif.: Rand Corp.

Hall, P.
1981 Urban Change: Some International Evidence. Unpublished paper, University of California, Berkeley.

Hansen, A., and H. Perloff
1944 *State and Local Finance in the National Economy.* New York: W. W. Norton.

Hanson, R.
1982 *The Evolution of National Urban Policy, 1970–1980: Lessons from the Past.* Washington, D.C.: National Academy Press.

Harrison, B.
1972 *Education, Training, and the Urban Ghetto.* Baltimore: The Johns Hopkins University Press.

Hatry, H.
1981 *Maintaining the Existing Infrastructure: Current "State-of-the-Art-and-Practice" of Local Government Planning.* Washington, D.C.: The Urban Consortium.

Haveman, R.
1982 *European and American Labor Market Policies in the Late 1970s: Lessons for the United States.* Report T-82-1. Washington, D.C.: National Commission for Employment Policy.

Hicks, D.
1982 Urban and economic adjustment to the post-industrial era. Pp. 552–558 in U.S. Congress, Joint Economic Committee, *The Administration's 1982 National Urban Policy Report* Part 2. Washington, D.C.: U.S. Government Printing Office.

Howell, J.
1981 Testimony. Pp. 345–350 in U.S. Congress, House Subcommittee on Economic Development, *Hearings: Overview and Assessment of Economic and Regional Development Programs Under the Jurisdiction of the Subcommittee on Economic Development.* Washington, D.C.: U.S. Government Printing Office.

Hutchinson, P.
1978 Transportation, segregation, and labor force participation of the urban poor. *Growth and Change* 9:31–37.

Ingraham, S.
1982 The Urban Distribution of Service Activities: U.S. Government Data Sources. Paper prepared for the Committee on National Urban Policy, National Research Council, Washington, D.C.

Jackson, G., G. Masnick, R. Bolton, and S. Bartlett
1981 *Regional Diversity: Growth in the United States, 1960–1980.* Boston: Auburn House.
Jones, B.
1979 Utilization of black human resources in the United States. *Review of Black Political Economy* 10(1):92.
Jorgenson, D.
1980 Interview. *Challenge* (November):11–25.
Kasarda, J.
1982 Urban Industrial Transformation and Minority Opportunity. Washington, D.C.: Unpublished paper prepared for the U.S. Department of Housing and Urban Development.
Knight, R.
1977 *The Cleveland Economy in Transition: Implications for the Future.* Cleveland: Cleveland State University, College of Urban Affairs.
1980 *The Region's Economy: Transition to What?* Cleveland: Cleveland State University, College of Urban Affairs.
1982a Changes in the Economic Base of Urban Areas: Implications for Urban Public Transportation. Paper prepared for the Transportation Research Board Conference on the Future of Urban Public Transportation, National Research Council, Washington, D.C.
1982b City development in advanced industrial societies. Chapter 3 in G. Gappert and R. Knight, eds., *Cities in the 21st Century.* Beverly Hills, Calif.: Sage.
Kolderie, T.
1982 *Many Producers, Many Providers.* Minneapolis: Hubert H. Humphrey Public Policy Institute, University of Minnesota.
Kutscher, R., and J. Mark
1982 The service-producing sector: some common perceptions. *Monthly Labor Review* 106(4):21–24.
Landau, R.
1982 *Technology, Economics, and Politics: Observations of an Entrepreneur.* Washington, D.C.: National Academy of Engineering.
Leone, R., and S. Bradley
1981 Toward an effective industrial policy. *Harvard Business Review* 59:91–97.
Levitan, S.
1975 Does public job creation offer any hope? *The Conference Board* (8):58.
Levitan, S., and C. Johnson
1982 The future of work: Does it belong to us or to the robots? *Monthly Labor Review* 105(9):10–14.
Levy, V.
1981 *Economic Development Programs for Cities, Counties, and Towns.* New York: Praeger Special Studies.
Long, J.
1981 *Population Deconcentration in the United States.* Special Demographic Analysis CDS-81-5. Washington, D.C.: Bureau of the Census.
Lucke, R.
1982 Rich states-poor states: inequalities in the federal system. *Intergovernmental Perspective* 8(2):22–28.
Lyall, K.
1982 A bicycle built for two: public-private partnerships in Baltimore. Pp. 17–58 in R. Foster and R. Berger, eds., *Public-Private Cooperation in American Cities: Seven Case Studies.* Lexington, Mass.: Lexington Books.

Magarell, J.
1983 Governors see higher education as key to economic recovery. *The Chronicle of Higher Education* (February 23):1, 12–13.

Mangum, G.
1982 CETA as a "second chance" system for disadvantaged youth. Ch. 7 in R. Taylor, O.H. Rosen, and F. Pratzner, eds., *Job Training for Youth*. Columbus, Ohio: National Center for Research in Vocational Education.

Mansfield, E.
1982 Tax policy and innovation. *Science* 215:1365.

Mare, R., and C. Winship
1979 Changes in race differentials in youth labor force participation. In *Expanding Employment Opportunities for Disadvantaged Youth: Sponsored Research*. Washington, D.C.: National Commission on Employment Policy.

Marshall, R.
1982 Youth employability: the social and economic context. Ch. 3 in R. Taylor, H. Rosen, and F. Pratzner, eds., *Job Training for Youth*. Columbus, Ohio: National Center for Research in Vocational Education.

Metropolitan Council
1982 *Competitive Advantages of the Twin Cities Economy*. Minneapolis: Twin Cities Metropolitan Council.

Meyer, J., ed.
1982 *Meeting Human Needs: Toward a New Public Philosophy*. Washington, D.C.: American Enterprise Institute.

Michalski, W.
1982 Structural change: positive adjustment policies—key to economic recovery. *The OECD Observer* (119):6–7.

Mills, D.
1981 The human resource consequences of industrial revitalization. Ch. 12 in M. Wachter and S. Wachter, eds., *Toward a New U.S. Industrial Policy?* Philadelphia: University of Pennsylvania Press.

Mirengoff, W., L. Rindler, H. Greenspan, and S. Seablom
1980a *CETA: Assessment of Public Service Employment Programs*. Washington, D.C.: National Academy of Sciences.

Mirengoff, W., L. Rindler, H. Greenspan, S. Seablom, and L. Black
1980b *The New CETA: Effect on Public Service Employment Programs*. Final Report. Washington, D.C.: National Academy of Sciences.

National Academy of Engineering
1983 *U.S. Leadership in Manufacturing*. Washington, D.C.: National Academy Press.

National Academy of Sciences
1983 *Strengthening the Government-University Partnership in Science*. Report of the Ad Hoc Committee on Government-University Relationships in Support of Science. Committee on Science, Engineering, and Public Policy. Washington, D.C.: National Academy Press.

National Academy of Sciences-National Academy of Engineering
1982 *Science and Mathematics in the Schools: Report of a Convocation*. Commission on Behavioral and Social Sciences and Education. Washington, D.C.: National Academy Press.

National Commission for Employment Policy
1979 *Fifth Annual Report: Expanding Employment Opportunities for Youth*. Washington, D.C.: National Commission for Employment Policy.

National Research Council (NRC)

1982a *Critical Issues for National Urban Policy*. Committee on National Urban Policy, Commission on Sociotechnical Systems. Washington, D.C.: National Academy Press.

1982b *National Policy and the Post-Industrial City: An International Perspective*. Committee on National Urban Policy, Commission on Behavioral and Social Sciences and Education. Washington, D.C.: National Academy Press.

1983 *The Competitive Status of the U.S. Machine Tool Industry: A Study of the Influence of Technology on International Competitive Advantage*. Committee on Technology and International Economic and Trade Issues and the Office of the Foreign Secretary, National Academy of Engineering. Washington, D.C.: National Academy Press.

Nelson, R.

1982 *Government and Technical Change: A Cross-Industry Analysis*. New York: Pergamon Press.

Nevins, A.

1976 *John D. Rockefeller: The Heroic Age of American Enterprise*. 2 vols. Millwood, N.J.: Kraus Reprint.

Newman, G.

1978 *The Labor Market Consequences of Trade Displacement: Evidence from the Trade Adjustment Assistance Program of 1962*. Philadelphia: Institute for Policy Research and Evaluation, Pennsylvania State University.

Norris, W.

1982 A New Role for Corporations. Address to Conference on Social Needs and Business Opportunities, Minneapolis, September 21.

Norton, R. D., and J. Rees

1979 The product cycle and the spatial decentralization of American manufacturing. *Regional Studies* 13:141–151.

Noyelle, T., and T. Stanback

1983 *Economic Transformation of American Cities*. Totowa, N.J.: Allanheld and Rowman.

O'Day, K., and L. Neumann

1984 Assessing need: the state of the art. Ch. 2 in *The Adequacy and Maintenance of Urban Public Facilities: A Symposium*. Washington, D.C.: National Academy Press.

Oreskes, M.

1982 Retraining of workers becomes a priority. *The New York Times—Special Supplement: Careers '83—The Marketplace* (October 17):Sec. 12, p. 5.

Palmer, J., and I. Sawhill, eds.

1982 *The Reagan Experiment*. Washington, D.C.: The Urban Institute Press.

Perloff, H.

1981 *Planning the Post-Industrial City*. Chicago: Planners Press.

Perry, D., and A. Watkins, eds.

1977 *The Rise of the Sunbelt Cities*. Beverly Hills, Calif.: Sage.

Personick, V.

1981 The outlook for industry output and employment. *Monthly Labor Review* 104(8):35–38.

Peterson, G.

1984 Financing the nation's infrastructural requirements. Ch. 3 in National Research Council, *The Adequacy and Maintenance of Urban Public Facilities: A Symposium*. Washington, D.C.: National Academy Press.

Peterson, G., N. Humphrey, M. Miller, and P. Wilson

in *The Future of America's Capital Plant*. Washington, D.C.: The Urban Institute
press Press.

Piore, M.
1981   The Theory of Macroeconomic Regulation and Current Economic Crisis in the United States. Working paper no. 285. Cambridge, Mass.: Massachusetts Institute of Technology.

Pred, A.
1977   City Systems in Advanced Economics. New York: John Wiley & Sons.

President's Commission for a National Agenda for the Eighties
1980   Urban America in the Eighties: Perspectives and Prospects. Washington, D.C.: U.S. Government Printing Office.

Prial, F.
1982   Lots of jobs, but skills are missing. The New York Times—Special Supplement: Careers '83—The Marketplace (October 17):Sec. 12, p. 15.

Public Technology, Inc.
1980   Urban Infrastructure: Assessing Its Condition and Developing Policies and Methods for the Future. Washington, D.C.: The Urban Consortium-Public Technology, Inc.

Rader, L.
1982   Computer literacy: option or imperative? The Bridge 12(3):14–19.

Rasmussen, D.
1981   Testimony. In U.S. Congress, House Subcommittee on Economic Development, Hearings: Overview and Assessment of Economic and Regional Development Under the Jurisdiction of the Subcommittee on Economic Development. Washington, D.C.: U.S. Government Printing Office.

Rees, J.
1979a Regional industrial shifts in the U.S. and the internal generation of manufacturing in growth centers of the southwest. Pp. 51–73 in W. C. Wheaton, ed., Interregional Movements and Regional Growth. Washington, D.C.: The Urban Institute.

1979b Technological change and regional shifts in American manufacturing. The Professional Geographer (February):45–54.

1980   Government policy and industrial location in the United States. In U.S. Congress, Joint Economic Committee, State and Local Financial Adjustments in a Changing Economy. Washington, D.C.: U.S. Government Printing Office.

1983   Industrial Innovation and the Appropriate Role for Regional Policy in the American and European Contexts. Working paper. Vienna, Austria: International Institute for Applied Systems Analysis.

Reich, R.
1982   Why the U.S. needs an industrial policy. Harvard Business Review 60(1):74–81.

Reiner, T., and J. Wolpert
1981   The non-profit sector in the metropolitan economy. Economic Geography 57:23–33.

Renaud, B.
1982   Structural Changes in OECD Economies and Their Impact on Cities in the 1980s. Washington, D.C.: Urban Development Department, The World Bank.

Rudnick, A.
1982   The American University in the Urban Context: A Status Report and Call for Leadership. Washington, D.C.: Division of Urban Affairs, National Association of State Universities and Land Grant Colleges.

Rumberger, R.
1981   The changing skill requirements of jobs in the U.S. economy. Industrial and Labor Relations Review 34(4):578–590.

Rutter, M., et al.
1979   *Fifteen Thousand Hours: Secondary Schools and Their Effects on Children*. Cambridge, Mass.: Harvard University Press.

Salamon, L.
1983   The New Federalism, the Federal Budget, and the Nonprofit Sector. Testimony before the Joint Economic Committee, U.S. Congress, April 14. Washington, D.C.: U.S. Government Printing Office.

Salamon, L., and A. Abramson
1982   *The Federal Budget and the Nonprofit Sector*. Washington, D.C.: The Urban Institute.

Salinas, P.
1980   Sub-Employment and the Urban Underclass: A Policy Research Report. Prepared for the Economic Development Administration, U.S. Department of Commerce.

Savas, E.
1982   *Privatizing the Public Sector: How to Shrink Government*. Chatham, N.J.: Chatham House.

Schriber, J.
1982   Whatever happened to Akron? *Forbes Magazine* (November 22):170–177.

Schwartz, G.
1982   Local Infrastructure Planning in Maryland. Paper prepared for the Maryland State Department of Planning, Baltimore.
1983   Revitalizing cities through sectoral strategies. In D. Hicks and N. Glickman, eds., *Transition to the 21st Century: Prospects and Policies for Economic and Urban-Regional Transformation*. Greenwich, Conn.: J.A.I. Press.
in   Where the jobs will be. In G. Schwartz and B. Neikirk, eds., *The Work Revolution*.
press New York: Rawson Associates, Inc.

Schwartz, G., and P. Choate
1980   *Being Number One: Rebuilding the U.S. Economy*. Lexington, Mass.: Lexington Books.

Science
1982   Electronics firms plug into universities. (August 6):217.

Scott, R., and D. Brower, eds.
1976   *Management and Control of Growth*. 4 vols. Washington, D.C.: Urban Land Institute.

Sekcenski, E.
1981   The health services industry: a decade of expansion. *Monthly Labor Review* 104(5):9–15.

Sheppard, H.
1969   *The Nature of the Job Problem and the Role of Public Service Employment*. Kalamazoo, Mich.: W. E. Upjohn Institute.

Sheridan, R.
1982   *Ohio Tomorrow: State Economic Growth and Development and the Role of Higher Education*. Part I: A perspective; Part II: The problem and alternate solutions. Cleveland: College of Urban Affairs, Cleveland State University.

Sherman, S., ed.
1983   *Education for Tomorrow's Jobs*. Report of the Committee on Vocational Education and Economic Development in Depressed Areas, National Research Council. Washington, D.C.: National Academy Press.

Sinclair, A.
1981   *Corsair: The Life of J. Pierpoint Morgan*. Boston: Little, Brown.

Singelmann, J.
  1978   *From Agriculture to Services: The Transformation of Industrial Employment.* Beverly
         Hills, Calif.: Sage.
Southern Growth Policies Board
  1981   *Report of the Task Force on Southern Cities.* Triangle Park, N.C.
Stanback, T., and M. Drennan
  1978   *The Transformation of the Urban Economic Base.* Special Report No. 19. Washington,
         D.C.: National Commission for Manpower Policy.
Stanback, T., and T. Noyelle
  1982   *Cities in Transition: Changing Job Structure in Atlanta, Denver, Buffalo, Phoenix,
         Columbus (Ohio), Nashville, and Charlotte.* Totowa, N.J.: Allanheld, Osmun.
Stanback, T., P. Bearse, T. Noyelle, and R. Karasek
  1981   *Services: The New Economy.* Totowa, N.J.: Allanheld, Osmun.
Steinman, S., and J. Tarr
  1982   Four decades of public-private partnerships in Pittsburgh. Pp. 59–128 in R. Foster and
         R. Berger, eds., *Public-Private Cooperation in American Cities: Seven Case Studies.*
         Lexington, Mass.: Lexington Books.
Sternlieb, G., and J. Hughes
  1975   *Post-Industrial America: Metropolitan Decline and Inter-Regional Job Shifts.* New
         Brunswick, N.J.: Center for Urban Policy Research.
Sternlieb, G., and D. Listokin
  1981   *New Tools for Economic Development: The Enterprise Zone, Development Bank and
         RFC.* Piscataway, N.J.: Center for Urban Policy Research.
Storey, J.
  1982   Income security. Ch. 12 in J. Palmer and I. Sawhill, eds., *The Reagan Experiment.*
         Washington, D.C.: Urban Institute Press.
Szanton, P.
  1981   *Not Well Advised.* Beverly Hills, Calif.: Sage.
Tarr, J.
  1984   Perspectives on the development of the urban infrastructure in the 19th and 20th
         centuries. In *The Adequacy and Maintenance of Urban Public Facilities: A Symposium,*
         National Research Council. Washington, D.C.: National Academy Press.
Thompson, W.
  1969   The economic base of urban problems. In N. Chamberlain, ed., *Contemporary Eco-
         nomic Issues.* Homewood, Ill.: Richard D. Irwin, Inc.
  1977   Land management strategies for central city depopulation. Pp. 67–78 in U.S. Congress,
         House Subcommittee on the City, *How Cities Can Grow Old Gracefully.* Washington,
         D.C.: U.S. Government Printing Office.
  1980   The durable past of the urban future. Pp. 27–39 in M. Harding and M. Osmun, eds.,
         Explorations in Public Policy: Essays in Celebration of the Life of John Osmun.
         Memphis, Tenn.: Southwestern at Memphis.
Treiman, D., and H. I. Hartmann, eds.
  1981   *Women, Work, and Wages: Equal Pay for Jobs of Equal Value.* Report of Committee
         on Occupational Classification and Analysis, Assembly of Behavioral and Social Sci-
         ences. Washington, D.C.: National Academy Press.
Trescott, P.
  1982   *Financing American Enterprise; The Story of Commercial Banking.* Westport, Conn.:
         Greenwood Press.

U.S. Congress, Joint Committee on Taxation
  1982   *Description of S. 2298, Enterprise Zone Act of 1982.* Washington, D.C.: U.S. Government Printing Office.
U.S. Congress, Joint Economic Committee
  1974   *Federal Subsidy Programs.* Washington, D.C.: U.S. Government Printing Office.
  1981a *The Regional and Urban Impacts of the Administration's Budget and Tax Proposals.* Washington, D.C.: U.S. Government Printing Office.
  1981b *Trends in the Fiscal Condition of Cities.* Washington, D.C.: U.S. Government Printing Office.
  1982   *Location of High Technology Firms and Regional Economic Development.* Washington, D.C.: U.S. Government Printing Office.
U.S. Department of Housing and Urban Development
  1980   *The President's National Urban Policy Report, 1980.* Washington, D.C.
  1982   *The President's National Urban Policy Report, 1982.* Washington, D.C.
Vaughan, R.
  1977   *The Urban Impacts of Federal Policies: Vol. 2—Economic Development.* Santa Monica, Calif.: Rand.
Venture
  1982   Breathing life back into U.S. cities. (August):33–38.
Westat, Inc.
  1981   Job Search and Relocation Assistance Project (JSRA): Final Report. Prepared for the Office of Policy Evaluation and Research, Employment and Training Administration, U.S. Department of Labor, Washington, D.C.
Wolman, H.
  1982   *European Central Government Policies Toward Declining Urban Economies.* Washington, D.C.: The Urban Institute.
Wolpert, J., and T. Reiner
  1982   The Not-for-Profit Sector in Stable and Growing Metropolitan Areas. Woodrow Wilson School, Princeton University.
Woodson, R.
  1981   *Summons to Life: Mediating Structures and the Prevention of Youth Crime.* Washington, D.C.: American Enterprise Institute.
Wurzburg, G.
  1978   *Improving Job Opportunities for Youth: A Review of Prime Sponsor Experience in Implementing the Youth Employment and Demonstration Projects Act.* Washington, D.C.: National Council on Employment Policy.
Ylvisaker, P.
  1981   Philanthropy as triage. *Foundation News.*
Zimmerman, H.
  1981   *Studies in Comparative Federalism: West Germany.* Washington, D.C.: U.S. Advisory Commission on Intergovernmental Relations.

Biographical Sketches
of Committee Members
and Staff

PAUL N. YLVISAKER is Charles William Eliot Professor of Education at
the Graduate School of Education, Harvard University. He received his
B.S. degree from Mankato State College (1942) and his M.P.A. (1945)
and Ph.D. (1948) degrees in political economy and government from
Harvard University. Ylvisaker began his teaching career at Bethany College and has taught at Harvard University, Swarthmore College, Princeton
University, and Yale University. In addition, he has served in a variety
of government positions and on advisory groups, including executive
secretary to the mayor of Philadelphia, commissioner of the New Jersey
Department of Community Affairs, and chairman of a presidential task
force on cities. From 1955 to 1967 he was a member of the staff of the
Ford Foundation, directing its public affairs program from 1959 to 1967.
He serves on a number of corporate, foundation, community, and educational boards. Ylvisaker's writing and research include works on urban
affairs, planning, education, and philanthropy.

BRIAN J. L. BERRY is dean of the School of Urban and Public Affairs,
Carnegie-Mellon University. He received a B.S. degree (1955) from University College, London, and his M.A. degree (1956) and Ph.D. degree
(1958) in geography from the University of Washington. He also received
an honorary A.M. degree from Harvard University in 1977. Berry was
an instructor at the University of Washington before joining the geography
faculty of the University of Chicago in 1958, where he became Irving B.
Harris Professor of Urban Geography, director of the Center for Urban

Studies, and chair of the Department of Geography. In 1976 he was appointed Williams professor of city and regional planning at Harvard University, where he also served as chair of the Ph.D. program in urban planning, director of the Laboratory for Computer Graphics and Spatial Analysis, fellow of the Institute for International Development, and professor of sociology. A member of the National Academy of Sciences, Berry is the author of many books and articles on urban affairs.

HARVEY BROOKS is Benjamin Pierce Professor of Technology and Public Policy at Harvard University. He holds an A.B. degree in mathematics from Yale University (1937) and a Ph.D. degree in physics from Harvard University (1940). He was a Henry fellow of Cambridge University (1937-1938) and has received honorary degrees from a number of universities. The positions he has held include assistant director, Advance Research Laboratory, The Pennsylvania State University, and professor of engineering research; lecturer, Salzburg Seminar in American Studies; Phi Beta Kappa Visiting Scholar; Gordon McKay Professor of Applied Physics, Harvard University; and Guggenheim fellow. He has been a member of the faculty of government at Harvard since 1961. A member of the National Academy of Sciences, Brooks has served as chair of the Commission on Sociotechnical Systems. He has also served as chairman of the board of the German Marshall Fund of the United States, chairman of the American Physical Science Society panel on public affairs, and consultant to the Science and Technology Policy Office, National Science Foundation.

KENNETH B. CLARK is the president of Clark, Phipps, Clark, and Harris of New York City. He received his A.B. degree from Howard University (1935) and his M.S. degree (1936) and Ph.D. degree (1940) in psychology from Columbia University. He joined the faculty of the City College of New York in 1942, where he taught social psychology, becoming professor emeritus in 1975. From 1967 to 1975 he was concurrently president of his consulting firm and president of Metropolitan Applied Research Center, Inc. Clark served as president of the American Psychological Association in 1971. He has practiced and written extensively on child, social, and clinical psychology; race relations; education; and human relations.

JOHN M. DEGROVE is director of the Joint Center for Environmental and Urban Problems at Florida Atlantic University. He also serves as chair of the department of political science and as provost of the Broward County campus of Florida Atlantic. He received his B.A. degree from Rollins College (1953), his M.A. degree from Emory University (1954), and his

Ph.D. degree in political science from the University of North Carolina (1958). From 1958 to 1964 he was a member of the political science faculty of the Unversity of Florida. He became professor of political science at Florida Atlantic University in 1964, also serving as dean of the College of Social Science from 1964 to 1978. DeGrove has been a member of the President's Commission on Urban Problems; the executive committee of the Southern Growth Policies Board; the Florida Constitutional Revision Commission and chairman of its local government committee; chairman of the Panel on State Urban Policy, National Academy of Public Administration; special adviser to the governor of Florida; and special adviser to the White House Conference on Strategic Planning. He has written books and articles on urban problems, state government, regionalism, and the environment.

JAMES M. HOWELL is senior vice-president and head of the economics department of the First National Bank of Boston. He holds a B.A. degree from Texas Agriculture and Mechanical College (1956) and a Ph.D. degree in economics from Tulane University (1963). Howell has served as economist for the Federal Reserve System; economic adviser to the Republic of Chile; and economist for the Office of the Secretary of Commerce. He joined the First National Bank in 1970. He was also professor of economics at the University of Maryland and has taught at The George Washington University.

HARVEY S. PERLOFF was dean of the School of Architecture and Urban Planning at the University of California, Los Angeles, from 1968 until his death in 1983. He received a B.A. degree (1935) from the University of Pennsylania. After graduate study at the London School of Economics, he received a Ph.D. degree in economics from Harvard University (1940). From 1941 to 1943 he was an economist for the Board of Governors of the Federal Reserve System. He then served as consultant to the government of Puerto Rico; as associate professor and head of the Program of Education and Research in Planning at the University of Chicago; and as director of the Program of Urban and Regional Studies at Resources for the Future, Inc. From 1962 to 1964 Perloff was the U.S. member of the Committee of Nine of the Alliance for Progress. He was a consultant to many U.S., foreign, and international organizations and served as a member of a wide variety of committees concerned with urban and regional problems. Perloff was president of the American Planning Association. He was a member of the Commission on Sociotechnical Systems of the National Research Council, chair of the Advisory Committee for the United Nations program of Training and Research in Regional Planning and

Development, and a member of the Executive Committee, Western Center, American Academy of Arts and Sciences. Perloff wrote many books and articles on planning, urban problems, economics, and regional issues.

GEORGE E. PETERSON is principal research associate and director of the public finance program of The Urban Institute. He holds a B.A. degree in history from Amherst College (1963); B.A. and M.A. degrees in politics, philosophy, and economics from Oxford University (1965), where he was a Rhodes scholar; and a Ph.D. degree in economics from Harvard University (1973). He has been a member of the staff of The Urban Institute since 1972, directing studies of urban land development patterns, central-city housing markets, impacts of tax policy on urban development, urban capital investment and financing, economic and fiscal monitoring systems, and compensation programs. He has written books and articles on public finance.

GAIL GARFIELD SCHWARTZ is president of Garfield Schwartz Associates, Inc., an economics consulting firm. She received her B.A. degree in political science from Smith College (1955), an M.A. degree in planning and public administration from New York University (1969), and a Ph.D. degree in urban and regional economics from Columbia University (1972). From 1971 to 1974 she was deputy director of the division of economic planning and development of the New York City Planning Department and became its director in 1974, serving until 1977 when she became a senior fellow of the Academy for Contemporary Problems, a position she held until 1981. During this period, she was also a senior research scientist at the Center for Metropolitan Planning and Research, visiting professor of planning at the University of North Carolina, and visiting professor of public policy at Johns Hopkins University.

ROBERT C. WOOD is Henry R. Luce Professor of Democratic Institutions and Social Order at Wesleyan University. He received his B.A. degree from Princeton University (1946) and his M.P.A. (1947), M.A. (1948), and Ph.D. (1950) degrees in political economy and government from Harvard University. After serving from 1949 to 1951 as assistant director of the Florida Legislative Research Bureau, Wood joined the staff of the U.S. Bureau of the Budget, leaving in 1953 to join the government faculty at Harvard University, where he taught until 1957. From 1957 to 1966 he was a member of the faculty of political science at Massachusetts Institute of Technology (MIT), where he served as head of the political science department from 1965 to 1966. In 1966 he was appointed under-secretary of the U.S. Department of Housing and Urban Development. In 1969 he directed the Joint Center for Urban Studies, Harvard-MIT, before becoming president of the University of Massachusetts, holding that position until 1977 when he returned to the Joint Center as a senior associate. From 1978 to 1980 he was superintendent of the Boston public schools. During the year 1980-1981 he was visiting professor of political science at MIT and visiting professor of education at Harvard University. From 1981 to 1983 he was professor of political science at the University of Massachusetts, Harbor Campus. Wood has written many books and articles on urban government and policy and urban education.

ROYCE HANSON was the study director of the Committee on National Urban Policy. He received his B.A. degree in economics from Central State University of Oklahoma (1953). His M.A. degree (1957) and Ph.D. degree (1963) in government and public administration and his J.D. degree (1983) are from The American University. Hanson was a member of the faculty of The American University's School of Government and Public Administration from 1957 to 1972. From 1966 to 1971 he served as president of the Washington Center for Metropolitan Studies. In 1971-1972 he was director of the New Communities Study Center of Virginia Polytechnic Institute and State University at Reston, Virginia. He was a visiting professor of urban affairs at the University of Maryland in 1971. From 1972 to 1981 he was chairman of the Montgomery County, Maryland, Planning Board of the Maryland-National Capital Park and Planning Commission. He is now associate director of the Hubert H. Humphrey Institute of Public Affairs at the University of Minnesota. He is the author of books and articles on urban affairs, planning, intergovernmental relations, and constitutional law.

GORDON L. CLARK is associate professor of geography at the University of Chicago. During 1981–1982 he was a National Research Council fellow working with the Committee on National Urban Policy. He received a B.Ec. degree (1973) and an M.A. degree (1975) in geography from Monash University, Melbourne, Australia. In 1978 he received his Ph.D. degree in geography from McMaster University, Hamilton, Ontario. From 1978 to 1983 he was an assistant professor at the John F. Kennedy School of Government, Harvard University. Clark held a Ford fellowship in urban studies in 1976-1978 and has received research grants from the National Science Foundation and the W. F. Milton Fund. He has written extensively on problems of labor markets, interregional migration, and the structure and functions of local governments.

JOHN REES, a National Research Council fellow for 1983, is associate professor of geography at the Maxwell School of Citizenship and Public Affairs, Syracuse University. He holds a B.A. degree (honors) from the University of Wales (1969), an M.A. degree from the University of Cincinnati (1971), and a Ph.D. degree from the London School of Economics (1977). From 1975 to 1983 he was on the faculty of the University of Texas at Dallas and from 1980 to 1982 served on the Economic Advisory Council of the North Texas Commission. Since 1977 Rees has received a number of research awards from the National Science Foundation and has conducted studies for government agencies, including the Joint Economic Committee of Congress, the Office of Technology Assessment, the General Accounting Office, and the U.S. Department of Housing and Urban Development. He has written articles on industrial location, technological change, and regional development.

Index

205